International Financial System

Policy and Regulation

KLUWER LAW INTERNATIONAL

International Financial System

Policy and Regulation

Ross P. Buckley

Wolters Kluwer
Law & Business

AUSTIN   BOSTON   CHICAGO   NEW YORK   THE NETHERLANDS

Published by:
Kluwer Law International
PO Box 316
2400 AH Alphen aan den Rijn
The Netherlands
Website: www.kluwerlaw.com

Sold and distributed in North, Central and South America by:
Aspen Publishers, Inc.
7201 McKinney Circle
Frederick, MD 21704
United States of America
Email: customer.care@aspenpubl.com

Sold and distributed in all other countries by:
Turpin Distribution Services Ltd.
Stratton Business Park
Pegasus Drive, Bigglewade
Bedfordshire SG18 8TQ
United Kingdom
Email: kluwerlaw@turpin-distribution.com

ISBN 978-90-411-2868-3

©2009 Kluwer Law International BV, The Netherlands

All rights reserved. No part of this publication may be reproduced, stored in a retrieval system, or transmitted in any form or by any means, mechanical, photocopying, recording or otherwise, without prior written permission of the publishers.

Permissions to use this content must be obtained from the copyright owner. Please apply to: Permissions Department, Wolters Kluwer Law & Business, 76 Ninth Avenue, 7th Floor, New York, NY 10011-5201, United States of America. Email: permissions@kluwerlaw.com.

*To the lights of my life, Ariella, Tara and Marcus;
and to the lighthouse, Rashelle.*

Table of Contents

About the Author xv

Preface xvii

Acknowledgements xix

Introduction xxi

Chapter 1
History of the Global Financial System 1
1.1 History 1
1.2 The Bretton Woods System 5
    1.2.1 Pressures on the Bretton Woods System 7
    1.2.2 Collapse of the Bretton Woods Exchange Rate System 9
    1.2.3 The International Monetary Fund Today 11
    1.2.4 The World Bank 13
    1.2.5 The World Trade Organization 13
1.3 The System Today 14

Chapter 2
Globalization and Global Capital Flows 15

Chapter 3
The Latin American and African Debt Crisis of 1982 21
3.1 The Debt Crisis of 1982 21
3.2 The Loans of the 1970s: Their Origins
    and Destinations 23
    3.2.1 The Lenders 24
    3.2.2 The Borrowers 25

3.3	Causes of the Latin American and African Debt Crisis		25
	3.3.1 Recycling of OPEC Funds		26
	3.3.2 Bank Behaviour		27
		3.3.2.1 Time and Ignorance of History	28
		3.3.2.2 Inexperience of the Banks	29
		3.3.2.3 Bank Profitability and Market Share	30
		3.3.2.4 The Promotion of Bankers' Careers	31
		3.3.2.5 Strong Debtor Economies	31
		3.3.2.6 Syndicated Lending	32
		3.3.2.7 Floating Interest Rates	32
		3.3.2.8 The Position of US Banks at Home	32
	3.3.3 Debtor Nation Policies		33
		3.3.3.1 Large Budget Deficits	33
		3.3.3.2 Overvalued Exchange Rates	33
		3.3.3.3 Anti-export Trade Regimes	33
		3.3.3.4 Capital Flight	34
		3.3.3.5 Corruption	34
	3.3.4 External Factors		35
		3.3.4.1 Interest Rate Increases	35
		3.3.4.2 Adverse Exchange Rate Movements	35
		3.3.4.3 Falls in Commodity Prices	36
		3.3.4.4 The Worldwide Recession	36
		3.3.4.5 Cessation of Petrodollar Recycling	36
		3.3.4.6 Conclusion on External Factors	36

Chapter 4
The Brady Plan   39
4.1 Background to the Brady Plan   39
4.2 The Baker Plan   40
4.3 The Brady Plan   40
    4.3.1 Mexico's Brady Restructuring   41
    4.3.2 The Phillipines Brady Restructuring   47
    4.3.3 Venezuela's Brady Restructuring   48
    4.3.4 Uruguay's and Chile's Restructurings   50
    4.3.5 Brazil's Brady Restructuring Initiated   50
    4.3.6 Argentina's Brady Restructuring   50
    4.3.7 Brazil's Brady Restructuring is Completed   51
    4.3.8 Collateralizing Brady Bonds   52
    4.3.9 Conclusions Regarding the Brady Plan   53

Chapter 5
The Asian Economic Crisis of 1997   55
5.1 The Crisis Erupts   55
5.2 Causes of the Asian Economic Crisis   56

Table of Contents xi

	5.2.1	Type of Indebtedness	57
	5.2.2	Extent of Indebtedness	57
		5.2.2.1 Excess Liquidity in the Developed World	58
		5.2.2.2 The Central Role of Crossover Investors	59
	5.2.3	Financial Sector Weaknesses	60
		5.2.3.1 Failure to Intermediate Capital Flows Effectively	60
		5.2.3.2 The Premature Liberalization of Local Financial Markets	61
	5.2.4	Fixed Exchange Rates	61
	5.2.5	Region-Wide Loss of Confidence	62
5.3	Conclusion and Lessons		63
	5.3.1	The Benefits of Floating Exchange Rates	64
	5.3.2	The High Risks of Foreign Currency Borrowing	64
	5.3.3	The Need for Long-Term Local Currency Capital	65
	5.3.4	International Capital Flows as a Product of Developed World Liquidity	65
	5.3.5	The Urgent Need for a New Perspective on Responsibility in International Lending and Investment	65
5.4	The Role and Impact of the IMF in the Asian Crisis		66
	5.4.1	Misdiagnosis	67
	5.4.2	Excessive Conditionality	68
	5.4.3	Protection of the System and of Creditors	69
	5.4.4	Mishandling of Market Expectations	70
	5.4.5	Social Costs of IMF Policies	70
5.5	Conclusions on the IMF's Role in the Asian Crisis		71

Chapter 6
Let's all Cry for Argentina   75
6.1 The Argentine Experience   75
6.2 Causes of the Argentine Crisis   77
     6.2.1 The Peso-Dollar Peg   77
     6.2.2 Excessive Indebtedness   78
     6.2.3 Corruption   79
     6.2.4 IMF Policies   80
6.3 The Restructuring of Argentina's Indebtedness   81

Chapter 7
Debt Relief for Poor Countries and for Iraq   85
7.1 Debt Relief   85
7.2 The US Approach to Iraqi Debt   86
7.3 Debt-for-Development Exchanges   93

Chapter 8
Measures Available to Debtor Nations — 97
- 8.1 Rigorous Local Prudential Regulation — 97
- 8.2 Debt Policy — 99
  - 8.2.1 Borrow Less Foreign Currency Debt — 99
  - 8.2.2 Issue Less Short-Term Debt — 100
  - 8.2.3 Issue More Long-Term Local Currency Denominated Debt — 100
- 8.3 Exchange Rate Policies — 101
- 8.4 Capital Controls — 104
  - 8.4.1 Chile's Controls — 107
  - 8.4.2 Malaysia's Controls — 108
  - 8.4.3 The Uses of Inflow Controls — 109
  - 8.4.4 The Uses of Outflow Controls — 110
  - 8.4.5 Inflow and Outflow Controls Compared — 111
  - 8.4.6 Inflow Controls in Developed Countries — 111
  - 8.4.7 Conclusion on Capital Controls — 112
- 8.5 Be More Willing to Play the Default Card — 112

Chapter 9
Global Measures to Improve the System — 121
- 9.1 The National Balance Sheet Problem — 121
  - 9.1.1 The Volatility Machine — 122
  - 9.1.2 Original Sin — 123
  - 9.1.3 Currency Mismatches — 124
  - 9.1.4 Local Currency Bond Markets — 125
  - 9.1.5 An International Solution — 127
    - 9.1.5.1 Changing the Lending Policies of Multilateral Development Banks — 129
    - 9.1.5.2 Local Currency Solutions — 130
    - 9.1.5.3 Re-orienting the Paris Club — 130
  - 9.1.6 Conclusion on National Balance Sheet Structures — 131
- 9.2 A Tax on International Currency Transactions — 132
- 9.3 A Global Financial Regulator — 135
- 9.4 A Lender of Last Resort — 135
- 9.5 A Sovereign Bankruptcy Regime — 137
  - 9.5.1 The Benefits of Bankruptcy Regimes — 138
  - 9.5.2 Why Is There No Global Sovereign Bankruptcy Regime? — 139
    - 9.5.2.1 Absence of an Overarching Need – until Relatively Recently – for a Sovereign Bankruptcy Regime — 140
    - 9.5.2.2 Difficulties of Creating International Institutions — 140
    - 9.5.2.3 Perceived Interests of Creditors — 141
  - 9.5.3 The Details of a Global Sovereign Bankruptcy Regime — 142

Table of Contents xiii

9.6	Collective Action Clauses	143
9.7	The IMF Proposal: The SDRM	145
	9.7.1 Would the SDRM Have Served the Debtors?	148
9.8	Benefits of a Global Sovereign Bankruptcy Regime	151
	9.8.1 Conclusion on Systemic Measures	152

Chapter 10
The Way Forward **155**

10.1 The Socialization of Private Sector Debt	156
10.2 The Future of the IMF	158
10.2.1 The IMF and Poverty in Africa	165
10.2.2 The Fund's Inability to Reinvent Itself	166

List of References **171**

Index **191**

About the Author

Ross Buckley is a Professor in the Faculty of Law at the University of New South Wales in Sydney, Australia, an Australia 21 Fellow, and a Senior Fellow of the Tim Fischer Centre for Global Trade & Finance at Bond University. He is the founding Series Editor of the *Global Trade Law Series* of Kluwer of The Hague, Series Co-Editor of Kluwer's *International Banking and Finance Law Series*, and founding editor of the Overseas Law column of the *Australian Law Journal*. He has taught as a Visiting Professor at Northwestern University, Chicago and has consulted to the US Department of Justice, the US Securities and Exchange Commission, Vietnam's Ministry of Trade, Indonesia's Ministry of Finance, and the Australian Tax Office.

Preface

> Lawyers and legal academics are largely absent from the debate about financial crises. The commentary is dominated by economists, many of whom unfortunately vastly oversimplify or even misunderstand the role of law in recent crises.
>
> Frank Partnoy[1]

Partnoy's complaint is a good one.

Lawyers need to get involved. Law schools need more scholars teaching and researching international finance law. Around the world, law schools that believe they ought to teach international trade law, do not teach international finance law. Yet financial flows far exceed trade flows, by a factor of over sixty to one; international financial transactions represent a far greater proportion of the practice of most major law firms than do trade transactions; and international finance, when it goes wrong, brings appalling suffering to the poorest citizens of poor countries. International finance law is important; it is only neglected because it is not understood.

I have written this book for a few reasons. One is to address this widespread lack of understanding with a hopefully accessible and interesting book. Another is to provide a general introduction to the international financial system and its regulation to assist students studying the topic. A third reason is to articulate my take on the system as one that works much to the detriment of the poor nations and the benefit of rich nations, and in particular to the detriment of the poor within poor nations and the benefit of the rich within rich and poor nations alike.

---

1. F. Partnoy, 'Why Markets Crash and What Law Can Do about It' (1999–2000) 61 *University of Pittsburgh Law Review*, 741.

In general, this book seeks to learn from history. For, as John Kenneth Galbraith said, '[h]istory has a way of repeating itself in financial matters because of a kind of sophisticated stupidity'.[2] If this book seeks anything, it seeks to work against this sophisticated stupidity for mistakes in the finance of developing countries sacrifice the lives of thousands and the futures of millions.

---

2. J. Galbraith, *The Sunday Times*, 25 October 1987. The more well known, similar quotation is from George Santayana, 'Those who cannot remember the past are condemned to repeat it.': Santayana, *Life of Reason* (1950–1956), vol.I, ch.xii.

Acknowledgements

I would like to thank the inimitable 'Dr P', Haig Patapan, who by serving as an unerring sounding board has had much to do with the birth and realization of this project. I would also like to thank Peter Dirou, for allowing me to reuse some of the material from an article we wrote together; and my two research assistants, Hernan Pintos-Lopez and David Yang, whose efforts contributed much towards getting this manuscript finished, and on time.

The publisher and I would like to thank the publishers of the following books and journals for their permission to use in this book parts of the material written by me (and in one case Peter and I) and published in these chapters and articles: 'How to Strengthen the International Financial System by Improving Sovereign Balance Sheet Structures' (2006) 2 *Annals of Economics and Finance*, 257 (with P. Dirou); 'Why Some Developing Countries Are Better Placed than the International Monetary Fund to Develop Policy Responses to the Challenges of Global Capital' 15 *Tulane Journal of International and Comparative Law*, Winter 2006, 121; 'Iraqi Sovereign Debt and Its Curious Global Implications', chapter in *Beyond the Iraq War: The Promises, Perils and Pitfalls of External Interventionism*, Heazle and Islam (eds) (London, Edward Elgar, 2006), 141; 'The Role of the Rule of Law in the Regulation of Global Capital Flows', chapter in *Globalisation and the Rule of Law*, Zifcak (ed.) (Oxford, Routledge, 2005), 140; 'Why Are Developing Nations So Slow to Play the Default Card in Renegotiating Their Sovereign Indebtedness?' [2005] *Chicago Journal of International Law*, 347; 'How the International Financial System, to Its Detriment, Differs from National Systems, and What We Can We Do About It' (2004) 34 *University of Hong Kong Law Journal*, 321; 'Do Cry for the Argentines: An Analysis of Their Crisis' (2003) 17 *Banking & Finance Law Review*, 373; 'The IMF's Proposal for a Sovereign Debt Restructuring Mechanism: An Australian Assessment' [2003] *Australian Journal of International Law*, 1; 'Sovereign Bankruptcy' (2003) 15 *Bond Law Review*, 86; 'The Fatal Flaw in

International Finance: The Rich Borrow and the Poor Repay' XIX No 4 *World Policy Journal*, Winter 2002/2003, 59; 'A Tale of Two Crises: The Search for the Enduring Lessons of International Financial Reform' (2001) 6 *UCLA Journal of International Law and Foreign Affairs*, 1; 'An Oft-Ignored Perspective on the Asian Economic Crisis: The Role of Creditors and Investors' (2000) 15 *Banking and Finance Law Review*, 431; 'The Role of Capital Controls in International Financial Crises' (1999) 11 *Bond Law Review*, 231; 'The Facilitation of the Brady Plan: Emerging Markets Debt Trading from 1989 to 1993' (1998) 21 *Fordham International Law Journal*, 1802 and 'The Transformative Potential of a Secondary Market: Emerging Markets Debt Trading from 1983 to 1989' (1998) 21 *Fordham International Law Journal*, 1152.

Introduction

> Something is wrong with the global financial system. One might think the system would shift money from rich countries, where capital is in abundance, to those where it is scarce, while transferring risk from poor countries to rich ones, which are most able to bear it... The current global financial system does none of these things.[1]
>
> Joseph Stiglitz, Nobel Laureate in Economics, former Chief Economist of the World Bank, in 2003.

It is a mistake to think that our international financial system was designed to deal with today's international capital flows. It was not.

When in 1944 John Maynard Keynes and Harry Dexter White proposed three international organizations to guide and assist the international economy, the international financial system was utterly different to the one we have today. Nations existed largely as financial islands. Capital flows between them were miniscule by contemporary standards.[2] Capital controls were in place between national economies to regulate and often prevent transnational capital flows.

Today finance is perhaps our most globalized activity. The price of credit in the US affects the interest rates offered to home buyers in Australia. A currency crisis in Thailand and Hong Kong almost instantly affects share prices in Turkey and Hungary. The economic collapse of Russia sends the values of the 30-year US Treasury Bond to unprecedented highs. These changes have come about

---

1. J. Stiglitz, 'Dealing With Debt: How to Reform the Global Financial System' (2003) 25 *Harvard International Review* 54, 54.
2. Total debt flows were USD 13.4 billion in 1970, USD 272 billion in 2000 and USD 647 billion in 2006: *Global Development Finance 2002* (Washington DC, World Bank, 2002), p. 246 and *Global Development Finance* 2007, available at http://siteresources.worldbank.org.

principally due to capital account liberalization, the process by which barriers to capital flows between nations are eliminated and financial globalization thus facilitated.

This book has deliberately not addressed the many soft-law regulatory initiatives of the past decade. Much has been done, in the decade following the Asian crisis, in promulgating standards and formulating codes of conduct, that are available for adoption by national regulators. I have not dealt with these developments for two reasons. First, Doug Arner has done a splendid job of doing so in *Financial Stability, Economic Growth and the Role of Law*[3] and reinventing the wheel did not appeal. Secondly, as this book makes clear, I firmly believe that these initiatives, while worthy, are not being made at a sufficiently fundamental level to redress the systemic weaknesses of the international financial system. They are improvements, but to the edges, not the core of the problem.

The book focuses upon why we have a system that is so fundamentally deficient for debtors, but also for creditors, and what can be done about it, both by the debtor nations themselves, and at a system-wide level.

---

3. Cambridge University Press, 2007.

Chapter 1
History of the Global Financial System

1.1   HISTORY

Before we consider our current international financial architecture, it is useful to review a little history.

Sovereign debt crises are nothing new. Spain in the sixteenth century and France in the eighteenth are the most commonly cited examples. The sixteenth century King of Spain would sporadically receive shipments of bullion and treasure from his overseas empire. These he used to finance fighting in Italy, France and Holland. Alas, engaging in a war is like building a house, it usually costs more than you intended and can afford. The Spanish King made up the difference by borrowing from banking houses. Periodically, he could not afford the repayments and there was, in modern parlance, a combination of rescheduling and debt relief – maturities were extended and interest rates reduced. This happened more than once: in 1557, 1575, 1596, 1607, 1627 and 1647; to be precise. Yet the bankers had lent so much their fortunes were linked umbilically to those of the Hapsburg Empire and thus they continued to lend. The sixteenth century debt crisis lasted a century.[1]

In the eighteenth century, France funded its repeated and costly wars with England by borrowing from Swiss and Dutch bankers. After almost a century of a similar pattern of defaults, reschedulings and debt relief, the limits of the lenders were reached and the loans stopped. The French monarchy collapsed a few years later.

---

1. H. James, 'Deep Red – The International Debt Crisis and Its Historical Precedents' *The American Scholar* 331, 334–336 (Summer 1987). Modern national names are used for convenience to describe geographical regions.

The history of Latin American debt crises coincides with the rise of independent nations in the region in the 1820s. Most Latin American nations except Brazil engaged in large bond issuances in London in the 1820s. By 1828 all were in default.[2] A pattern soon emerged in lending to the region. Once the previous default had been resolved and capital was again abundant in Europe it would find its way to Latin America, usually by Europeans purchasing Latin bonds. Within a decade, the debtors would be unable to service the bonds and would default. For instance, capital flowed south in the 1860s. The collapse came in 1873. It flowed to Argentina in the 1880s, and led to the crisis of 1890. It again went to the region in the 1920s, and, with the Great Depression, almost 70% of Latin American sovereign dollar-denominated bonds and almost 90% of municipal, provincial and corporate bonds were in default by the mid-1930s.[3] The two principal exceptions to this region-wide default following the Great Depression were Argentina and Venezuela. Argentina sold off much of its gold reserves to service its national government bonds although it had to default on many of its provincial and municipal bonds. Venezuela had prepaid most of its debt before the Great Depression and did not default. Argentina honoured its national obligations to the letter throughout the 1930s and 40s. It never took advantage of the substantial concessions that were extended to Brazil and would have been forthcoming had Argentina threatened to default. Argentina repaid its national debts in full in gold and yet when capital did flow to the region, it did not receive access to it any earlier than its neighbours or at preferential interest rates.[4] Argentina did the right thing in the 1930s and 1940s for no reward.

In the overwhelming majority of sovereign debt crises, from the sixteenth century to the mid-twentieth century, sovereign debtors defaulted on their debts.

More recently, this pattern has changed, which is a theme to which we will return much later. But it is time to begin to understand where we are today, and to do that we must focus on the events of 1944.

With the end of World War II in sight, the Allied powers began to chart the post-war global economy. Foremost in their minds were two periods. From 1873 until World War I had been a period of general prosperity characterized by ever increasing trade and capital flows. The decade after World War I was, in sharp contrast, characterized by isolationism between countries and declining trade and

---

2. C. Marichal, *A Century of Debt Crises in Latin America* (Princeton, NJ, Princeton University Press, 1989), p. 43; and F.G. Dawson, *The First Latin American Debt Crisis: The City of London and the 1822–1825 Loan Bubble* (New Haven, Yale University Press, 1990).
3. Marichal, *A Century of Debt Crises in Latin America*, pp. 95, 96, 99, 120 and 149–150; D. Delamaide, *Debt Shock* (London, Weidenfeld & Nicholson, 1984), pp. 53–54; and M.E. Skiles, 'Latin American International Loan Defaults in the 1930s: Lessons for the 1980s?', Research Paper No. 8812 given at the Federal Reserve Bank of New York (New York, April 1988), pp. 1, 15.
4. J.D. Sachs, *Developing Country Debt and the World Economy*, J.D. Sachs (ed.), (Chicago, University of Chicago Press, 1989), p. 23; Marichal, *A Century of Debt Crises in Latin America*, p. 218; and P.H. Lindert and P.J. Morton, 'How Sovereign Debt Has Worked', in *Developing Country Debt and the World Economy*, J.D. Sachs (ed.), (Chicago, University of Chicago Press, 1989), pp. 231–232.

capital flows, and this led to the Great Depression of 1929. The Depression in many ways persisted until the advent of World War II. So it was to the forefront of the minds of those who designed the post-war system.

Because the architecture of the post-war financial system was designed principally by the US and UK it reflected rich country perspectives on the world economy and was designed to safeguard their economic interests. However, it also represented a rare moment of altruism: both nations were genuinely concerned with building a more prosperous and secure world. In President Harry S. Truman's words:

> A just and lasting peace cannot be attained by diplomatic agreement alone, or by military cooperation alone. Experience has shown how deeply the seeds of war are planted by economic rivalry and by social injustice. [. . .] [The UN Charter] has set up machinery of international cooperation which men and nations of good-will can use to help correct the economic and social causes for conflict.[5]

The highest priority of those who had lived through the Great Depression and the Second World War was to ensure that such a depression and war would never happen again. This spurred unprecedented cooperation that allowed the creation of new international institutions, including the United Nations, the World Bank and the International Monetary Fund. In addition to the scarring experience of the war, the Great Depression had a profound effect on those who lived through it. In the United States, for example, national income and production declined by 50% between 1929 and 1932 which rendered more than 14 million people unemployed. Accordingly, the delegates at Bretton Woods sought to create a stable international financial system upon which could be built a new post-war prosperity and full employment.[6]

Of particular relevance to lawyers is Bretton Woods' contribution to the general acceptance of a multilateral, rules-based approach to international economic relations. Notwithstanding humanity's long history of conflicts between nations over economic relations, 'the existence of a rules-based framework for the resolution of international economic conflicts can help promote cooperation'[7] and Bretton Woods was, in many ways, the first such framework to endure.

The architects of Bretton Woods were Britain's John Maynard Keynes and the United States' Harry Dexter White. Keynes was the most influential economist of his time, an Honorary Adviser to the British Treasury, and a regular advisor to the

---

5. Text of address to the plenary conference that created the United Nations, in S. Schlesinger, *Act of Creation: The Founding of the United Nations* (Cambridge, Westview Press, 2004), pp. 292–293.
6. A. Endres, *Great Architects of International Finance: The Bretton Woods Era* (London, Routledge, 2005).
7. R. Lastra, 'The Bretton Woods Institutions in the XXIst Century' in *The Reform of the International Financial Architecture*, R. Lastra (ed.) (London, Kluwer Law International, 2001), p. 69.

former US President, Franklin Delano Roosevelt. White was a former academic economist and Assistant to the Secretary of the US Treasury, Henry Morgenthau.[8]

From 1941, the two men independently started developing plans for the postwar economic order. They began to share their ideas from mid-1942 and, although the initial plans differed considerably in relation exchange rate flexibility and capital mobility, agreement was eventually reached on a joint plan, which was published in April 1944. This proposal formed the basis for negotiations with other nations at Bretton Woods. The final version was largely modelled on White's approach, which envisaged a stabilization fund to regulate exchange rate stability and address balance of payments problems and a global bank for reconstruction and development.[9]

It is not surprising that the final proposal was closer to White's version than Keynes' as the United States was the dominant partner in the wartime alliance and the stronger economic power. In 1945 it produced nearly half the world's industrial production.

The International Monetary and Financial Conference of the United and Associated Nations was held at Bretton Woods, New Hampshire, in July 1944 to formulate the ground rules for the new international financial system. It was attended by delegates from 45 nations. Developing and least developed nations had very little input at the conference, certainly relative to the input they seek to have today in the policy settings and operations of the IMF, World Bank and WTO. At the conference, there was a high degree of consensus among delegates about the problems of the interwar years. Conflict in international economic relations between the wars had often been characterized by the use of currency devaluations as a trade weapon and the imposition of trade restrictions.[10] Hence exchange rate stability was a particular focus of the new system, as was the need to guard against volatile capital flows.

The most difficult issue in Keynes' view was to determine the level of discretion nations should be allowed. The model agreement sought to strike a balance between facilitating international financial stability and allowing the accommodation of domestic policy priorities. Such trade-offs are rarely easy: rules are that overly rigid may leave nations little choice but to leave the international system, which is not conducive to international order. Yet a lack of rules may lead to international financial chaos. The final Anglo-American proposal opted for a strong element of national discretion: it included some strict requirements but most of the proposed articles of agreement were closer to guidelines.

---

8. *Ibid.*, p. 71; A. Van Dormael, *Bretton Woods: Birth of a Monetary System* (London, MacMillan Press, 1978), p. 42.
9. H. James, *International Monetary Cooperation Since Bretton Woods* (Oxford, International Monetary Fund and Oxford University Press, 1996), pp. 35–46.
10. V. Argy, *The Postwar International Money Crisis – An Analysis* (London, George Allen & Unwin, 1981), p. 2.

1.2 THE BRETTON WOODS SYSTEM

The delegates at Bretton Woods believed predictable exchange rates facilitated trade and yet sought to avoid the absolute rigidity of the gold standard under which currencies' values were tied to gold absolutely – a system that had broken down in the chaos that followed the onset of the Great Depression

The approach adopted at Bretton Woods was not as rigid as the gold standard but far less flexible than leaving rates to the market. A central feature was a system of fixed exchange rates that could be adjusted only in exceptional circumstances. This was enshrined in Article IV of the IMF Articles of Agreement, which provided that each member of the Fund agreed to maintain a fixed par value for its currency, expressed in gold or US dollars. Nations were expected to intervene in foreign exchange markets to keep the value of their currency within 1% of the par value. Par values could be changed but only to address a 'fundamental disequilibrium' and any proposed change of more than 10% from initial parity would require IMF approval. In addition, under Article VIII, the system would require nations to refrain from restricting current account convertibility, although Article XIV allowed for a transition in the removal of controls over currency transactions.[11]

The arrangements for exchange rate stabilization and multilateral currency convertibility were important pre-conditions for enhanced international trade in goods and services. However, both Keynes and White were deeply suspicious of international capital flows, especially where these resulted from speculative activity. Hence it was always envisaged that exchange rate stability would require nations to maintain capital controls.[12]

Based on the Anglo-American proposal, the Bretton Woods conference created two enduring international institutions: the IMF and the International Bank for Reconstruction and Development. The IBRD later became part of the World Bank group (a group of five related development institutions). The IBRD was to be 'a conduit for world capital intended for long-term investment projects'.[13] The IMF was to have a short-term, financial focus but the need for a mechanism for addressing balance of payments problems and a regulator to enforce the rules about adjustments meant that for Keynes and White the IMF was a critically important institution.

The importance of the third Bretton Woods institution – which would promote trade liberalization – was recognized prior to the conference within the

---

11. International Monetary Fund, 'What is the IMF?'; Endres, *Great Architects of International Finance*, pp. 14, 22–23; Argy, *The Postwar International Money Crisis – An Analysis*, p. 24.
12. Endres, *Great Architects of International Finance*, p. 19; James, *International Monetary Cooperation Since Bretton Woods*, pp. 38–39; Lastra, 'The Bretton Woods Institutions in the XXIst Century', p. 77.
13. Endres, *Great Architects of International Finance*, p. 22; see also World Bank, 'World Bank History' <web.worldbank.org>, 3 July 2007.

Anglo-American alliance and by conference participants. However conference negotiations did not address the creation of such a body:

> Certainly the most important ingredient of [US Secretary of State Cordell Hull's] vision of liberalization was the one that received least limelight at Bretton Woods: trade and the threat of protectionism. [. . .] Only in December 1945, well after the end of the war, did the US government launch an initiative for an International Trade Organization (ITO). By then it was too late.[14]

Ironically, US congressional support for the IMF was enhanced by including the promotion of trade as one of the Fund's objects, yet it was the US Congress that later effectively killed off the International Trade Organization by refusing to ratify the 1948 Havana Charter. The General Agreement on Tariffs and Trade (GATT) was salvaged from the wreckage of the ITO project but it was not until 1995 that the original vision was realized with the creation of the World Trade Organization (WTO).[15]

Of the two Bretton Woods institutions, the IMF is by far the most important for the functioning of the international financial system. The World Bank is a development institution focused on alleviating global poverty. The actions of the IMF have far greater effect on international finance. The aims of the IMF agreed at Bretton Woods were:

(i) To promote international monetary cooperation through a permanent institution which provides the machinery for consultation and collaboration on international monetary problems.

(ii) To facilitate the expansion and balanced growth of international trade, and to contribute thereby to the promotion and maintenance of high levels of employment and real income and to the development of the productive resources of all members as primary objectives of economic policy.

(iii) To promote exchange stability, to maintain orderly exchange arrangements among members, and to avoid competitive exchange depreciation.

(iv) To assist in the establishment of a multilateral system of payments in respect of current transactions between members and in the elimination of foreign exchange restrictions which hamper the growth of world trade.

(v) To give confidence to members by making the general resources of the Fund temporarily available to them under adequate safeguards, thus providing them with opportunity to correct maladjustments in their balance of payments without resorting to measures destructive of national or international prosperity.

(vi) In accordance with the above, to shorten the duration and lessen the degree of disequilibrium in the international balances of payments of members.[16]

---

14. Endres, *Great Architects of International Finance*, pp. 52–53.
15. Lastra, 'The Bretton Woods Institutions in the XXIst Century', p. 69.
16. International Monetary Fund, 'Articles of Agreement of the International Monetary Fund' <www.imf.org/external/pubs/ft/aa/index.htm>, 3 July 2007.

The IMF Articles of Agreement included rules for the adjustment mechanism to correct balance of payments imbalances and rules governing the provision of credit to member countries. An important feature was the creation of a quota system. Quotas were calculated primarily on the basis of each member country's national income, trade and international reserves. Under Article 3, members were required to pay their quota into the fund, with 25% payable in gold or US dollars and the remainder in the member's own currency. Most of the negotiations at Bretton Woods centred on the size of quotas, which were linked to voting power in relation to the Fund. Given the size of their economies, the United States and Britain had between them more than 40% of the total vote. Quotas were also significant because they determined the pool of resources from which the fund, under Article V, could provide assistance to members to address temporary financial difficulties.[17]

The IMF began to operate in 1946 and the IBRD provided its first loan in 1947. Yet their initial impact was somewhat muted. The IMF, for example, was initially hampered in its operations by the world's practical dependence on key currencies, especially the US dollar, and only really became significant with the achievement of full currency convertibility at the end of 1958. In addition, the main vehicle for post-war European reconstruction became the Marshall Plan rather than the IBRD, which played a strategic but limited role in providing loans to a few European countries, but far more quickly than initially intended began to work mostly with poor countries.[18]

1.2.1   PRESSURES ON THE BRETTON WOODS SYSTEM

The Bretton Woods system functioned effectively until the early 1970s. However, the par value system of managed exchange rates had defects: in particular, it was too rigid. Countries were reluctant to devalue in response to external imbalances, partly because devaluation was regarded as an admission of economic failure and partly because the Article IV requirement to notify the IMF might leave them vulnerable to currency speculation. The par value requirements discouraged countries from adjusting their exchange rates: they could not make significant changes in the absence of a 'fundamental disequilibrium' and hence were restrained in seeking to anticipate and head off problems. Small changes were unattractive because they might be insufficient to address underlying imbalances and yet would still signal an inclination towards further devaluations: hence such measures could be inherently destabilizing and provoke capital outflows.

---

17. James, *International Monetary Cooperation Since Bretton Woods*, p. 48; Argy, *The Postwar International Money Crisis – An Analysis*, pp. 23–25; Lastra, 'The Bretton Woods Institutions in the XXIst Century', pp. 80–81.
18. Argy, *The Postwar International Money Crisis – An Analysis*, pp. 22–23; James, *International Monetary Cooperation Since Bretton Woods*, pp. 66, 73, 84; World Bank, 'World Bank History'.

The limitations of rigid exchange rates became more evident with the growth of capital mobility and increasing porousness of capital controls.

Two political considerations also deserve mention. First, the emergence of the Cold War so soon after the end of the Second World War placed limitations on the degree of economic cooperation that could be achieved. Although the Soviet Union had been envisaged as an important member of the IMF, with one of the largest quotas, it never joined. Some Eastern bloc countries joined the IMF but later either left (e.g., Poland, Cuba) or were expelled (e.g., Czechoslovakia). As a result, a number of Communist countries were unable to benefit from the expansion of international trade in the post-war period.

Secondly, decolonization in the 1950s and 1960s resulted in the creation of many new nations, especially in Asia and Africa. Many of these former colonies required access to significant amounts of capital for economic development and therefore had a particular interest in World Bank assistance. However, they could not access World Bank assistance without joining the IMF. This period saw the greatest expansion of IMF membership: today the IMF has 184 members as compared to the 29 countries that signed the original Articles of Agreement in 1944.[19]

In the 1960s a new problem emerged due to the importance of the dollar for the world economy and its convertibility to gold under the IMF Articles of Agreement. The Triffin dilemma, named after Yale economist Robert Triffin, was a function of the fact that the Bretton Woods system effectively encouraged non-US reserve banks to accumulate dollar reserves in order to meet any excess demands. Such accumulation only made sense if convertibility could be guaranteed. However, the greater the accumulation of dollars relative to US gold reserves, the greater the potential threat to that guarantee.

The response to this problem was the development of new forms of international liquidity, in the form of Special Drawing Rights. However, Special Drawing Rights were initially opposed by strong currency countries and, by the time they became effective in the late 1960s, further liquidity was unhelpful given growing inflationary pressures.

In summary, Bretton Woods has become synonymous with the post-war expansion, yet in the eyes of some the history of the post-war period highlights the tensions that arose from reconstruction and the limitations of the system adopted:

> The institutions created at Bretton Woods were fundamentally unsuited to the combination of the international political climate of the early Cold War and the prevalence and persistence of the managed exchange and trade regimes inherited from the 1930s and the experience of war. The Marshall Plan and the initiatives associated with it, especially the European Payments Union, produced a much more effective immediate mechanism for promoting recovery and creating incentives for the earliest steps toward trade liberalization.[20]

---

19. International Monetary Fund, 'What is the IMF?'.
20. James, *International Monetary Cooperation Since Bretton Woods*, p. 83.

Nevertheless, the system was able to continue throughout the first two decades after World War Two, largely due to the strength of the US economy and the recoveries in Europe and Japan. Given the importance of the US dollar to the Bretton Woods system, for the system to be stable the US had a responsibility to maintain responsible fiscal and monetary policies. In the second half of the 1960s, such responsibility could no longer be assumed.

1.2.2 COLLAPSE OF THE BRETTON WOODS EXCHANGE RATE SYSTEM

Nations faced with a balance of payments imbalance have various responses available to them: they can devalue their currency, impose restrictions on the current account, impose capital controls, encourage trading partners to reduce trade barriers or adopt deflationary fiscal and monetary policies.

Only some of these options were practically available to nations of the Bretton Woods era. The scope to adjust currency values was restricted by the Bretton Woods exchange rate system. Nor did nations have much enthusiasm for increasing interest rates or curbing spending: in many Western countries, the post-war political consensus was based on increased social spending as a trade-off against wage demands. While a nation might be able to improve access to foreign markets, trade liberalization was typically a slow process.

Prior to current account convertibility, restrictions on the current account were the normal national response. However, this option was foreclosed by the move to current account convertibility. Although capital controls were permitted under the Bretton Woods system, capital controls were proving increasingly difficult to apply in practice because of growing capital mobility, especially given the growth of multinational corporations. At any rate, capital controls were not an effective adjustment mechanism: they might provide temporary respite but did not necessarily change the underlying rationale for capital outflows.

Hence in the 1960s balance of payments problems became increasingly difficult to manage without recourse to unpopular deflationary measures or changes to exchange rates of the kind that Bretton Woods was designed to avoid. It is therefore remarkable that the Bretton Woods exchange rate system survived as long as it did. One of the main reasons for its survival was the level of international cooperation between governments and central banks. Yet this cooperation came under increasing strain as the decade progressed. Leading economies and key US trading partners in Europe had an interest in maintaining stability and had been willing to resist pressures created by the increasing real value of gold against the dollar. However, because the dollar price of gold was fixed at USD 35 per ounce, the more the real value of gold exceeded this artificial peg, the stronger was the incentive for central banks to demand gold for dollars from the US Treasury. Furthermore, other countries became less enthusiastic about supporting the dollar (e.g., by selling their own gold reserves) when the US did not appear to be willing to contain its military and social spending to sustain the dollar price of gold.

Three factors came together to force the end of the Bretton Woods system: the inherent rigidity of the system itself, US spending on the Vietnam War and social programs, and the divergence of national responses. Had US trading partners like Germany and Japan been willing to accept higher rates of inflation, the system could have continued. In James' words,

> The crisis of the Bretton Woods system can be seen as a particular and very dramatic instance of the clash of national economic regulation with the logic of internationalism. In the circumstances of 1971, the disruption of the system followed very obviously and directly from the policies of the United States. [...] Once one country (the United States) decided to use the system for the sake of power politics, other members would legitimately object, the markets would realize the unsustainability of the divergent national positions, and begin to prepare for a collapse of the parity structure.[21]

Matters came to a head in 1971 because of massive flows away from the dollar and towards the deutsche mark. Inflationary fears in Germany stopped it from intervening to keep the mark down. Other European currencies also appreciated in value. The United States responded by suspending the convertibility of gold. The main western industrial nations tried to keep the system going by negotiating a new agreement on reform of the international monetary system at the Smithsonian Conference in late 1971. However, this agreement did not address underlying problems, such as the Triffin dilemma. The revaluation of the European currencies improved the competitiveness of US exports but this provided only temporary relief. A sell-off of sterling in 1972 forced Britain to float its currency outside the newly agreed band. This was followed by two further rounds of dollar flight because of an expectation of further US devaluations. The US negotiated devaluations against the major European currencies and the yen. However, as the sell-off of the dollar continued, Germany and other European nations jointly floated their currencies, effectively signalling the demise of the Bretton Woods accord.

Since then, the international financial system has been based on floating exchange rates. In due course, IMF members amended Article IV to specify that countries are free to choose any form of exchange arrangement they wish, provided they do not peg their currency to gold, including floating their currency or pegging its value to another currency or currencies.[22]

Although the par value system is gone, the IMF has developed new roles for itself in the post-Bretton Woods world economic order. The IMF is no longer a stabilization fund but has instead become a broader international financial institution focused on debtor nation crisis management, surveillance, conditional financial support and technical assistance. Not surprisingly, IMF financial support is of most relevance to developing nations, including those that swelled its ranks in the 1960s and again in the 1990s with the collapse of the Soviet Union.

---

21. James, *International Monetary Cooperation Since Bretton Woods*, p. 207.
22. Lastra, 'The Bretton Woods Institutions in the XXIst Century', p. 75; International Monetary Fund, 'What is the IMF?'.

History of the Global Financial System 11

1.2.3 THE INTERNATIONAL MONETARY FUND TODAY

The IMF plays a pivotal role today in shaping the interaction between developing countries and global capital. The IMF advises countries upon when and how to liberalize their financial systems and open up to global capital. In addition, for countries with an IMF program in place, the Fund has direct input into the fiscal and monetary policy settings of the country.

More than 90 IMF member states have sought loans or technical assistance from the IMF.[23] In the Debt Crisis that commenced in 1982, most African and Latin American countries sought IMF assistance. In recent years the IMF arranged bailout packages in the wake of the Asian crisis of 1997 and offered assistance following crises in Russia, Brazil, Turkey and Argentina. Countries that approach the IMF for assistance are often already in considerable financial difficulty and suffering from macroeconomic mismanagement.[24] The IMF provides loans to states to seek to correct balance of payments problems and promote economic growth by implementing adjustment policies and reforms. The IMF also offers technical assistance, aiding states in formulating and managing economic policy, and advising upon domestic banking systems, fiscal policy and management of public finances. Technical assistance is usually implemented by placing IMF staff in the relevant government departments of the recipient country and by training nationals of the recipient country (the IMF has established regional training centres in Africa, the Caribbean and the Pacific). Countries that adhere to IMF policy recommendations are eligible for assistance from the Fund's Poverty Reduction and Growth Facility.[25]

The IMF's financial support is contingent upon entering an 'arrangement' with the Fund. The arrangement requires that policies designed to restore financial balance be implemented. The country seeking assistance must provide the IMF with a 'Letter of Intent' that outlines the policies it intends to implement. The IMF website states that the policies are formulated by the country seeking financial assistance 'in consultation with the IMF'.[26] However the policies and procedures are often effectively imposed upon member states, leaving domestic governments with little scope for input. A government must demonstrate its commitment to the implementation of these economic policies.[27] The recommended policies are

---

23. International Monetary Fund, 'How the IMF helps to resolve economic crises' <www.imf.org/external/np/exr/facts.crises.htm>, 3 July 2007.
24. K. Rogoff, 'The IMF Strikes Back' <www.imf.org/external/np/vc/2003/021003.htm>, 4 December 2007; and J.P. Joyce, 'Through a glass darkly: New questions (and answers) about IMF programs' (Working Paper 2002–04, Wellesley College, 2002), pp. 2–3.
25. International Monetary Fund, 'Policy Statement on IMF Technical Assistance' <www.imf.org/external/pubs/ft/psta/index.htm>, 4 December 2007; and Joyce, 'Through a glass darkly: New questions (and answers) about IMF programs', p. 4.
26. International Monetary Fund, 'IMF Lending' <www.imf.org/external/np/exr/facts/howlend.htm>, 4 December 2007.
27. International Monetary Fund, 'IMF Conditionality: A Factsheet' <www.imf.org/external/np/exr/facts/conditio.htm>, 4 December 2007.

intended to reduce public debt and bring about economic stability. The prescriptions are well-intended; however they take decision-making out of the domestic realm. Domestic policymaking is replaced by policies imposed by IMF economists.[28]

Stiglitz suggests the IMF has overstepped its mandate by viewing all matters of domestic policy as factors that potentially contribute to economic instability, and thereby claiming input into a very wide range of domestic structural issues. These policies invariably impose the 'harsh fiscal austerity'[29] of the 'Washington Consensus'. The 'Washington Consensus' describes the policies advocated by the IMF, the World Bank and the United States Treasury, which include reduction of public expenditure, privatization of public enterprises, deregulation of financial systems and removal of barriers to trade. These policies reflect a quite extreme free market ideology. Stiglitz suggests these policies do not address the root causes of financial strife, which vary among countries. IMF policies regularly fail to address human rights issues such as healthcare and food shortages. Nonetheless, less-developed countries accept IMF prescriptions due to their weak bargaining power and acute financial need. IMF policies attract vigorous and increasing criticism regarding their formulation, implementation, lack of transparency and lack of accountability.[30]

Furthermore, if a country rejects IMF policies it will forfeit its right to assistance from the World Bank. The World Bank only offers credit to countries that comply with IMF policy prescriptions.[31]

Nonetheless, over the years several developing countries have chosen not to follow IMF prescriptions. China has enjoyed strong economic growth for two decades by charting its own, unique, economic course. China has a high degree of autonomy in setting its own policies due to the capital controls that isolate its financial system from the vagaries of global capital, the domestic ownership of its financial system, and the strong desire of foreign corporations to do business in China irrespective of the policy environment. Malaysia, Hong Kong, Chile and Colombia have also effectively implemented locally determined policies. These countries have all implemented policies the IMF would have opposed, such as capital controls, restrictions on speculative trading, and the retention and development of state-owned assets.

---

28. C. Santiso, 'Good Governance and Aid Effectiveness: The World Bank and Conditionality' (2002) 7 *Georgetown Public Policy Review* 1.
29. Rogoff, 'The IMF Strikes Back'.
30. S. George, 'A short history of neo-liberalism: Twenty years of elite economics and emerging opportunities for structural change', paper presented at the Conference on Economic Sovereignty in a Globalizing World (Bangkok, 24–26 March 1999) <www.zmag.org/CrisesCurEvts/Globalism/george.htm>, 4 December 2007; Joyce, 'Through a glass darkly: New questions (and answers) about IMF programs', p. 2; and K. Raffer, 'International Financial Institutions and Financial Accountability' (2004) 18 *Ethics and International Affairs*, 61.
31. World Bank, 'About Us' <www.worldbank.org/about>, 15 October 2003.

1.2.4 THE WORLD BANK

The World Bank (which includes the IBRD) still has a role in reconstruction, especially helping nations to rebuild after wars or natural disasters, but its main focus has long been on poverty alleviation, providing longer term funds for economic development. In the Bank's own words, 'its primary focus is on helping the poorest people and the poorest countries'.[32]

1.2.5 THE WORLD TRADE ORGANIZATION

Since 1995, the World Trade Organization has stepped into the role originally intended for the ITO but in a world in which the volume of world trade is far beyond anything the delegates at Bretton Woods might have imagined. In its words, the WTO 'is the only international organization dealing with the global rules of trade between nations. Its main function is to ensure that trade flows as smoothly, predictably and freely as possible'.[33]

The WTO was born out of the Uruguay Round of Multilateral Trade Negotiations that concluded in 1994. The Uruguay Round expanded the global trade regime from goods into services and intellectual property by virtue of GATS, the General Agreement on Trade in Services, and TRIPS, the Agreement on Trade Related Aspects of Intellectual Property Rights. Previously, intellectual property issues had been dealt with in UNCTAD, the United Nations Commission on Trade and Development, and WIPO, the World Intellectual Property Organization. The protection of intellectual property only enhances the economic development of a nation when the advantages of being able to produce goods, pharmaceuticals, movies and music by copying those produced in the developed world are no longer greater than the disadvantages of not protecting locally produced intellectual property and of foreign investment not being accompanied by the latest technology. This is quite a sophisticated level of development, so, understandably, in UNCTAD and WIPO the vast majority of developing countries voted against America's consistent attempts to improve intellectual property protection globally.[34]

Shifting the forum for intellectual property protection from UNCTAD and WIPO to the WTO was a clever move by the US but one that still required the assent of the developing countries by way of their agreement to TRIPS. This agreement was obtained as a *quid pro quo* for the promise by the US and EU of greatly liberalized access to their markets for the agricultural produce of developing countries. Yet once TRIPS was in place and enforceable, the promised access did not materialize for a host of reasons. Today the US and EU still subsidize their

---

32. World Bank, 'About Us'.
33. World Trade Organization, 'The WTO...in brief' <www.wto.org/english/thewto_e/whatis_e/inbrief_e/inbr00_e.htm>, 15 October 2003.
34. For an excellent account of this process, see J. Braithwaite and P. Drahos, *Global Business Regulation*, (Cambridge, Cambridge University Press, 2000), pp. 61–65.

agricultural producers extensively to the great detriment of developing country exporters. The WTO and TRIPS were founded on, as lawyers would put it, a consideration that failed – the full price for the promise was never received.

1.3 THE SYSTEM TODAY

The global economy has changed profoundly. In 1970 the capital that moved around the globe to support trade in goods and services far exceeded that which moved to support direct and portfolio investment. Today capital flows outweigh trade flows by a factor of over 60 to one.[35]

Yet this extraordinary statistic tells only part of the story of the profound, unprecedented changes in the world in which we live. You may have read that financial globalization currently is yet to reach the heights reached between 1870 and 1913. And it is true that the capital exports of the world's then capital-exporting countries, Britain, The Netherlands, France and Germany, were a larger proportion of their GDP than capital exports are today of the GDP of capital exporting countries. However these statistics tell only one-half of the story. For in the last years of the 19th century and the first of the 20th capital flows were all in the direction one would expect – from the capital-rich (such as Britain, France, Germany and Holland) to the capital-poor countries (such as Australia, Argentina, Canada and New Zealand). The truly surprising thing, and the reason the current globalization of capital flows is without historical precedent, is that today there are major capital flows from poor to rich countries (as rich individuals and companies in poor countries invest in developed countries), as well as from rich countries to poor countries.

If Keynes and White had looked out and seen the truly global financial system in place today, in which nearly all the economically significant nations are open to the inflow and outflow of global capital, it is reasonable to suppose they would have crafted for this system some of the institutions which each national financial system had, and has, in place:

(1) a bankruptcy regime;
(2) a financial regulator with enforcement powers; and
(3) a lender of last resort.

Yet none of these institutions exist at the global level. Their absence in the Keynes and White architecture was reasonable, for the world Keynes and White looked out upon was one of capital controls, and very limited transnational capital mobility. Their absence in today's highly globalized financial system is far more problematic, a theme we'll return to later in this book.

Before we consider how to improve the international financial architecture, however, it is important to understand how globalization has utterly transformed, and been itself shaped by, contemporary global capital flows.

---

35. P. Sutherland (1998) 'Managing the International Economy in an Age of Globalisation' (The 1998 Per Jacobsson Lecture, annual meeting of the IMF and the World Bank).

Chapter 2
Globalization and Global Capital Flows

Globalization can be defined in numerous ways. It has been said to be 'the development and deepening of world markets in capital, in goods and in services by the increasing occurrence of commercial exchanges across international boundaries' and 'the increasing tendency toward an interconnected worldwide investment and business environment'.[1]

My favourite definition of globalization comes from a former colleague, John Farrar, who said, simply, that globalization is all about convergence: convergence in markets in capital, goods, services and manufacturing methods, and convergence in cultures. Convergence, I find, is the most helpful way to think about this phenomenon. Globalization is very highly developed in finance, well developed in the trade of commodities and goods, and less so in services.

Globalization is about convergence, but it is not uniform or consistent. Capital markets, commodities markets, goods markets and cultures are all converging. However, wealth is not converging under globalization. The richest 20% of humanity owned 60 times as much as the poorest 20% in 1990, and 74 times as much in 2000.

Technology is not converging under globalization. In 2005, 86% of patents granted at the US, European and Japanese patent offices were granted to entities from only six countries: the US, Japan, Germany, Korea, France and the UK.[2] From 1977 to 2006, the least developed countries taken together were granted 48 patents by the US Patents and Trademark Office, which represented 0.0014% of

---
1. M. Warby, 'Review', *The Australian Financial Review*, 22 September 2000, p. 6 and Investorwords investing glossary <www.investorwords.com.html>, respectively.
2. OECD, *Compendium of Patent Statistics, 2007*, available at <www.oecd.org>, 13 Dec 2007.

total patents granted.[3] Less than 19% of the world's people have access to the internet, with access rates ranging from 70% in North America to 5% in Africa.[4]

Labour markets are not converging under globalization. As the wealth differential between rich and poor countries widens, so do the barriers keeping people out of the rich countries rise. In the previous period of strong financial globalization, from 1873 to 1913, an individual's mobility between nations was basically unimpeded. Globalization today favours free movement of capital, but not of labour. It allows capital to go where labour is cheap but doesn't allow labour to move to where the capital and expertise are located and where wages and work conditions are better.

So globalization is a very partial phenomenon. It is partial in that it affects some aspects of economies and societies profoundly and other aspects hardly at all. It also is partial in that it favours some nations over others and some people within a nation over others in that nation.

Globalization finds perhaps its fullest expression in global capital flows and capital markets. The level of financial integration within, and across, the international economy is high and increasing because capital is perfectly suited to a global market – it moves around the world at the touch of a keyboard, and in response to information that comes in, principally, on a computer screen. It is difficult to think of any other product for which the global market is more integrated, and for which events in one part of the world will almost instantly cause repercussions in other parts of the world.

Globalization is a product of two technological revolutions and an ideological one. The technological revolutions are in information and telecommunications – each of which, of course, is underpinned by the computing revolution. The ideological revolution is the victory of free market capitalism in the contest of ideologies – and, more specifically, the idea that free markets lead to an optimal allocation of resources and the highest levels of economic efficiency and growth. While these revolutions are recent, globalization is not a new phenomenon. The Roman Empire was the most important force for globalization the world had seen[5] and globalization introduced numerous Chinese initiatives to Europe in the 11th Century. In the words of Nobel laureate, Amartya Sen:

> high technology in the world of 1000 AD included paper and printing, the crossbow and gunpowder, the clock, the iron chain suspension bridge, the kite, the magnetic compass, the wheelbarrow and the rotary fan. Each one of these examples of high technology... a millennium ago was well-established and extensively used in China and... practically unknown elsewhere. Globalization spread them across the world, including Europe.[6]

---

3. Brooks World Poverty Institute, University of Manchester, *Ending World Poverty*, available at <http://povertyblog.wordpress.com/implementing-the-mdgs-and-other-statistics/>, 12 Dec 2007.
4. Internet World Stats, *Internet Usage Statistics*, available at <www.internetworldstats.com/stats.htm>, 12 Dec. 2007.
5. J. Braithwaite and P. Drahos, *Global Business Regulation*, pp. 40–45.
6. A. Sen, 'Global Doubts as Global Solutions' (Alfred Deakin Lecture, Melbourne, 15 May 2001) <www.abc.net.au/rn/deakin/stories/s296978.htm>, 4 December 2007.

Nonetheless, we live in a most unusual, and utterly unprecedented, world today: a world in which the poor lend money to the rich,[7] a world in which over one billion people struggle to survive on less than USD 1 per day yet massive amounts of capital slosh around the globe looking for productive uses, a world in which foreign capital pours into poor countries in good times and promotes growth in those countries, and then later withdraws leaving debt that typically severely damages the poor in these countries. As Sebastian Edwards has written,

> [e]conomists have long recognized that cross-border capital movements pose a difficult policy issue. In the absence of strong financial supervision in either lending or borrowing countries, unregulated capital flows may ... be misallocated, ... generating waves of major disruptions in the receiving nations.[8]

The globalization of capital flows and markets includes the following phenomena and trends:[9]

(1) Massive transnational capital flows are a fact of life and foreign investors in particular are opportunists. Foreign investors will move money into an economy quickly and in large quantities in good times and seek to remove it even more quickly when trouble looms.

(2) The nature and management of investors changed radically in the 1990s. The proportion of capital controlled by large institutional investors (mutual funds, pension funds, insurance companies etc) increased substantially. For instance, US mutual funds assets increased over four times between 1990 and 1997 from USD 1,067 billion to USD 4,490 billion.[10] Hedge funds brought aggressive new investment techniques to bear. More significantly, but with less publicity, virtually all major commercial and investment banks and securities firms established departments that function virtually as hedge funds, making extensive use of leverage and derivatives and the capacity to move in to and out of markets swiftly. Indeed, since the early 1990s, the entire money management industry has become far more performance-driven, less risk averse and more inclined to use leverage heavily.

(3) Access to up to the minute information facilitates investment decisions at great distances and foreign investors receive relatively homogenized information. Before the communications revolution, long-term investment was often the only sensible approach to foreign investment. Today an investment portfolio abroad can be managed as aggressively and

---

7. Or, at least, rich individuals and companies in poor countries invest in and lend to entities in rich countries.
8. S. Edwards 'How Effective Are Capital Controls?' (Working Paper No. 7413, National Bureau of Economic Research, November 1999) <www.nber.org/papers/w7413>, 20 March 2000.
9. The following factors owe much to H. Kaufman, 'Protecting against the next financial crisis: the need to reform global financial oversight, the IMF, and monetary policy goals' (1999) 34 *Business Economics* 56.
10. US Department of Commerce, *Statistical Abstract of the United States 1998* (118th ed.), p. 533.

intensively as if it is one's own country. Yet the sources of information for such investment decisions will be far less diverse than if it was in one's own country, with volatility-enhancing consequences for investor behaviour.

(4) Modern financial derivatives provide tremendous opportunities for hedging risks, but are perhaps more often used to facilitate speculation and as integral elements of volatility inducing activities.

(5) Liquidity is often illusory but temptingly easy to believe in. Capital markets that are deep and efficient in good times can rapidly become thin, volatile and illiquid in bad times. This is especially true of secondary markets in emerging markets debt and of access by developing countries to new money through debt issues.

(6) Due to the above factors, capital markets in the debt and equity of developed and developing nations are integrated and interdependent today to an unprecedented degree.

Each of these aspects of globalization increases the volume of capital flows to emerging market nations and the volatility of such flows.

The origin of the term 'emerging market' is a story that deserves telling. The term was coined in about 1984 by the International Finance Corporation, the commercial arm of the World Bank, while it was seeking a title for a LDC investment fund. The IFC had previously promoted the Third World Investment Trust, but investors had been nonplussed, perhaps because its acronym was unhelpful. So the IFC renamed the fund, The Emerging Markets Growth Fund, which proved to be a marketable name. The name began to increase in popularity and by the early 1990s had gained broad appeal as a non-pejorative alternative to 'third world' or 'less developed countries'.[11]

Globalization is a broad church, a process with many facets. One facet worth examining is its impact on human rights in developing countries. Globalization tends to increase the volume of portfolio capital flows to emerging market nations and the volatility of such flows. Indeed, there is considerable evidence that the globalization of financial markets increases the volatility of such markets.[12] In good times, these flows support growth in developing countries. In bad times they can cause appalling human suffering.

The globalization of capital markets gives countries access to new sources of capital. There is much evidence that capital markets discharge critical functions in

---

11. A. Soulard, 'The Role of Multilateral Financial Institutions in Bringing Developing Companies to U.S. Markets' (1994) 17 Fordham International Law Journal 145, p. 147.
12. J. Ayuso and R. Blanco, 'Has Financial Market Increased during the 1990's?', paper presented at the International Financial Markets and the Implications for Monetary and Financial Stability conference of the Bank for International Settlements (Basel, 25–26 October 1999); and P. Bustelo, C. Garcia and I. Olivie, 'Global and Domestic Factors of Financial Crisis in Emerging Economies: Lessons from the East Asian Episodes' (Working Paper No. 16, Instituto Complutense De Estudios Internationales, November 1999), p. 68.

the efficient allocation of capital,[13] that capital markets promote economic growth,[14] and that effective financial systems and access to foreign capital are critical to development. Indeed, an innovative and effective financial system was central to the growth and modernization of history's most successful 'emerging market', the United States of America in the first half of the 19th century.[15]

However, as all the economic crises since 1982 have demonstrated, generous access to foreign capital is often far from a good thing for developing countries. A slick intellectual trick is often perpetrated here. Free trade in goods and services is generally accepted among economists as welfare enhancing. It tends at times to cause severe change and economic dislocation in countries, but overall the result of free trade is a wealthier world. The trick is to assert that what holds for goods holds for money. Isn't money just another good? Legally it is often treated as such.[16] Experience tells us otherwise. The difference is that capital has to be repaid.

Capital is only welfare enhancing if put to productive uses that generate returns in excess of the cost of the capital. The failure by Latin America to do this with the massive loans of the 1970s led to the debt crisis of the 1980s. The inability of the East Asian financial systems to channel the increased capital flows of the early and mid-1990s into productive uses contributed significantly to the Asian crisis of 1997. The Asian economies were performing strongly before foreign capital flows to the region increased due to local capital market liberalization, surplus liquidity in the US, and the dissuasive effect the Mexican peso crisis in late 1994 had on further capital flows to Latin America.[17] It is therefore not surprising that the increased capital flows of the 1990s ended up fuelling speculative bubbles in stock and real estate markets in Asia. Likewise, Argentina's excessive borrowing in the 1990s for general revenue purposes (with which the IMF agreed) was a major contributor to that country's economic collapse at the end of the decade.

The clearest lesson of the recent economic crises is that unfettered capital mobility is not necessarily welfare enhancing and not an unmitigated good.[18]

---

13. J. Wurgler 'Financial Markets and the Allocation of Capital' (2000) (unpublished manuscript). Wurgler found the efficiency of capital allocation to be positively correlated with the amount of firm-specific information in local stock markets and with the legal protection of minority shareholders.
14. R.G. King and R. Levine, 'Finance and Growth: Schumpeter Might Be Right' (1993) 108(3) *The Quarterly Journal of Economics*, 717; R.G. King and R. Levine, 'Finance, entrepreneurship and growth' (1993) 32 *Journal of Monetary Economics*, 513; and R. Levine and S. Zervos 'Stock Markets, Banks, and Economic Growth' (1998) 88(3) *The American Economic Review*, 537.
15. P.L. Rousseau and R. Sylla, 'Emerging Financial Markets and Early U.S. Growth' (Working Paper No. 7448, National Bureau of Economic Research, December 1999).
16. F.A. Mann, *The legal aspect of money: with special reference to comparative private and public international law* (Oxford, Clarendon Press, 5th ed., 1992).
17. R.P. Buckley, 'An Oft-Ignored Perspective on the Asian Economic Crisis: The Role of Creditors and Investors' (2000) 15 *Banking and Finance Law Review*, 431.
18. R.P. Buckley, 'International Capital Flows, Developing Countries and Economic Sovereignty' *Yearbook of International Economic and Financial Law 1999* (London, Kluwer Law International, 2001); N. Lustig, 'Crises and the Poor: Socially Responsible Macroeconomics' (Presidential Address to the Fourth Annual Meeting of the Latin American and Caribbean Economic Association, Santiago, Chile, 22 October 1999).

The huge loans to Latin America of the 1970s brought 'massive returns to the rich'.[19] However, when these loans had to be repaid in the 1980s they were repaid by increasing taxes, reducing price supports on essential items and cutting spending on public health care, public education and public infrastructure. The rich benefited from the loans, the common people and the poor repaid them.

Likewise in Asia the boom in portfolio capital flows and lending to the region in the early to mid-1990s principally benefited the rich. The dislocation and impoverishment brought on by the crisis in 1997 has, however, fallen far more heavily on the shoulders of the common people and the poor. With the exception of Indonesia, Asia recovered far more quickly from its crisis than Latin America and sub-Saharan Africa were able to recover from the 1982 crisis. Nonetheless, the profound difference between those who benefit when international capital flows in, and those who suffer when it flows out, has been maintained.

As Nora Lustig has written, 'Macroeconomic crises, with the exception of wars, are the single most important cause of large increases in ... poverty'.[20] In Charles Calomiris' words, 'When the crisis has passed, the big winners are the wealthy, politically influential risk takers, and the biggest losers are the taxpayers in countries like Mexico or Indonesia'.[21]

This transfer of responsibility onto the poor is depressingly consistent and is examined in some detail in the final chapter of this book.

The role of the creditors and investors in the creation of the excessive indebtedness is widely overlooked. This is unsurprising. Most commentators on the international financial system, academic and journalistic, are from developed countries and that they should, in the main, incline to the creditors and investors' perspective is to be expected. As a result, it is this perspective that tends to dominate the national debate on these matters. (Furthermore, the quickest research for scholars to write is that which systematizes, interprets and analyses the ideas of others: groundbreaking research that challenges the orthodox view requires extensive support from statistics and data whereas research that confirms the orthodox view needs merely to cite the work of others. A scholars' career is more likely to be served by subscribing to the orthodox views than by challenging them. Accordingly, considerable pressures within academe conspire to promote the production of essentially derivative scholarship and thus reinforce the tendency for one perspective to dominate the literature in developed countries.)

It is time for a new framework for understanding responsibility in international lending. Lending and borrowing are joint activities, one cannot occur without the other, but in the international context the prevailing presumption is that bad loans and bad investments are entirely the debtors' fault. This is a convenient fiction for international banks and investors, but it is a fiction with severe consequences, as the next chapter establishes.

---

19. 'A Survey of Latin America', *The Economist* (United Kingdom), 13 November 1993.
20. Lustig, 'Crises and the Poor: Socially Responsible Macroeconomics'.
21. C.W. Calomiris, 'The IMF's Imprudent Role as Lender of Last Resort' (1998) 17 *Cato Journal*, 275, pp. 276–277.

Chapter 3
The Latin American and African Debt Crisis of 1982

3.1 THE DEBT CRISIS OF 1982

The debt crisis that erupted in 1982 was the most damaging and far reaching financial crisis of the post-war 20th century.[1] Since then we have had major crises in Mexico in 1994, East Asia in 1997, Russia in 1998 and Argentina in 2001 as well as a host of more localized crises. These have superseded the debt crisis in the public imagination to the extent that the Asian crisis was described, by no less than the Managing Director of the IMF, as 'the most severe crisis of the last fifty years'.[2] This is plain silly. The debt crisis brought the international financial system to the edge of total collapse – the Asian crisis had no such effect. The total exposure of US banks to developing countries at year-end 1982 was 287.7% of total capital. Exposure to Latin America alone represented some 176.5% of bank capital. The 1983 exposure of the nine largest US banks to only three countries, Mexico,

---

1. D. Delamaide, *Debt Shock* (London, Weidenfeld & Nicholson, 1984); J. Levinson, 'The International Financial System: A Flawed Architecture' (1999) 23 *Fletcher Forum of World Affairs*, 1; Marichal, *A Century of Debt Crises in Latin America*, p. 95; United Nations Economic Commission for Latin America and the Carribbean & United Nations Centre on Transnational Corporations (ECLAC/CTC), *Transnational Bank Behaviour and the International Debt Crisis* (Santiago, Chile, United Nations, 1989); and P.A. Wellons, *Passing the Buck – Banks, Governments and Third World Debt* (Boston, Harvard Business School Press, 1987).
2. M. Camdessus, 'Development and Poverty Reduction: a Multilateral Approach' (Address by the Managing Director of the IMF at the Tenth United Nations Conference on Trade and Development, Bangkok, Thailand, 13 February, 2000); and see Gengatharen who spouts the nonsense that the Asian crisis is probably the worst economic crisis on record and worse than the Great Depression: R. Gengatharen, 'Destabilising Financial Flows: Are Capital Controls the Solution?' [1999] *LAWASIA Journal*, 12, 13.

Brazil and Argentina, was 115% of the capital of those banks.[3] A repudiation by one major debtor at this time could readily have led to a total collapse of the short-term interbank market upon which most banks relied for liquidity.

Likewise, the impact of the debt crisis on the debtor nations was far more widespread, severe, and long-reaching than that of the Asian crisis. The debt crisis affected all of Latin America and most of sub-Saharan Africa. The Asian crisis affected Indonesia, Korea, Malaysia, the Philippines and Thailand. The debt crisis lasted much longer and was much more severe. The debt crisis lasted from 1982 until around 1993 for most Latin American countries and until the debt relief initiatives of 1999 for sub-Saharan Africa. In contrast, by the end of 1999 only Indonesia was not well on the way to recovery from the Asian crisis of 1997.[4]

One estimate puts the economic cost of the Latin American debt crisis in the 1980s at over two percentage points of growth per year.[5] In human terms, the 1980s was a lost decade in Latin America. In one commentator's words, writing in 1995:

> the region [is] burdened with a crumbling infrastructure of potholed roads, electricity blackouts and water shortages which will take decades to make good...and terrible damage [has been inflicted] on the poor. By 1993, 60 million more Latin Americans had been driven below the poverty line, bringing the total to nearly half of the population.[6]

During the 1980s, spending per capita on health care decreased by 50% in 37 poor countries.[7] UNICEF has calculated that in 1988 alone about 500,000 young children died due to the debt crisis and its domestic and international management.

The principal cause of the debt crisis was simple. The borrowers borrowed too much and the lenders lent too much. In particular, the borrowers failed to put the borrowed funds to work to earn a return higher than the interest rate on the funds; as is required if debt is to be repaid. And the lenders lent knowing that the funds, in the main, were not being put to such productive uses. The debt crisis was most aptly named – it was primarily a crisis brought on by too much borrowing and too much lending.

The massive flows of debt began in earnest to Latin America in the early 1970s and already by mid-1974 some bankers were expressing grave concerns. In the

---

3. J.D. Sachs, 'Introduction', in *Developing Country Debt and the World Economy*, J.D. Sachs (ed.) (Chicago, University of Chicago Press, 1989), p. 11; and Aronson, 'International Lending and Debt' (1983) 6:4 *The Washington Quarterly*, 62, 68.
4. East Asia Analytical Unit, *Asia's Financial Markets: Capitalising on Reform* (Canberra, Dept of Foreign Affairs and Trade, 1999), p. 37.
5. B. Eichengreen, *Financial Instability* (Paper prepared on behalf of the Copenhagen Consensus, 2004).
6. D. Green, 'Hidden fist hits the buffers', *New Internationalist*, October 1995, 35.
7. Testimony of Dr R. Jolly, Deputy Executive Director for Programmes, United Nations Children's Fund, before the House Committee on Banking, Finance and Urban Affairs hearings on the *International Economic Issues and Their Impact on the U.S. Financial System*, 4 January 1989, 101st Congress First Session, 14, 15.

words of David Rockefeller, Chairman of Chase Manhattan Bank, as reported on the front page of *The Wall Street Journal*, 6 June 1974:

> Channeling massive flows of oil dollars from dollar-rich to dollar-poor countries once seemed easily manageable. But now it looks more troublesome... My own view... is that the process of recycling through the banking system may already be close to the end for some countries, and in general it is doubtful this technique can bridge the [payments] gap for more than a year or at the most 18 months.[8]

Likewise, in 1976 Emma Rothschild wrote that, 'The question for the financial system is not whether these debts will be dishonored. Rather, it is an issue of when, and how, and where.'[9]

But I am ahead of myself. Let's go back to the beginning: to the origins of the loans.

3.2 THE LOANS OF THE 1970s: THEIR ORIGINS AND DESTINATIONS

The traditional sources of foreign capital for the region before 1970 were foreign investment in bonds, direct investment, official loans and supplier's credits.[10] In this regard, the development of South America parallels that of North America. The development of the United States in the nineteenth century was mainly financed by issuing bonds, principally to European non-bank investors, and the defaults, of which there were plenty, therefore did not threaten the financial system.[11]

In the early 1970s major commercial banks began to lend to Latin America. The lenders were now banks, not investors in bonds, projects or exports. For the first time in history the major thrust of development finance was commercial bank lending.[12] The stakes had suddenly been dramatically increased and few seemed

---

8. C. Stabler, 'Mideast Oil Money Proves Burdensome', *The Wall Street Journal* (New York), 6 June 1974, 1, 29 (as reproduced in Wellons, *Passing The Buck – Banks, Governments And Third World Debt*, p. 23. Of course, other bankers were of a different view. Walter Wriston, Chairman of Citibank, was quoted in the same *Wall Street Journal* article as saying, 'The Great Crisis... ain't going to happen'.
9. As quoted in D. Delamaide, *Debt Shock: The Full Story of the World Credit Crisis* (Garden City, NY, Doubleday, 1984), p. 15.
10. F.G. Dawson, *The First Latin American Debt Crisis: The City of London and the 1822–1825 Loan Bubble* (New Haven, CT, Yale University Press, 1990), p. 237; R.A. Debs, D.L. Roberts and E.M. Remolona, *Finance for Developing Countries – Alternative Sources of Finance – Debt Swaps* (New York and London, Group of Thirty, 1987), p. 10.
11. C. Lewis, *America's Stake in International Investments* (Washington, DC, Brookings Institute, 1938) pp. 17–24, 30, 35, 36–39, 45–48.
12. B. Eichengreen and R. Portes, 'After the Deluge: Default, Negotiation, and Readjustment during the Interwar Years', in *The International Debt Crisis in Historical Perspective*, B. Eichengreen and P.H. Lindert (eds) (Cambridge, MIT Press, 1989), pp. 40–41; and

aware of the change. Any major default would now hurt a relatively small group of major banks and the repercussions could potentially disable the entire international financial system.

3.2.1 THE LENDERS

So which banks were making these loans? A United Nations study identified three groups of lenders – leaders, challengers and followers – in these terms:[13]

> The 'leader' banks were all United States banks and essentially dominated syndicated lending in the 1970s. They were Citicorp, Chase Manhattan, BankAmerica, J.P. Morgan and Manufacturers Hanover.
>
> The 'challenger' banks were from North America, Europe and Japan and competed aggressively with the leaders for the lending business. They included Lloyds, Bank of Montreal, Bank of Tokyo, Bankers Trust, Chemical, Canadian Imperial Bank of Commerce, Toronto Dominion, Commerzbank, Bank of Nova Scotia and Long Term Credit Bank of Japan.
>
> The 'follower' banks were all non-US and had a strong interest in lending to the region without being as aggressive as the leaders and challengers. They included National Westminster, Deutsche Bank, Barclays, Dresdner, West Deutsche LB, Royal Bank of Canada, Midland Bank, Credit Lyonnais, Industrial Bank of Japan and Banque Nationale de Paris.

In addition, thousands of other banks participated in one or more syndicated loans to the region.[14] Different groups of lenders lent for different reasons. The leaders were very aggressive in marketing these loans and came to 'depend on income from special deals with riskier clients willing to pay higher fees, commissions and interest to gain market access.'[15] The lead banks in the 1970s became rather addicted to the 'profit hit' from fees from large syndicated loans. As Buchheit identified in 1983, " 'front-end' fees in international lending, when taken into bank income in the quarter or year in which they are charged, provide a potentially unhealthy added incentive for banks to seek out international loans in order to boost earnings immediately.'[16] The leaders lent principally to maximize this quarter's profits and less to gain market share. In contrast, the challenger banks, seeking

---

R.A. Debs, D.L. Roberts and Remolona, *Finance for Developing Countries – Alternative Sources of Finance – Debt Swaps*, p. 10.
13. ECLAC/CTC, *Transnational Bank Behaviour and the International Debt Crisis*.
14. Brazil had over 450 bank creditors in 1982 (see United Nations Centre on Transnational Corporations, *Debt Equity Conversions – A Guide for Decision-makers* (New York, United Nations, 1990), p. 23 (hereafter 'UNCTC')) and over 1,500 US banks were involved in lending to the region.
15. UNCTC, *Debt Equity Conversions – A Guide for Decision-makers*, p. 24.
16. L.C. Buchheit, 'Tightening controls on international lending by US banks' (May 1983) *International Financial Law Review*, 14, 15.

a higher international profile, were more motivated by increased market share than by profits.[17]

The leader banks opened up most of these markets. Initially, they led the charge in lending to Argentina, Brazil and Mexico. The challengers soon acquired proficiency in this business and began to acquire market share by undercutting interest rates and fees. Rather than compete too aggressively on the basis of price, the leaders established new markets by lending to nations such as Bolivia, Peru and Uruguay and to private sector corporations.[18]

3.2.2   THE BORROWERS

The nature of the lenders in the 1970s was not the only factor without significant historical precedent. In earlier lending booms, such as the 1920s, the majority of loans were to national, provincial or municipal governments.[19] In the 1970s the majority of loans were to the major industrial, petroleum and energy corporations of the region (many of which were wholly or partially state-owned). The other major borrowers were the state-owned development banks which sought foreign funds to relend in their own countries on a wide range of industrial projects as Latin America strove to fulfill its promise as the world's new economic powerhouse.[20]

3.3   CAUSES OF THE LATIN AMERICAN AND AFRICAN DEBT CRISIS

Many commentators are in no doubt as to the causes of the crisis – it is simply that they disagree one with the other.[21] The consensus of many bankers is well expressed by Rimmer de Vries:

> The attention lavished on LDC debt problems since 1982 has built a consensus on the root causes of the trouble – the debtor's inappropriate demand

---

17. UNCTC, *Debt Equity Conversions – A Guide for Decision-makers*, p. 23.
18. ECLAC/CTC, *Transnational Bank Behaviour and the International Debt Crisis*, pp. 89 and 105.
19. Marichal, *A Century of Debt Crises in Latin America*, p. 235; E. Jorgensen and J.D. Sachs, 'Default and Renegotiation of Latin American Foreign Bonds in the Interwar Period', in *The International Debt Crisis in Historical Perspective*, Eichengreen and Lindert (eds), p. 53.
20. Marichal, *A Century of Debt Crises in Latin America*, p. 235. The most important corporate borrower in the international financial markets in this period was Pemex, the Mexican oil company, and other major borrowers, were Petrobras and Electrobras of Brazil, Ecopetrol of Columbia, Agua y Energia of Argentina and Petroperu.
21. Few topics engender such polarized debate as the causes of the crisis. Some writers even disagree with themselves: 'The US [financial community], however, deserves very little direct blame for the debt problem... To be sure, many US banks behaved irresponsibly in the 1970s by making vast sums of credit available to Latin American countries which were becoming ever less credit worthy': E.W. Hannan and E.L. Hudgins, 'A U.S. Strategy for Latin America's Debts', *The Backgrounder*, No. 502, 7 April 1986 (The Heritage Foundation, Washington, DC).

management and resource allocation policies prior to 1982, and their inadequate adjustment to the adverse global environment that followed.[22]

Fifteen years after the debt crisis, the initial response of the IMF and the creditors to the Asian crisis echoed the same 'blame-the-debtors' sentiments. To pretend the loans and investments were sound when made and have since gone off the rails due to the debtors' fault is a convenient fiction for creditors and investors. However, from a broader perspective, the causes of the debt crisis are more numerous and varied. Four are generally identified: petrodollar recycling, bank behaviour, debtor nations' policies, and external factors such as interest and exchange rates. Each will be considered.

3.3.1 Recycling of OPEC Funds

In 1974 a new reason for lending to Latin America came out of the east – the Organization of Petroleum Exporting Countries (OPEC) cartel. The quadrupling of oil prices by OPEC in 1973–74[23] resulted in a large transfer of funds to OPEC which, in turn, deposited them in western banks. By the end of 1975, USD 13.8 billion had flowed from OPEC into the six largest US banks.[24] The oil price rises had initiated a recession in industrial countries so demand for these funds was weak. However, the banks found a market in the countries that then were known as less developed countries (LDCs) and now are called the emerging markets. While the industrial world adjusted and reduced its demand for oil, adjustment was far slower in LDCs that were bent on a path of industrialization, on 'catching up'. The process came to be known as recycling. Funds flowed from Latin America and the developed nations to OPEC as payments for oil; from OPEC to the major banks as Euromarket deposits, and from the banks to Latin America as loans. Once again, a surplus of capital in creditor countries was funding a lending boom in Latin America.[25]

This recycling of OPEC funds was presented as a positive social good for the world economy: 'banks were applauded for smoothing the transition to higher oil prices'.[26] Yet there was another aspect to it. The trade and lending policies that France, Germany, Japan, and the United Kingdom adopted in response to the first oil shock were designed to improve their trade balances and generate the funds for

---

22. R. de Vries, Chief Economist, Morgan Guaranty Trust Company, 'Economic and trade adjustment in the United States and other industrial countries and The LDC debt issue: problems and prospects' (Statement to The Asahi-Zeit Symposium, Tokyo, 29–30 March 1988), p. 21.
23. The price of oil was USD 3.01 per barrel in July 1973. It was raised by OPEC to USD 11.65 effective from 1 January 1974: 'Selected Statistics on World Oil', HBS Case Services, No. 380-144.
24. P.A. Wellons, *World Money and Credit – The Crisis and Its Causes* (Boston, Division of Research, Harvard Business School, 1983), p. 23.
25. Marichal, *A Century of Debt Crises in Latin America*, pp. 95 and 41–42; and B. Stallings, *Banker to the Third World: U.S. Portfolio Investment in Latin America, 1900–1986* (Berkeley and Los Angeles, University of California Press, 1987), pp. 294–295.
26. Aronson, 'International Lending and Debt', 66.

oil.[27] Much of the export drive of these nations was aimed at LDCs, 'in effect shifting to them the G-5 trade deficits with OPEC and using bank credits to make the shift possible'.[28] For example, France in 1973, before the oil shock, had a trade surplus of USD 500 million with its former colonies in Africa. Five years later France had a trade surplus of USD 2.2 billion with the same former colonies. The massive southward flow of funds in the 1970s permitted the LDCs to increase imports from the developed nations which sustained economic growth in the developed world.

In short, in the 1970s LDCs chose to consume goods from the developed world and oil from OPEC nations on a deferred payment plan. The banks, with encouragement from their home governments,[29] chose to fund this deferred payment plan. The banks, their home governments and the borrowers all benefited from the plan in the short-term. No one gave much attention to the question of repayment.

3.3.2 BANK BEHAVIOUR

The leader banks identified earlier contributed directly to the lending boom of the 1970s. As a United Nations study discovered:

> leaders showed a greater tendency to aggressively sell higher priced loan packages to borrowers traditionally denied access to international credit markets altogether or who were at least denied such large amounts of funds. Although there was no alteration in the risk characteristics which relegated them to the margin of international borrowing, these borrowers suddenly found leaders seeking to persuade them to take on huge credits which they had not contemplated borrowing.[30]

Put more pithily, 'the banks sent salesmen to Mexico, not analysts.'[31] As one international loan officer in the 1970s reflected:

> As a domestic credit analyst, I was taught to develop reasonable asset security for all loans unless the borrower was of impeccable means and integrity. As an international loan officer, I was taught to forget about that, and instead to develop a set of rationales that would make the home office feel good about the loan, even though, technically, it was "unsecured".[32]

---

27. Wellons, *Passing The Buck – Banks, Governments And Third World Debt*, pp. 58–63. The fifth G-5 nation, the United States opted for an inflationary response to the oil shock: *ibid.*, p. 59.
28. *Ibid.*, p. 61–62.
29. Wellons argues persuasively that the role of the G-5 governments is often understated in analyses of the debt crisis: *Ibid.*, p. 53.
30. ECLAC/CTC, *Transnational Bank Behaviour and the International Debt Crisis*, pp. 11–12.
31. Delamaide, *Debt Shock: The Full Story of the World Credit Crisis*, p. 102. On the issue of aggressive salesmanship of these loans, see also Pieder Konz, 'The Third World Debt Crisis', (1989) 12 *Hastings International and Comparative Law Review* 527, 528.
32. S.C. Gwynne, 'Adventures in the Loan Trade', *Harpers'*, September 1983, 22, 24.

This behaviour accorded with history. In investigating a spate of loans to Latin America that all rapidly went into default in the mid-1870s, a subcommittee of the English House of Commons found that banks 'seem to have been regardless of the financial resources of the borrowing State; such resources, if inquired into, would have been found to have been totally inadequate to meet the liabilities incurred.'[33] The lending booms of the 1870s[34] and 1920s were fuelled by hard salesmanship, paid agents and bribes to officials of borrowing countries. Bribery was so common in the 1920s that only two major US banks refrained from it.[35]

In hindsight, the overlending of the banks to the region was a major cause of the debt crisis.[36] Many commentators believe that the banks consciously overlent to the region. In the words of Jeffrey Sachs,

> Few banks, apparently, were concerned with the question of whether the debtor countries would be willing and able to service their debts if debt servicing had to come out of national resources rather than out of new loans. This issue seemed to be an abstract concern, at least through the end of the 1970s.... New lending to repay old loans made sense in the circumstances.[37]

There were many reasons for the lending boom of the 1970s. One of the principal ones – surplus capital in the northern hemisphere – has already been considered. There are at least another eight: the passage of time and ignorance of history, the inexperience of the banks, the quest for greater profits, the promotion of individual bankers' careers, the strength of the borrowers' economies, the rise of syndicated lending, the innovation of floating rate interest and the position of US banks at home. Each will be considered.

3.3.2.1   Time and Ignorance of History

Enough time had elapsed since the defaults of the 1930s for a new generation of bankers to be in control of lending and to 'rediscover' Latin America.[38] Banking, as an industry, has a short memory,[39] and international financial history is not part of the education of most bankers. In the words of Frank Griffith Dawson:

> the semi-comic, semi-tragic first Latin American debt crisis and its aftermath demonstrate that when financiers and investors choose to ignore

---

33. The *Report from the Select Committee on Loans to Foreign States* (1875) at xlvi. These words, perfectly apposite in 1985, are from an investigation in 1875 into the lending frenzy of 1870–1873.
34. L. Jenks, *The Migration of British Capital to 1875* (New York, Knopf, 1927), pp. 292–293.
35. Skiles, 'Latin American International Loan Defaults in the 1930s: Lessons for the 1980s?', p. 10.
36. ECLAC/CTC, *Transnational Bank Behaviour and the International Debt Crisis*, pp. 50–51.
37. Sachs, 'Introduction', in *Developing Country Debt and the World Economy*, p. 9.
38. Dawson, *The First Latin American Debt Crisis: The City of London and the 1822–1825 Loan Bubble*, p. 237.
39. Eichengreen and Lindert, *The International Debt Crisis in Historical Perspective*, p. 4.

history, they are destined to repeat the disasters of the past on an even grander scale.[40]

The indisputable fact that, 'since independence, debt crises have been a permanent feature of the history of Latin America, being linked to the boom and bust cycles of the economies of the region'[41] did nothing to slow the lending frenzy of the 1970s.

3.3.2.2 Inexperience of the Banks

It is easy to assume the bankers making the massive loans of the 1970s were experienced in lending to LDC sovereigns and corporations. Usually they were not. In the early 1980s the chief economist of the Bank for International Settlements said

> Banks have had a hundred years to learn how to make a loan to the butcher on the corner. They've had only ten years to learn how to evaluate a sovereign risk.[42]

Gwynne, in analyzing the loan selling industry of the 1970s said:

> The world of international banking is now full of aggressive, bright, but hopelessly inexperienced lenders in their mid-twenties... Their bosses are often bright but hopelessly inexperienced twenty-nine year old vice presidents with... so little credit training they would have trouble with a simple retail installment loan. Their bosses, sitting on the senior loan committee, are pragmatic, nuts-and-bolts bankers whose grasp of local banking is profound, ... [but who] are fish out of water when it comes to international lending.[43]

In particular, the banks overlooked the extraordinarily high performance correlations between debtors across the LDC sector which mean that when defaults occur, they tend to occur across the sector. This is a classic error in modern portfolio theory and banks should have had a far closer eye on their overall portfolio risk.

Most of the creditor banks had taken their first steps in the early 1970s into a whole new field of lending.[44] Many of the smaller banks were simply playing 'follow the leader'. They entered into a new field of lending with little capacity to make independent credit decisions. Many of the smaller banks had little, if any, appreciation of Latin America and the complexities of lending to sovereigns and corporations in LDCs and little, if any, capacity in-house to analyse the issues in

---

40. Dawson, *The First Latin American Debt Crisis: The City of London and the 1822–1825 Loan Bubble*, p. 236.
41. Marichal, *A Century of Debt Crises in Latin America*, p. 238.
42. Statement of Alexandre Lamfalussy, quoted in Delamaide, *Debt Shock*, p. 50.
43. S.C. Gwynne, *Adventures in the Loan Trade*, Harpers', September 1983, p. 23.
44. R.D. Sloan, 'The Third World Debt Crisis: Where We have Been and Where We Are Going' (Winter 1988) *The Washington Quarterly*, 105.

this international context.[45] They simply relied on the large lead banks. In the words of an OECD study, 'there is ample evidence that during the boom of the international syndicated loan market many banks participated in lending syndicates on the basis of inadequate independent loan evaluation but relying on the assessment of lead managers'.[46] After 1982 many smaller banks felt misled by their bigger brethren and strongly resisted subsequent extensions of credit as part of the rescheduling process.[47]

The definitive expression of this collective inexperience was the now famous credo of the leading international banker of the day. Walter Wriston was Chairman of Citicorp when he made the pronouncement that was to influence more international lending decisions in the 1970s than any credit analysis: 'Countries never go bankrupt'.[48] Never was a statement more true in form and false in substance.[49] Sovereigns do not become legally insolvent, because there are no legal rules to effect a sovereign insolvency, but sovereigns can be reduced to servicing their debt only by imposing unconscionable hardship on their people, and only by borrowing the funds to do so from the banks.

3.3.2.3 Bank Profitability and Market Share

The leader banks went south looking for profits and the challenger banks went south looking to become leader banks, i.e., in search of increased market share. Each had other motivations – the leader banks were losing market share in the domestic market and the challengers certainly sought profits – but these were the two principal motivations of the groups of banks that led the charge into Latin America, and profits and market share they found. For instance, Citibank derived a remarkable 72% of its overall earnings in 1976 from its international operations[50] and derived more profits in 1977 from its Brazilian business than from its entire United States operations.[51] The margins on these loans in the early 1970s were up to two percentage points above banks' costs of funds.[52] This was lucrative business, in the short-term.

---

45. Wellons, *Passing The Buck – Banks, Governments And Third World Debt*, pp. 231–235.
46. OECD, *Prudential Supervision in Banking*, (Paris, OECD, 1987), p. 125.
47. ECLAC/CTC, *Transnational Bank Behaviour and the International Debt Crisis*, p. 61.
48. Sachs, 'Introduction', in *Developing Country Debt and the World Economy*, p. 8.
49. S.S Golub, 'The Political Economy of the Latin American Debt Crisis' (1991) 26(1) *Latin American Research Review*, 177.
50. Sachs, 'Introduction', in *Developing Country Debt and the World Economy*, p. 8.
51. Delamaide, *Debt Shock*, p. 117.
52. Evidence to Subcommittee on Financial Institutions Supervision, Regulation and Insurance of the House Committee on Banking, Finance and Urban Affairs, Washington, DC, 21 April 1983 (C.T. Conover, Comptroller of the Currency); see also Lindert and Morton, 'How Sovereign Debt Has Worked', in *Developing Country Debt and the World Economy*, p. 230.

3.3.2.4 The Promotion of Bankers' Careers

A grossly undervalued contributor to the lending boom was the career reward structure for individual bankers. Employees are very efficient at identifying, and doing, precisely what gets rewarded in an organization, irrespective of the stated policies of the organization. Bonuses were large and promotion quick for bankers in the 1970s, and bonuses and promotions were based on the amount of business done,[53] not the quality of that business. In the mid-1970s bankers could lend aggressively secure in the knowledge that the resulting boost to their careers would see them promoted, possibly to another country and often in another bank, before the risks of those loans crystallized.[54] In analyzing a loan to a Filipino company, Gwynne noted that,

> by the time the borrower suspended its debt payments [some two and a half years into the loan], *all* of the loan officers who had worked on it had moved on to other banks. Such rapid job movement is common in banking... Thus many of the people who make the big international loans are not around to collect them when they go bad.[55]

When errors of judgment do not become apparent for many years the normal primary sanction for error – being identified with the mistake – fails to exert much influence. Careful, sober, boring risk analysis was vital in the 1970s and the behaviour least likely to advance a bankers' career.

3.3.2.5 Strong Debtor Economies

The region had been showing impressive economic growth for a number of years and was commonly thought to be the next economic powerhouse. Many believed that Argentina, Brazil and Mexico in particular would industrialize and enjoy the sort of sustained economic growth that in fact occurred in South-East Asia. The major Latin American nations were perceived to enjoy the same cheap educated workforce as the Asian nations, with a generous dollop of natural resources and proximity to Western markets thrown in for good measure.[56] These views were not without foundation. Mexico's economy had grown on average 6% per annum from 1940 until 1970, and Brazil's had boomed from 1968 until 1973, growing at an average annual rate of 11%.[57] The flaws in the economic systems of these countries, while serious, were not apparent.

---

53. Gwynne, *Adventures in the Loan Trade*, Harpers', September 1983, p. 25.
54. Levinson, 'The International Financial System: A Flawed Architecture', 5.
55. Gwynne, *Adventures in the Loan Trade*, Harpers', September 1983, p. 26.
56. D. Green, *Silent Revolution – The Rise of Market Economics in Latin America* (London, Cassell, 1995), p. 17.
57. J.F. Torres and R. Landa, 'The Changing Times: Foreign Investment in Mexico' (1991) 23 *Int'l Law & Pol*, 814; and Delamaide, *Debt Shock*, pp. 55–56.

3.3.2.6 Syndicated Lending

The development of syndicated lending enabled banks to assemble the vast amounts of funds required. Syndicated lending originated in the US domestic market and first appeared in the London Eurocurrency market in the late 1960s.[58] Before syndication, such massive loans were beyond the capacity of any one bank and so bond issues were the traditional debt finance vehicle. Syndication was very profitable for the lead banks due to the raft of fees involved, such as an agent's fee for administering the loan and a commitment fee for making the facility available.

3.3.2.7 Floating Interest Rates

The other technical innovation that made possible the use of loans for development finance was floating interest rates. Borrowers sought funds for five to seven years. Banks could fund themselves in the Euromarkets to make these loans for periods of only up to six months. The solution was to set the interest rate on the loans as a floating rate that is reset every three or six months at some specified margin over the bank's cost of funds in the euro market – usually represented by LIBOR (the London Interbank Offered Rate).[59] From the bank's perspective, this solution neatly transferred the interest rate risk to the debtors.

3.3.2.8 The Position of US Banks at Home

In the early 1970s the major US banks were losing market share in their home markets which made expansion abroad attractive.[60] This factor in the lending frenzy is overlooked by most commentators but the effect of the US banking system reforms implemented in response to the financial crisis of the 1930s meant growth opportunities for US banks in the US were severely constrained.[61] The Glass-Steagall Act[62] separated investment banking from commercial banking. While this prohibition did not extend to the actions of US banks abroad,[63] it severely restrained the growth of US banks domestically. The other troublesome legacy of post-1929 banking reform was the prohibition on inter-state banking. In the case of Citibank and Chase Manhattan, for instance, the recession in their home state, New York, severely limited lending opportunities there. As the rest of

---

58. J.N. Brooks, 'Participation and Syndicated Loans: Intercreditor Fiduciary Duties for Lead and Agent Banks under US Law', *Butterworths Journal of International Banking and Financial Law*, June 1995, 275.
59. Levinson, 'The International Financial System: A Flawed Architecture', 3.
60. Wellons, *World Money and Credit – The Crisis and Its Causes*, p. 27.
61. Dawson, *The First Latin American Debt Crisis: The City of London and the 1822–1825 Loan Bubble*, p. 237.
62. The principal provisions of the Glass Steagall Act are in sections 16, 20, 21 and 32 of the Banking Act of 1933.
63. Regulation K of the Federal Reserve, section 211.

the country and new lines of business were closed to them, overseas operations were the obvious avenue for growth.

For these eight reasons, the banks overlent grossly to the region. Let's consider now the part the debtors played in the creating the crisis.

3.3.3 DEBTOR NATION POLICIES

There was a common pattern of economic policies and factors among the debtor nations that contributed to or worsened the crisis. These included bloated budget deficits, overvalued exchange rates, anti-export trade regimes, capital flight and corruption. Each will be considered.

3.3.3.1 Large Budget Deficits

Great inequalities of personal income characterize most Latin American economies. The resulting fierce political conflicts too often lead to high budget deficits as governments struggle to resist the claims of pressure groups and to tax appropriately the economic elites. Foreign borrowing in the 1970s provided a way to bridge the gap between excessive government spending and inadequate taxation revenues.

3.3.3.2 Overvalued Exchange Rates

Overvalued exchange rates favour urban workers and local manufacturing at the expense of the agricultural sector and tend to restrict inflation.[64] Leaving their exchange rates overvalued therefore neatly reflected the political power realities of most of the debtor nations, and tended to restrain one of the region's recurring nightmares, hyperinflation. Accordingly many of the debtor nations' exchange rates were overvalued for most of the 1970s. Overvalued exchange rates also encourage import-consumption and the acquisition of foreign assets by private citizens (capital flight) and these effects were to prove very costly for the region's economies.

3.3.3.3 Anti-export Trade Regimes

Most debtor countries had pursued a policy of economic self-sufficiency and promoted import reduction over export expansion.[65] Import-substitution and economic self-sufficiency fitted well with the nationalistic pride of most of the debtor nations and protection of local industries was a common response to local political conflicts and demands. Protectionist policies discourage exports and encourage the production of import-competing goods. Unfortunately these policy choices are not economically efficient. This is borne out by comparing Latin America's economic

---

64. Sachs, 'Introduction', in *Developing Country Debt and the World Economy*, p. 15.
65. R. de Ruyter van Steveninck, 'Import Substitution and the Debt Crisis in Latin America', (1991) 3(2) *Tinbergen Institute Research Bulletin*, 133.

performance to East Asia's. East Asia also borrowed recycled petro-dollars at this time but tended to invest the money in export-oriented industries, which generated the funds to service the debt, and grew their economies.[66]

3.3.3.4 Capital Flight

Capital flight refers to the accumulation of foreign assets by the private sector (often at the same time as the public sector is incurring increasing foreign debt). Thus in the 1970s Mexico accumulated some USD 75 billion of foreign debts, while its private sector accumulated perhaps USD 40 billion of foreign assets.[67] In 1980–1981, 84% of the tremendous increase in foreign loans to Argentina was offset by the outflow of private capital, and for Venezuela the figure was over 100%, i.e. the outflow of private capital from Venezuela in those two years exceeded the inflow of foreign loans.[68] The World Bank estimated that for the three countries with the most severe problem, Argentina, Mexico and Venezuela, capital flight in the period 1979–1982 amounted to an astonishing 67% of capital inflows. This was partly the result of overvalued exchange rates: astute locals knew the cyclical nature of Latin American economies far better than did the international banks and preferred to keep their riches abroad. Another reason capital moved offshore was to distance itself from its tainted origin.

3.3.3.5 Corruption

There is a pattern in many Latin American countries, which amounts almost to a tradition, of corruption in government and major projects. As Carlos Marichal has said, '[i]t is well known that the principal beneficiaries were the technocrats, generals, and businessmen who received secret commissions and contracts on the huge flow of foreign funds. In no period of modern Latin American history has financial corruption reached such heights'.[69] Statistics are understandably scant, but a significant portion of the foreign loans were never put to their intended productive uses which made more difficult the task of earning sufficient foreign exchange to repay the loans.

In summary, the debt crisis would never have eventuated if the loans had been put to productive uses that generated returns in foreign currency greater than the cost of debt service. For the reasons enumerated above, that was rarely the case, and efficient use of such vast sums was always going to be highly improbable and in direct contradiction to the region's history.

---

66. United States International Trade Commission (USITC), *The Effect of Developing Country Debt–Servicing Problems on U.S Trade*, A Report to the Subcommittee on Trade of the House Ways and Means Committee, Investigation No. 332–234, USITC Pub No. 1950, 3.
67. Sachs, 'Introduction', in *Developing Country Debt and the World Economy*, p. 12.
68. Sachs, 'Introduction', in *Developing Country Debt and the World Economy*, p. 9. See also, World Bank, *World Development Report* (New York, Oxford University Press, 1985), p. 64.
69. Marichal, *A Century of Debt Crises in Latin America*, p. 238.

The Latin American and African Debt Crisis of 1982

3.3.4 EXTERNAL FACTORS

There are five external factors which precipitated the debt crisis. However, by 1982 debt levels were so high that while these factors determined the timing of the outbreak of the crisis, they were not the cause of it. A crisis was inevitable.[70] The five external factors are: interest rate increases, exchange rate movements, falls in commodity prices, a worldwide recession, and the cessation of petrodollar recycling. Authors invariably cite the first three factors. The fourth – the worldwide recession – receives less attention and the fifth – the cessation of petrodollar recycling – receives almost none. Each will be considered here.

3.3.4.1 Interest Rate Increases

Euromarket interest rates doubled between 1978 and 1981.[71] This was a direct result of the stringent monetary policy adopted by the developed countries in response to the second 'oil shock' in 1979–80.[72] As Robert Pastor said, 'The effect on the borrowing developing nations was catastrophic, but few realized it until it was too late'.[73] This factor is included as an external cause of the crisis because it is customary to do so. However, the interest rate rises were a direct result of monetary policy in developed countries, particularly the United States, and so were external only to the debtors.

3.3.4.2 Adverse Exchange Rate Movements

While less than half of the loans came from US commercial banks, nearly all were denominated in US dollars. The strong appreciation of the US dollar against the currencies of other developed countries from late 1980 until early 1985 meant that

---

70. M.B. Goldman, 'Confronting Third World Debt: The Baker and Brady Plans', *Backgrounder* No. 559, 22 January 1987 (Washington DC, The Heritage Foundation, 1987); R. Dornbusch, 'Debt Problems and the World Macroeconomy', in *Developing Country Debt and the World Economy*, p. 310; and C. Huhne, 'Some Lessons of the Debt Crisis: Never Again?', in *International Economics and Financial Markets – The AMEX Bank Review Prize Essays* (Oxford, Oxford University Press, 1989), p. 85.
71. H. Askari, *Third World Debt and Financial Innovation – The Experiences of Chile and Mexico* (Paris, Development Centre of the OECD, 1991), p. 20. Eurodollar rates peaked at 19.5% in March 1980: USITC, *The Effect of Developing Country Debt-Servicing Problems on U.S Trade*, p. 4. Calculations of the real interest rates at this time (the nominal rates adjusted for the rate of inflation in world trade) show that the real Libor passed 18% in late 1981: see Dornbusch, 'Debt Problems and the World Macroeconomy', in *Developing Country Debt and the World* Economy, p. 302.
72. R.A. Pastor, 'The Debt Crisis: A Financial or a Development Problem?', in *Latin America's Debt Crisis – Adjusting to the Past or Planning for the Future*, R.A Pastor (ed.) (Boulder and London, Lynne Rienner Publishers, 1987), pp. 7–8; Sachs, 'Introduction', in *Developing Country Debt and the World Economy*, p. 8; and USTIC, *The Effect of Developing Country Debt-Servicing Problems on U.S Trade*, p. 4.
73. Pastor, 'The Debt Crisis: A Financial or a Development Problem?', p. 8.

the debtor nations had to export ever greater amounts to non-US markets to earn the same amount of US dollars to service the loans.

3.3.4.3 Falls in Commodity Prices

Decreasing commodity prices are routinely listed as one of the major external contributors to the crisis. Commodity exports were vital to the economies of the region and prices had declined on average some 33% by 1982.[74] But it is in the nature of commodity prices to fluctuate widely. Such prices rose steadily throughout the 1970s.[75] Their steep fall was virtually assured in the next recession. The decline in commodity prices in the early 1980s was not so severe so as to be an immediate cause of the crisis.

3.3.4.4 The Worldwide Recession

The severe tightening of monetary policy in most developed countries in response to the second dramatic oil price rise in 1979 and 1980, plunged the developed world into an economic downturn in 1980 which reached its low point in 1982.[76] The quantities and prices of debtor nations' exports of both commodities and goods therefore decreased, at precisely the time interest rates were increasing.

3.3.4.5 Cessation of Petrodollar Recycling

Net bank deposits from OPEC revenues were USD 40 billion in 1980; USD 2.5 billion in 1981; and negative USD 10 billion in each of 1982 & 1983, i.e., OPEC investors withdrew USD 10 billion each year.[77] This drying up of the source of the capital flow to Latin America receives surprisingly little attention in most analyses of the debt crisis. Yet it certainly contributed to higher interest rates and to the banks turning off the flow of funds so quickly in 1982.

3.3.4.6 Conclusion on External Factors

All of the external factors had some role to play in bringing about the crisis in late 1982 and the most significant was the dramatic rise in interest rates. Yet this factor was external only to the debtor nations. It was the direct result of policy decisions in the US and other OECD nations. The developed world, in acting to prevent

---

74. Delamaide, *Debt Shock*, p. 28. Wheat and copper's prices were down about 25%, coffee was down over 30% and sugar had fallen a precipitous 70%: see USITC, *The Effect of Developing Country Debt–Servicing Problems on U.S Trade*, p. 4.
75. Dornbusch, 'Debt Problems and the World Macroeconomy', in *Developing Country Debt and the World* Economy, p. 303.
76. Torres and Landa, 'The Changing Times: Foreign Investment in Mexico', 820; and USITC, *The Effect of Developing Country Debt–Servicing Problems on U.S Trade*, p. 5.
77. USITC, *The Effect of Developing Country Debt–Servicing Problems on U.S Trade*, p. 4.

domestic inflation, imposed a frightful cost on the less developed world under the very loans the OECD governments had encouraged their banks to make.

Of all the external factors perhaps only the appreciation in the US currency and the cessation of petrodollar recycling would have been difficult to predict. Interest rates and commodity prices fluctuate greatly and the international economy periodically undergoes a recession. The direct causal links between interest rate rises and worldwide recession, and between worldwide recession and commodity prices, mean that this combination of external factors was predictable: the only uncertainty was when it would happen. The borrowers and the banks had together created an economic relationship that could not withstand the normal vicissitudes of international economic life.

The partial solution to their collective folly was to emerge from Sao Paulo and Mexico City.

Chapter 4
The Brady Plan

4.1   BACKGROUND TO THE BRADY PLAN

In early March 1989 the pages of the *Wall Street Journal* rang with the warning that '[w]hile the Bush administration searches for a new US policy on Third World debt, the red ink is turning to blood.'[1] The article told how over 300 people had died in riots in Venezuela protesting austerity measures imposed by the government at the behest of its creditors.[2] Political opposition to unrelieved debt service was growing strongly throughout the region. Tensions were also increasing in the US banking industry. In 1988 the negotiation of rescheduling packages with their attendant new money obligations had become very difficult and protracted in the face of stiff bank resistance. Increasing numbers of regional US and European banks were resisting advancing fresh funds.[3] The regional banks were, for the first time, starting to see how the lead US banks had managed the restructuring process to their own advantage, and the resulting resentment was souring attempts to elicit further new money and new money, and lots of it, was central to the Baker Plan.

---

1. W.S. Mossberg and P. Truell, 'Another Round: Bush Aides Are Likely to Offer a Plan Soon on Third World Debt', *The Wall Street Journal*, 9 March 1989.
2. The government reported 287 fatalities. Some commentators placed the death toll as high as 1500: see J. Ferguson, *Venezuela in Focus – A guide to the People, Politics and Culture* (London, Latin American Bureau, 1994), p. 5.
3. L.C. Buchheit, 'Whatever became of old new money?' (December 1990) *International Financial Law Review*, 11, 12; R. MacMillan, 'The Next Sovereign Debt Crisis' (1995) 31 *Stanford Journal of International Law*, pp. 328–329.

4.2 THE BAKER PLAN

This plan, initiated in 1985 and named after James A Baker, the then Secretary of the US Treasury, was premised on a view that the debtors could grow out of the debt crisis if sufficient new credit was advanced to make this possible.

Remarkably, James Baker was to reappear in international politics as President Bush's special envoy on Iraq's debts. He spent 2004 traversing the globe seeking to drum up support among rich nation creditors for the total cancellation of Iraq's debts. He succeeded in the main by securing the support of the principal creditor nations to Iraq to an utterly unprecedented cancellation of 80% of Iraq's debts.[4]

But first time around James Baker didn't succeed. Banks had wearied of forever advancing new funds. Countries had wearied of their ever-rising level of indebtedness. The Baker Plan failed, in part because the debt crisis involved a massive debt overhang which nothing less than a degree of debt forgiveness would redress, and partly because the commercial banks simply failed to advance the new money Baker was requiring.

IMF austerity programmes were no longer politically tenable in Latin America. Their continuation could have led to the overthrow of some of the democratic governments that had come to power during the 1980s and the return of totalitarian regimes to the region. Such developments would have been against US interests. A new approach was needed from the US government. The Brady Plan was that approach.

4.3 THE BRADY PLAN

The Brady Plan represented a sharp departure from the Baker Plan. That much initially was clear. However, little else was clear as Treasury Secretary Nicholas Brady was deliberately vague when he made his speech on 10 March 1989 to a joint meeting of the IMF and the World Bank in Seoul, South Korea.[5] His vagueness reflected the US Treasury's incapacity 'to orchestrate a full-scale "plan" and make it work'[6] and its unwillingness to be caught in the middle of the negotiations between creditors and debtors.

---

4. R.P. Buckley, 'Iraqi Sovereign Debt and Its Curious Global Implications', in *Beyond the Iraq War: The Promises, Perils and Pitfalls of External Interventionism*, Heazle and Islam (eds), (London, Edward Elgar, 2006), pp. 141–155.
5. N. Brady, 'Remarks to a Third World Debt Conference' sponsored by the Brookings Institute and the Bretton Woods Committee, 10 March 1989, reprinted in *Department of State Bulletin*, May 1989, pp. 53–56. See also 'Bankers are briefed on the Brady plan' 766 *IFR*, 11 March 1989, 28; and 'Washington's view on Brady' 767 *IFR*, 18 March 1989, 29; J. Calverley and I. Iversen, 'Banks and the Brady Initiative', in *Third World Debt – Managing the Consequences*, Griffith-Jones (ed.) (London, *IFR* Publishing Ltd, 1989), pp. 129, 133.
6. Calverley and I. Iversen, 'Banks and the Brady Initiative', p. 133.

Secretary Brady proposed a series of individual market-based transactions in which

- (i) creditors would be invited to participate voluntarily;
- (ii) debt relief would be tied into the conversion of loans into collateralized bonds;
- (iii) debtor nations would be permitted to repurchase their own discounted debt on the secondary market; and
- (iv) debt-equity schemes would be promoted.[7] The proposal was seen as an expression of increased urgency from the US government about the resolution of the debt crisis, a strong call for the development of capital-market-based solutions, and an official acceptance that some debt forgiveness was essential. At long last, it seemed, the calls for debt relief were to be heeded.

To the chagrin of many commercial bankers, the Brady proposal dealt only with debt to commercial banks. It made no call for debt forgiveness by official lenders. Many commercial bankers felt being asked to carry alone the burden of debt forgiveness was unfair when official lending accounted for around 40% of total emerging market loans. In 1990 these criticisms were met to a very limited extent when the association of official lenders, the Paris Club, permitted debt relief in the form of principal or interest rate reductions or very long maturities in the restructuring of the official indebtedness of severely-indebted low income countries. These were principally the poorer African nations. Bolivia was the only Latin American nation to be granted such relief. The Brady Plan thus offered very little to African nations that were not desperately poor but of which the principal indebtedness was to official agencies, development banks and other governments.[8]

4.3.1 Mexico's Brady Restructuring

The first Brady-style restructuring was of Mexico's debt. Mexico's strategic importance to the US was seen as likely to result in the most favourable precedent for other debtor nations. Negotiations began in earnest between Mexico and its commercial bank creditors in May, 1989. An agreement in principle was announced in July, the terms sheet was settled and distributed to banks in September, the debt reduction package was signed in February 1990 and the bonds issued in late March 1990.[9] It was a slow process dragging hundreds of banks to the table

---

7. See L.C. Buchheit, 'The background to Brady's initiative' (April 1990) *International Financial Law Review*, p. 30; and L. Fraust, 'Debt Plan Spurs Interest in Securitizing LDC Loans', *The American Banker*, 28 March 1989, 55.
8. 'World Bank Report' (1991) 24 *LatinFinance*, 12; 'Africa's Unpayable Debts', *The Economist*, 2 November 1991, 18.
9. 'The Debt Agreement' *Mexico Service*, 27 July 1989; B. Wolfson, 'Paving the Paper Trail' (1991) 26 *LatinFinance*, 49; 'At Last?', *The Economist*, 13 January 1990, 94; and J. Hay and N. Paul, *Regulation and Taxation of Commercial Banks during the International Debt Crisis* (Washington DC, World Bank, 1991), U.S. Annex 1, p. 3.

when most were resisting strenuously. Mexico's Brady scheme represented a significant departure from Secretary Brady's proposals as it was a one-off scheme in which creditor participation was effectively compulsory. The US Treasury swiftly accepted the virtues of necessity and embraced the bonds as a product of the Brady proposals.[10] Many banks were reportedly 'disgusted' with the deal but in the end had to go along with it.[11] The die had been cast for future Brady style restructurings.

The banks were offered a choice from the following three options for their Mexican loans.

(1) The banks could have their loans converted into newly issued 30-year bonds paying Libor plus 13/16%. The principal of these bonds would be discounted 35% from the loans. Repayment of principal would be guaranteed by zero coupon bonds issued for the purpose by the US Treasury, acquired by Mexico and held in escrow. In addition, there would be a rolling guarantee of eighteen months interest.[12]

(2) The banks could have their loans converted into what became known as 'par bonds' – bonds with the same face value as the loans which paid interest at the discounted, fixed rate of 6.25%.[13] The term and collateral for these bonds were as for the discounted principal bonds considered above.

(3) The banks could elect to participate in new loans to Mexico in the coming four years to the extent of 25% of their medium and long-term exposure to Mexico.

The new money option contained a paradox. It was crucial that sufficient banks opt for new money as it was required to assist with the purchase of the required collateral, the payment of interest on the Brady bonds, and for the continued economic growth of Mexico. However, the extension of new money eroded the debt-reduction effect of the proposal and if too many banks opted for new money there may have been a net increase in Mexico's indebtedness.

The acquisition of the collateral for these bonds was funded by USD 1.3 billion from Mexico, USD 2 billion from Japan, and USD 3.7 billion from the IMF and the World Bank.[14]

This approach of offering the banks a range of restructuring options was known as the 'menu' approach. It allowed banks to choose the option that most

---

10. Buchheit, 'The background to Brady's initiative', 30.
11. 'Hurricane heading for Brady Plan' 794 *IFR*, 23 September 1989, 12; and 'Commercial bankers say Brady Plan is a non-starter' 795 *IFR*, 30 September 1989, 8.
12. 'The Debt Agreement', *Mexico Service*, 27 July 1989; and Santos, 'Beyond Baker and Brady: Deeper Debt Reduction for Latin American Sovereign Debtors' (1991) 66 *NYULR*, 79.
13. At the time of Mexico's restructuring agreement, July 1989, Libor was 8.81%. The usual interest rate on Mexico's debt was Libor plus 13/16th. The par bonds at 6.25%, fixed, thus represented an interest saving of nearly 3.4%. By way of comparison, 30-year US Treasury bonds were yielding 8.14%.
14. 'The Debt Agreement', *Mexico Service*.

suited their view on interest rates and debtor prospects and their individual tax, regulatory and accounting situation.[15]

The prospects of the Brady proposal were greatly enhanced by a letter of 14 July 1989 from the SEC to David Mulford, Under Secretary of the Treasury, which 'clarified' the application to the Mexican Brady restructuring of Financial Accounting Standards No. 15, 'Accounting by Debtors and Creditors for Troubled Debt Restructurings' (FAS 15).[16] The relevant part of FAS 15 provides that if, in full settlement of a debt, a creditor receives assets of which the fair value is less than the recorded value of the debt, then the creditor must record the shortfall as a loss. If an active market exists, fair value is market value. In the absence of such a market, fair value was to be estimated based on expected cash flows discounted for risk.

David Mulford is commonly regarded as the architect of the Brady Plan and he had requested, and doubtless shaped, the letter of 14 July 1989 from the SEC. In the name of applying FAS 15 to Mexico's restructuring, the SEC wrote that a loss need not be recognized if 'the total future undiscounted cash receipts specified by the new terms of the loan, including receipts designated as both principal and interest, equal or exceed the book value of the loan.'[17]

This letter is a remarkable document. Upon its manifestly clear meaning, FAS 15 does not mean to exclude the time value of money from the calculations nor to treat interest as principal. Compare the approach of the Bank of England: discount bonds were to be placed on bank books at their face value of 65% with the loss of 35% to be charged to provisions. Par bonds, on the other hand, could be recorded at face value provided the current provisions against Mexican debt were otherwise adequate.[18] Given that discount and par bonds were designed to be of equal value and were treated by the international banks as such, this approach, which lays great weight on the face value of the bond and ignores the interest rate, is quite artificial (although not nearly as artificial as the SEC's approach).

Because of this SEC letter, the banks could accept Mexico's Brady Bonds in exchange for their loans without having to recognize a loss[19] notwithstanding that shortly after issue the par bonds were trading at 42% of face value and the discount bonds at 63%. The analysis in this SEC letter represents the apotheosis of the popular debt crisis game of images and mirrors by treating interest as principal and

---

15. J. Clark, 'Debt Reduction and Market Reentry under the Brady Plan' 18(4) *FRBNY Quarterly Review*, Winter 1993–94, 44–45.
16. The text of this letter and its attachment is set out in Hay and Paul, *Regulation and Taxation of Commercial Banks during the International Debt Crisis*, pp. 126 et seq, 159–160.
17. SEC letter and attachment reproduced in Hay and Paul, *Regulation and Taxation of Commercial Banks during the International Debt Crisis*, p. 128.
18. See Hay and Paul, *Regulation and Taxation of Commercial Banks during the International Debt Crisis*, p. 43.
19. M. Monteagudo, 'The Debt Problem: The Baker Plan and the Brady Initiative: A Latin American Perspective', (1994) 28(1) *The International Lawyer*, pp. 74–75. The SEC was careful to point out that its analysis of FAS 15 did not derogate from the general requirements of FAS 5 that loan losses must be recognized when a loan (or bond) is determined to be uncollectible in whole or part: SEC letter and attachment reproduced in Hay and Paul, *Regulation and Taxation of Commercial Banks during the International Debt Crisis*, p. 129.

making the value of money in 30 years equal to its value today. By ensuring that Brady bonds could be accepted by banks without provisions or writedowns,[20] the SEC made the Mexican restructuring far more palatable for US banks; at the cost of turning reality on its head.

This restructuring was of all of Mexico's medium and long-term debt to the commercial banks (some USD 54 billion of debt). A great deal of arm-twisting by regulators was required to secure the participation of all banks. Many were very reluctant to participate but bankers usually find overt pressure from their home regulators difficult to resist. Banks elected to convert 41% of total indebtedness into discounted principal bonds, 49% into discounted interest ('par') bonds, and to advance new money for the remaining 10%.[21] Of the three options, new money was to prove by far the most lucrative and Citibank's foresight in taking that option exclusively was richly rewarded. Yet in 1990 substantial pressure was needed to make banks holding the required 10% of exposure agree to advance new money.

These overall figures mask dramatic differences between the banks of different countries, differences which serve to highlight just how much 'international banks' remain influenced by the nations of their birth.[22] The following table shows the total percentage of debt exchanged for par or discount bonds or left in place (from which base new money obligations were calculated) by banks from different countries:

Bank Choices in the Mexican Restructuring[23]

Country	Par Bond	Discount Bond	New Money
France	79%	9%	12%
United States	58%	24%	19%
Japan	18%	81%	0%
Canada	48%	52%	0%
Germany	80%	20%	0%
United Kingdom	48%	45%	6%

As the table demonstrates, there were dramatic differences between the choices of banks from different countries, with, for instance, Japanese banks choosing to take roughly 80% of their loans as discount bonds and the rest as par bonds and the

---

20. 'Banks were able to account for both the par and discount bonds issued in Mexico's 1990 debt exchange without recognizing a restructuring loss': Office of the Superintendent of Financial Institutions, Canada, 'Guideline: Exposure to Designated Countries, EDC 1990–10', Part E, reproduced in Hay and Paul, *Regulation and Taxation of Commercial Banks during the International Debt Crisis*, pp. 114–115.
21. Testimony of W.R. Rhodes, Federal News Service, 21 March 1990.
22. Wellons, *Passing The Buck – Banks, Governments And Third World Debt*.
23. This table is from Hay and Paul, *Regulation and Taxation of Commercial Banks during the International Debt Crisis*, p. 10.

German banks choosing to take 80% of their loans as par bonds with the rest as discount bonds. The reasons for these dramatic differences may be a combination of the variations in the regulatory and taxation regimes of countries[24] and the pressure brought to bear on US and French banks, in particular, to advance new money.

The terms of the bonds differed from the loans in a number of respects. The bonds were negotiable instruments designed to be traded, and the sharing clause and mandatory prepayments clause typical of syndicated bank loans were absent. Furthermore, there were some other less than usual provisions of this restructuring:

(i) the Mexican government agreed to permit USD 1 billion of debt-equity conversions per annum for the next three years; and
(ii) debt payments would be increased on discounted principal and par bonds if after July 1996 Mexico's earnings from oil exports exceeded 1989 levels in real terms or if the real price for Mexican oil after 1996 exceeded USD 14 per barrel.

These potential increases in debt payments were both capped and counterbalanced in a complex scheme. The increase in repayments due to improved oil exports was limited to 30% and interest rates on the par bonds were capped at 9.25%. Furthermore, if oil prices fell below USD 10 per barrel during the life of the agreement the banks could be required to advance further new funds of up to USD 800 million.[25]

This Mexican restructuring was perceived to be a crucial first test of the Brady initiative. Secretary Brady's proposals were generally treated in the press as entirely novel and without precedent but the idea had been considered for quite some time.[26] Indeed, the genesis of Brady's proposal was in Latin America not Washington: in the Aztec bonds, developed at Mexico's request, in 1988, and in even earlier proposals by Brazil to convert its foreign debt into 35-year bearer bonds with the same face value as the loans and below market fixed interest rates.[27] The agenda for this restructuring was established not in Washington, but in Sao Paulo and Mexico City. Indeed, the US government had initially been strongly resistant to the idea.[28] The receptive ear in Washington necessary for Mexico's ideas to gain credence was that of David Mulford, then Assistant Secretary of the

---

24. Hay and Paul, *Regulation and Taxation of Commercial Banks during the International Debt Crisis*, pp. 9–10.
25. 'The Debt Agreement', *Mexico Service*.
26. See 'Third World Debt – Watch out securitisation is on its way' 703 *IFR*, 12 December 1987, 3876; and 'Brazil – Time to securitise its debt' 663 *IFR*, 7 March 1987, 763; and 'LDC debt securitisation' 723 *IFR*, 7 May 1988, 1444.
27. 'LDC Debt – The deep discount bushfire' 690 *IFR*, 12 September 1987, 2947. Note, with the exception of collateral, how closely these bonds proposed by Brazil resemble the par bonds ultimately issued nearly three years later in Mexico's Brady style restructuring.
28. See Statement of Professor Luiz Carlos Bresser Pereira, *Solving the Debt Crisis: Debt Relief and Adjustment* (Statement delivered before the House Committee on Banking, Finance and Urban Affairs hearings on the 'Lesser Developed Countries' Debt Crisis'), 101st Congress First Session, 5 January 1989, 336–337, and Buchheit, 'The background to Brady's initiative', 30.

Treasury. To his credit, Mulford ran with Mexico's and Brazil's ideas and when Nicholas Brady became Treasury Secretary, Mulford had a superior who too was willing to listen.

A crucial element of the Mexican debt negotiation strategy was the insistence on debt reduction and interest relief. The international financial community resisted any debt relief vigorously. Nevertheless, the Plan has been severely criticized for affording inadequate debt relief,[29] criticisms with which this author agrees. With the benefit of hindsight, the banks gained so much from the Plan, they could have afforded to give more to get it.

The actual savings to Mexico from its Brady restructuring are difficult to assess. Different analysts produce very different assessments. At the wildly optimistic end of the range, Clark calculated savings of USD 21.1 billion in claims payable to banks by Mexico, which represents some 43.5% of the loans eligible for restructuring.[30] At the other end of the spectrum, some researchers claim Mexico's Brady restructuring left its total indebtedness unchanged: the debt relief afforded by the discount bonds was offset by the new money advanced.[31]

These disparate views can be reconciled to some extent. Clark's footnotes reveal that his figure for reduction in claims payable does not include the new money which was central to the restructuring and must be included in any analysis of its overall effect. Furthermore, about 60% of his calculated saving comes through lower interest payments on the par bonds calculated at the floating rates prevailing at the time of the restructuring. However, floating rates declined after the restructuring so that within a few years interest on Mexico's debt was about the same as if the restructurings had not occurred,[32] i.e. declines in floating interest rates had offset the interest rate savings on the fixed interest par bonds.

The Brady restructuring did benefit Mexico in one way: the nation was now more protected against interest rate rises as the restructuring corrected one of the anomalies of the lending boom of the 1970s by replacing some floating rate debts with fixed rate ones. Ironically, however, interest rates were to fall for the next six years. The restructuring also corrected the other major anomaly of the 1970s lending boom – the form of the credits as loans rather than bonds.

However, the Brady restructuring failed to help Mexico at all on one important measure. Mexico's net annual transfer to the banks before the restructuring was USD 3.24 billion. After the restructuring it was USD 3.59 billion.[33] This is because before Brady most of the interest payments were funded by new money. Once again, however, figures do not tell the full story. The Brady process served an important function in breaking the upward spiral of total indebtedness and in

---

29. Santos has described the Plan as 'irreparably flawed' for this and other reasons: Santos, 'Beyond Baker and Brady: Deeper Debt Reduction for Latin American Sovereign Debtors', 79–80.
30. Clark, 'Debt Reduction and Market Reentry under the Brady Plan', 46.
31. Monteagudo, 'The Debt Problem: The Baker Plan and the Brady Initiative: A Latin American Perspective', 80.
32. Clark, 'Debt Reduction and Market Reentry under the Brady Plan', 49.
33. Clark, 'Debt Reduction and Market Reentry under the Brady Plan', pp. 47–48.

reducing the demands on the scarce time of government ministers and civil servants which arose from the periodic restructurings of the 1980s. In Clark's words:

> The Brady restructurings did not achieve significantly more near-term cash flow relief for debtors than the previous approach. But they did provide a more stable long-run financial framework that, in combination with structural reforms by debtors and a favorable environment of lower global interest rates, helped to restore market access.[34]

Shortly after the Mexican restructuring, the commercial banks negotiated agreements with the Philippines, Costa Rica, Venezuela and Morocco in that order.[35]

4.3.2 THE PHILLIPINES BRADY RESTRUCTURING

At the time, the Filipino restructuring was referred to as a Brady scheme.[36] However, it was not a classic Brady style restructuring as discount and par bonds were absent. Banks were offered the choice between advancing new money or selling their current exposure back to the Philippines at around 50 cents on the dollar.[37] This restructuring resulted in a reduction of almost 13% of the Philippines external bank debt.[38] The Philippines government had indicated that over the following year or two there would be additional debt reduction initiatives, such as par bonds, in a series of voluntary, market based transactions[39] (true to the original spirit of Treasury Secretary Brady's proposals). However, when these further debt reduction initiatives were implemented they were in the form of a classic, Mexican-style, compulsory, one-off Brady scheme. This later restructuring was presented as if it were the Philippine's first Brady restructuring. This would have surprised those engaged in the 1989 exercise, but was tenable because the 1989 restructuring was such an atypical Brady restructure. The new menu offered to banks included collateralized 25-year interest reduction registered bonds, 15-year interest reduction bearer bonds with less collateral, or new money.[40] After the 1990 restructuring the

---

34. Clark, 'Debt Reduction and Market Reentry under the Brady Plan', p. 62.
35. Hay and Paul, *Regulation and Taxation of Commercial Banks during the International Debt Crisis*, pp. 5–6.
36. Hay and Paul, *Regulation and Taxation of Commercial Banks during the International Debt Crisis*, pp. 4–5.
37. Buchheit, 'The background to Brady's initiative', 31.
38. International Monetary Fund, *Annual Report*, 1990, pp. 28–32.
39. Buchheit, 'The background to Brady's initiative', 31.
40. The 25-year bonds had full collateral for principal and a rolling guarantee of 14 months interest and a fixed coupon of 4.25% in year one, rising progressively to 6.5% in year six and thereafter. The 15-year bonds had a rolling guarantee of 12 months interest for the first six years and fixed rates commencing at 4% in year one rising to 6% in year six and the floating rate of Libor plus 13/16th% for years seven to 15. Principal was not collateralized. The new money option was to advance new money equal to 25% of a bank's exposure. The new money would be in the form of 17-year bonds bearing interest of Libor plus 13/16%.

Philippines had USD 5.3 billion of bank debt. The second restructuring in early 1992 reduced this by a further USD 1.5 billion.

The original proposals of Secretary Brady had emphasized that debt relief and restructuring would be voluntary and Mexico's restructuring was religiously referred to by all involved as a voluntary exercise.[41] The first Filipino restructuring incorporated relatively less debt relief and more new money than Mexico's. The response to it was illuminating as 'bankers eagerly noted that the Philippine agreement is more "voluntary" than the Mexico settlement.'[42] Its other interesting aspect was that the Philippines were permitted to repurchase about USD 1.3 billion of its debt for roughly the debt's secondary market price.[43]

4.3.3 VENEZUELA'S BRADY RESTRUCTURING

Venezuela received the next Brady style restructuring because their economic program met with US approval.[44] Argentina and Brazil would have to adapt their domestic economic policies further towards the model of the Washington technocrats before either would be granted a Brady style restructuring.[45]

Venezuela's 'Brady' rescheduling was announced on 25 June 1990. The menu included the following five options:[46]

(1) The exchange of loans for 30-year collateralized principal discount bonds paying Libor plus 13/16%. The discount bonds had a face value of 70% of the amount of a bank's loans. Principal was secured by zero coupon US Treasury bonds and there was a 14 month rolling interest guarantee.

---

41. A. Masuda, 'Mexico's Debt Reduction Agreement and the New Debt Strategy' (1991) 11(1) *EXIM Review*, 30.
42. Hay and Paul, *Regulation and Taxation of Commercial Banks during the International Debt Crisis*, p. 5.
43. For an analysis of debt buy-backs as often not being in the debtor's best interests (an approach with which this author disagrees), see 'A taxing burden of debt', *The Economist*, 8 September 1990, p. 101. For the author's views on buy-backs, see R.P. Buckley, 'Debt Exchanges Revisited: Lessons from Latin America for Eastern Europe' (1998) 18 *Northwestern Journal of International Law and Business*, 655.
44. In the words of Barber Conable, President of the World Bank, 'it's absolutely essential to differentiate between debtors in terms of support': Mossberg and Truell, 'Another Round: Bush Aides Are Likely to Offer a Plan Soon on Third World Debt'. The then President of the World Bank is here emphasizing that support in the form of debt relief must be reserved, and used as a reward, for those debtor countries which toe the official line on economic policy.
45. Mossberg and Truell, 'Another Round: Bush Aides Are Likely to Offer a Plan Soon on Third World Debt'. At this time both Argentina and Brazil were substantially in arrears on their interest payments: P. Truell, 'Bolivia and Brazil Reach Accord on Plan to Cut $300 Million of Each Other's Debt', *Wall Street Journal*, 11 May 1990.
46. 'Evaluating the Venezuela 1990 Financing Plan – Choosing Among the Financing Options', Salomon Brothers Inc., July 1990, p. 5; P. Vankudre, 'Brady Bonds', (1991) 26 *LatinFinance*, 53; Hay and Paul, *Regulation and Taxation of Commercial Banks during the International Debt Crisis*, p. 6.

(2) The exchange of loans for 30-year collateralized par bonds paying a fixed rate of 6.75%. These par bonds had the same collateral as the discount bonds. Both the par and discount bonds provided for higher interest rates after 6 years if oil prices exceeded USD 26 per barrel
(3) The acquisition of new money bonds equal to 20% of a bank's loans[47] and conversion of those loans into debt-conversion bonds eligible for conversion into equity. The debt-conversion bonds had a 17 year term and a coupon of Libor plus 7/8%. The new money and debt-conversion bonds were bearer bonds, as opposed to the discount and par bonds that were registered. Bearer bonds are more attractive for some investors and are generally considered more difficult to restructure. For this reason rating agencies subsequently often rated bearer Brady bonds more highly than registered Brady bonds
(4) The exchange of loans for 17-year temporary interest reduction bonds. These bonds paid interest at 5% for two years, 6% for two years, 7% for one year then Libor plus 7/8% thereafter and had a rolling interest guarantee for the first five years.
(5) The sale, in effect, of loans to Venezuela for 45 cents on the dollar, roughly the price for Venezuelan debt at that time. This sale of loans was effected by the exchange of loans for a short-term, fully-collateralized, 91-day note equal to 45% of the amount of a bank's loans. This global note was collateralized by US Treasury bills and was simply a different way of structuring a buy-back option. There was, for obvious reasons, a cap on the amount of loans which could be tendered under this option, which was set at USD 5.5 bn, face value, of loans.

As is apparent, Venezuela's rescheduling was broadly similar to Mexico's, one year earlier, with the addition of temporary interest reduction bonds and the option of selling loans back to Venezuela at the secondary market price.[48]

Nonetheless, the banks made very different choices in Venezuela's Brady scheme than in Mexico's. Discounted principal bonds attracted only 9% of debt (as opposed to 41% for Mexico), par bonds 34% (49% for Mexico), new money 34% (10% for Mexico), temporary interest reduction bonds 11% and, finally, the holders of 9% of the debt sold it back to Venezuela.[49] As with Mexico's restructuring, over time the new money option was to prove the most financially

---

47. That is, if a lender acquired new money bonds, its entire portfolio of loans would be converted into bonds eligible to be swapped into equity. 40% of these new money bonds pay interest at Libor plus one%, the balance at Libor plus 7/8%.
48. As was the case with Mexico, an effective exemption from the Securities Act was obtained for this issuance of bonds in the US See letter of 17 October 1990 from Arnold & Porter for Venezuela and Milbank Tweed Hadley & McCoy for the bank advisory committee for Venezuela to the SEC and the SEC reply of 17 October 1990 (1990 SEC No-Act. LEXIS 1193).
49. C. Calderon and R. McCarthy, 'New Money for Old' (1990) 20 *LatinFinance*, 73; R. McCarthy, 'After Brady: the Debt Dust Settles' (1991) 24 *LatinFinance*, 30; and 'Venezuela signs final portion' 856 *IFR*, 8 December 1990, 28. The principal participants in the buyback option were Japanese banks and market traders.

rewarding, and with the Mexican experience behind them, far more banks took the risk and chose that option.

4.3.4 URUGUAY'S AND CHILE'S RESTRUCTURINGS

Subsequently, a Brady-style agreement was negotiated with Uruguay which involved a buy-back of much of Uruguay's debt. Banks were offered a simplified choice of 30-year par bonds with a 6.75% coupon and the usual collateral, new money equal to 20% of current loans with the current loans rendered eligible for conversion into equity, or a debt buyback option at 56 cents on the dollar. In December, 1990, banks chose to convert 33% of Uruguay's USD 1.64 bn of medium and long-term debt into par bonds, sell 39% back to Uruguay at 56 cents on the dollar and advance new money loans with respect to the balance of 28% of the nation's debt.

Chile's debt was also restructured but due to its relatively robust economic health no discount or par bonds were involved. Chile's restructuring was conventional and involved new money plus the right for debt buy-backs and debt-equity conversions. The assistance of a Brady-style restructuring was not required.

4.3.5 BRAZIL'S BRADY RESTRUCTURING INITIATED

Brazil's Brady scheme had a long and chequered history as the nation's economic policies and performance failed to satisfy the Washington-based decision makers at the IMF, World Bank and US Treasury. In August 1991, Brazil proposed a menu of options that included 30-year collateralized par bonds, 30-year collateralized discount bonds, two types of temporary interest reduction bonds and a new money option. The proposal was for the par bonds to bear a coupon of 4.8% and carry a guarantee of principal but no rolling interest guarantee (which had been the most difficult aspect of the earlier Brady bonds to price). The discount bonds were to be for 62.5% of the face value of the loans. The temporary interest reduction bonds were to carry reduced fixed interest rates for the first six years and, in one case, a fixed rate of 8% for the balance of the total term of 25 years, and in the other case an interest rate of Libor plus 13/16% for the balance of the total term of 15 years. The new money option was for a bank to advance new money to the extent of 25% of its current exposure. The announcement of the agreed terms of Brazil's restructuring was eagerly anticipated from August to October 1991 but never came.

4.3.6 ARGENTINA'S BRADY RESTRUCTURING

Argentina and its bank advisory committee announced their agreement in principle on this long-awaited restructuring on 7 April 1992. The terms were close to the

The Brady Plan

Mexican model with the banks being given the choice between 30-year fixed interest par bonds, 30-year discount bonds and new money loans.[50]

Interest rates decreased after this preliminary agreement with the result that the overwhelming majority of creditors chose par bonds. The restructuring was then delayed while Argentina tried to persuade its creditors to take 35% of their debt in discount bonds. Initially only 20% of Argentina's creditors had opted for discount bonds. Because par bonds leave principal unreduced, they require more funds for the acquisition of collateral than do discount bonds and Argentina could only afford the collateral if at least 35% of the bonds had discounted principal. Argentina was eventually able to persuade its creditors to take 35% of their exposure in discount bonds in time for a December, 1992 signing and an April, 1993 issuance of the Brady bonds.

4.3.7 BRAZIL'S BRADY RESTRUCTURING IS COMPLETED

Brazil and its creditors reached agreement on the terms of the long-awaited Brady style restructuring in mid-1992.[51] Again, as with Argentina, interest rates declined after the terms of the restructuring were set and before the banks were required to select their options from the menu. As a result, the selections were heavily biased in favour of par bonds and the acquisition of collateral required more funds than Brazil had available. Brazil sought to have creditors rebalance their selections of restructuring instruments; a process that proved to be very time-consuming: agreement on new options was not reached until July 1993.[52] Even then, the

---

50. The par bonds paid interest at 4% in year one rising progressively to 6% in year seven and thereafter. There was full collateral for principal and a 12 month rolling interest guarantee. The discount bonds had the standard 35% discount of principal, paid Libor plus 13/16th% and had the same collateral as the par bonds. The great majority of Argentina's USD 8 billion in interest arrears were converted into past-due interest bonds. These unsecured bonds paid a floating interest rate above Libor and had a term of twelve years.
51. 'Q&A: William Rhodes', (1992) 39 *LatinFinance*, 87; and 'Brazil signs US$44bn Brady deal' 937 *IFR*, 11 July 1992, 28. The menu Brazil agreed with its creditor banks included: 30-year discount bonds at Libor plus 13/16th%, with collateral for the principal and a 12-month rolling interest guarantee; 30-year par bonds paying 4% in year one rising progressively to 6% for years 7 to 30, and with the same collateral as the discount bonds; 15-year front-loaded interest reduction bonds (FLIRBs) paying 4% for years one and two, 4.5% for years three and four, 5% for years five and six, and Libor plus 13/16% thereafter, and collateral only for a 12-month rolling interest guarantee for the first six years; 18-year new money bonds equal to 18.18% of a bank's exposure and paying Libor plus 7/8%; new money loans with a tenor of 20 years, the same interest rate as the FLIRBs, and progressively higher repayments of principal; and 20-year capitalization bonds with the same interest rates as FLIRBs except that for years seven on the rate is 8% fixed, not a floating rate, and the difference between the lower interest rates for years 1 to 6 and 8% will be capitalized (these bonds have no collateral).
52. The commercial banks elected for almost 60% of the debt to be converted into the two available classes of par bonds, and for almost 20% to be converted into discount bonds. Brazil sought a maximum of 40% of par bonds and a minimum of 35% of discount bonds. See 'Brazil Asks to Extend Deal Closing to Nov 30', *LDC Debt Report*, 31 May 1993, 1; 'Brazil Brady on the way'

process was not over as Brazil was unable to obtain an IMF accord and funding by the November 30 deadline. A new deadline of 15 April 1994 was set for the completion of the rescheduling.

Unlike other debtors, Brazil did not need IMF funds to acquire the collateral for the Brady bonds. However, the US Treasury was not willing to sell the zero coupon bonds needed as collateral to Brazil without IMF approval and the restructuring agreement had been made conditional upon an IMF accord being in place. Cross-conditionality of official and commercial bank lending was alive and well. However, at the eleventh hour, when the IMF would still not commit its funds, Brazil revealed it had purchased the necessary US Treasury zero-coupon bonds in the open market and intended to proceed with the rescheduling anyway. Brazil then promptly obtained waivers of the term which made the IMF agreement a condition of the closing and Brazil's Brady restructuring was the first to proceed without the formal support of the IMF.[53]

In addition, in 1994–1995, Brady restructurings proceeded in Bulgaria, the Dominican Republic, Ecuador, Jordan, and Poland.[54]

4.3.8 COLLATERALIZING BRADY BONDS

The collateral for the repayment of principal of the Brady bonds was an essential part of the Brady Plan and a useful application of debtor funds, the collateral required for the provision of a rolling guarantee of interest was neither.

Brady bonds typically had full collateral for the repayment of principal, plus collateral sufficient to secure the payment of 12 or 18 months of interest instalments. The collateral for principal was an essential part of the Plan. The banks were deeply concerned that these loans would never be repaid and were becoming a form of perpetual debt. The collateral for principal addressed this concern by guaranteeing that in 30 years the bonds would be repaid. The collateral for principal was also relatively cheap to acquire, because of the long 30-year tenor of the bonds, and was also easily priced into the secondary market value of the bonds, and readily stripped out at later times and traded separately to the underlying bonds. This collateral was thus, for a number of reasons, an efficient use of funds.

The collateral that was held in escrow to provide security for the payment of, as the case may be, either 12, 15 or 18 months of interest payments was not able to be properly priced into the bonds in secondary market trading because the guarantee was a rolling guarantee, i.e. it applied to cover 12 or 18 months of

---

988 *IFR*, 17 July 1993, 45; 'Brazil: Rebalancing update' 981 *IFR*, 29 May 1993, 60; 'Brazil requests Brady extension' 997 *IFR*, 18 September 1993, 47; 'Brazil – Under Pressure' 998 *IFR*, 25 September 1993, 47; and 'Brazil – Critical mass reached' 1010 *IFR*, 18 December 1993, 48.
53. 'No IMF letter for Brazil' 1022 *IFR*, 19 March 1994, 49; and 'Brazil – Waiver approved' 1023 *IFR*, 26 March 1994, 46.
54. World Bank, *World Debt Tables, 1994–95*, (Washington DC, The World Bank), pp. 4–5, 27–29 and see pp. 68–75 for the detailed terms of each restructuring.

The Brady Plan 53

repayments whenever the debtor might stop making such repayments. The value of the guarantee thus depended upon when the debtor might default upon payments under the bonds, thereby activating the guarantee. Accordingly, the secondary market values of the bonds never fully reflected the value of this rolling guarantee. Furthermore, given prevailing interest rates, this collateral was substantially more expensive to acquire than that needed to secure the repayment of principal.

4.3.9   CONCLUSIONS REGARDING THE BRADY PLAN

It is today generally accepted that the securitization of loans into bonds under the Brady Plan served both the international banks and the debtor nations.

The Brady Plan served the banks in four ways:

(1) It gave the banks liquid bonds, rather than relatively illiquid loans, which facilitated the banks selling the assets.
(2) It triggered a turn-around in secondary market prices of these assets.
(3) It enabled debtor nations to start borrowing, and issuing bonds, again, from which the banks earned fees.
(4) It signaled the end of the debt crisis.

Each will be considered.

The Brady Plan gave the banks liquid bonds, rather than relatively illiquid loans.[55] Secondary market turnover of emerging markets bank loans was around USD 70 billion face value of loans in 1989 and about USD 100 billion in 1990. In the next five years the Brady Plan converted these loans into readily tradable bonds and the impact on secondary market turnover was dramatic. By 1997 USD 305 billions of loans, and a staggering USD 2,403 billion of Brady Bonds, were traded.[56] With bonds instead of loans, banks were able to sell distressed debt off their balance sheets and free up capital for more productive uses.

The Plan also triggered a turnaround in the secondary market price of the debt that improved the real value of the banks' portfolios dramatically.[57]

A Brady restructuring enabled debtor nations to return to the voluntary capital markets, from which the banks benefited by earning underwriting fees for bond issuances, and from other financial market activity. Finally, and more importantly, the Brady Plan benefited the banks as it signaled the end, from the perspective of

---

55. Loans could certainly be traded but it was not simple, and therefore relatively expensive, to do so. See R.P. Buckley, 'The Law of Emerging Markets Loan Sales' (1999) 14 *Journal of International Banking Law*, 110; R.P. Buckley, 'The Practice of Emerging Markets Loan Sales' (1999) 14 *Journal of International Banking Law*, 151.
56. 'Back to the Future' (1990) 16 *LatinFinance* 24; 'Brady's Bazaar', *Economist*, 12 May 1990, 81; B. O'Reilly, 'Cooling Down the World Debt Bomb', *Fortune*, 20 May 1991, 124; Voorhees, 'Doses of Reality' (1992) 40 *LatinFinance* 26; and Emerging Markets Traders Association, *1997 Debt Trading Volume Survey*, 25 February 1998, 7.
57. S.H. Lee and H. M. Sung, 'The Reactions of Secondary Market Prices of Developing Country Syndicated Loans to the Brady Plan', a paper dated 15 January 1993, Appendix at 19.

developed nations, of the debt crisis that had commenced in August, 1982 and that had, for over a decade, remained a live threat to the stability of the international financial system.

Given these four clear benefits to the international financial community from the Brady Plan it is important to note that the banks resisted the Plan at the time, fiercely. In the words of *The Economist*, 'the bosses of most of America's big money-centre banks bristle with rage at any mention of the Brady plan. They fume at the write-offs they have had to make on their developing-country debt portfolios.'[58]

At the time, the banks could not recognize what would prove to be in their own best interests.

The Brady Plan also served the debtor nations. The Plan signaled the end of the debt crisis, at least in the perception of the international financial community, and this perception mattered, because the change meant the debtor nations could return to the voluntary capital markets with bond issuances, particularly Eurobonds, and it also meant that foreign investment capital began flowing into the region, albeit slowly at first.

Whether the Plan actually resolved the debt crisis from the perspective of the debtors is another issue altogether. The debt is still there, being serviced today, in the form of Brady bonds along with the tremendous amounts of debt borrowed since. From the perspective of peasants in the fields of Mexico or Ecuador, who receive far poorer health services and education for their children than they would if such a high proportion of their government's income did not go in debt service, it is highly arguable that the debt crisis has never gone away. But the Brady Plan did resolve the crisis from the perspective of the creditors, and this was important in revitalizing the region through the stimulative effects of fresh capital flows.

---

58. 'Brady's Bazaar', *The Economist*, 81. See also the comments of Horst Schulman, Managing Director of the Institute of International Finance, who said, 'Forced debt forgiveness was not essential... All parties concerned might be better off today [without it]', reported in 'Schulman Speaks Out', *LDC Debt Report*, 21 September 1992, 4.

Chapter 5

The Asian Economic Crisis of 1997

5.1 THE CRISIS ERUPTS

The Asian problems first manifested clearly in Thailand in June 1997. Foreign money had flooded into Thailand and fuelled speculative markets in real estate and stocks and heavy domestic consumption that contributed to a massive current-account deficit.[1] (A current account deficit is the extent to which the value of imports of goods and services plus the net interest on foreign debts exceeds the value of exports of goods and services.) The current-account deficit and an over-valued currency linked Thailand's situation to that of Mexico's in late 1994; and the results were the same – Thailand spent most of its foreign exchange reserves defending the value of its currency against speculators before being forced to allow it to float on July 2. As with Mexico a few years earlier, the currency's value fell through the floor, losing some 40% in four months and 50% in six. In the following weeks the contagion spread to Malaysia and the Philippines.

Nonetheless, it was not until October that the currency crisis, as it was then termed, deepened across the sector. The precipitating event was intense speculation on the Hong Kong dollar which triggered a sustained plunge in Hong Kong share prices. East Asia's troubles have attracted numerous names. Initially it was termed a currency crisis, later briefly a debt crisis, then an economic crisis, and now most often is referred to simply as 'the Asian crisis'. How should it be characterized?

A currency crisis arises when a nation no longer has the wherewithal to intervene in the markets to support the value of its currency and the currency then has to be allowed to float. If its value has been supported by government intervention this almost always results in a sharp devaluation. Debt crises are the result of a nation's total indebtedness exceeding its capacity to meet repayments.

---

1. M. Feldstein, 'A Self-Help Guide for Emerging Markets', *Foreign Affairs*, March/April 1999, 93.

The resources available to meet repayments are foreign exchange reserves, export earnings and funds from refinancing – and the immediate cause of many debt crises is the cessation of the latter. The traditional measures of this capacity are debt export and debt service ratios. A debt export ratio is the ratio of a nation's total debt to its export earnings. A debt service ratio is the ratio of the sum of a nation's interest and principal amortization payments to its export earnings. These ratios are seen as a measure of a country's capacity to service its foreign debt as exports generate the ongoing foreign exchange used for this purpose.

Debt crises are generally characterized by debt export ratios over 200% and debt service ratios over 20%.[2] These ratios for the East Asia and Pacific region were 99% and 12% respectively in 1996,[3] whereas the debt service ratio for Latin America in 1996 was 30%. Regional averages can, of course, mislead. Indonesia's 1996 debt export ratio of 220% and its debt service ratio of 34% suggest a debt crisis for that country – which is one of the reasons that recovery from the Asian crisis has been so much slower in Indonesia than in the other Asian countries. However, the debt export ratios of Korea, Malaysia, and Thailand were all substantially lower than those of Argentina, Brazil and Mexico in 1996 and the debt export ratio for East Asia and the Pacific in 1997 was 103%, compared to Latin America's 193%. In addition, the debt export and debt service ratios for East Asia and the Pacific were substantially lower in 1997 than in 1992.[4] Accordingly, the Asian crisis was in no conventional sense a debt crisis. It also differed from the debt crisis of 1982 and the Mexican peso crisis of 1994–95 in that the troublesome indebtedness was that of the private, not the public or quasi-public, sector and that it occurred within 'a benign international environment with low interest rates and solid growth in output and exports'.[5] It was initially a currency crisis and developed into a more generalized economic crisis, at least for Indonesia, Thailand, and Korea, the three most severely affected countries.

5.2 CAUSES OF THE ASIAN ECONOMIC CRISIS

The five principal causes of the Asian economic crisis were:

(i) the type of indebtedness;
(ii) the extent of indebtedness;
(iii) financial sector weaknesses;
(iv) fixed local exchange rates; and
(v) a region-wide loss of confidence.

Each will be considered.

---

2. The view of a Morgan Guaranty study cited in Aronson, op cit n 1 at 68.
3. The World Bank, *Global Development Finance 1997*, Vol 1 (Washington, DC, World Bank, 1997), p. 160.
4. The World Bank, *Global Development Finance 1998*, Vol 1 (Washington, DC, World Bank, 1998), pp. 33, 124 and 128.
5. The World Bank, *Global Development Finance 1998*, Vol 1 (Washington, DC, World Bank, 1998), pp. 4, 30.

5.2.1 Type of Indebtedness

The particular type of debt that contributed significantly to East Asia's economic problems was short-term debt, particularly that denominated in local currency. We will commence by considering short-term debt, then add in the impact of it being in local currency.

Short-term indebtedness increased significantly in 1995 and 1996 across the region, with the increase concentrated in China, Indonesia and Thailand. The build up of short-term debt was not a region-wide phenomenon. The ratio of short-term to total debt in the countries of the region in mid-1997 ranged from 67% in Korea and 46% in Thailand, to 19% in the Philippines.[6]

The primary problem with foreign investment in the short-term debt of emerging markets nations is the fluidity of the investment. Adverse economic news is likely to result in the debt not being rolled over upon maturity and thus in net capital outflows. The secondary problem is that such capital outflows may foment a collapse in investor confidence in the economy.

When the short-term debt is denominated in local currency, volatility is heightened because a substantial devaluation will decimate a local currency portfolio. Accordingly, the first signs of a devaluation will prompt a severe sell-off. The reliance on local currency short-term bonds intensified the Asian economic crisis once it commenced. The World Bank has summarized the combined effect of short-term and local currency debt, in these terms: '[t]he build up of short-term, unhedged debt left East Asian economies vulnerable to a sudden collapse of confidence.... The loss of confidence led to capital outflows, and thus to depreciating currencies and falling asset prices, which further strained private balance sheets and so proved self-fulfilling'.[7]

5.2.2 Extent of Indebtedness

The extent of indebtedness which contributed to the Asian troubles was itself the product of

(i) excess liquidity in the developed world; and
(ii) the role of crossover investors.

Each will be considered.

---

6. The World Bank, *Global Development Finance 1997*, pp. 35, 160. For short-term debt 'accurate information is not widely available from debtors. By its nature, short-term debt is difficult to monitor [and] loan-by-loan registration is normally impractical': The World Bank, *Global Development Finance 1998*, pp. 24, 144. Nonetheless, this is no small market – it had a total capitalization of about USD 850 billion at year-end 1996: S. Kandler, 'Local Currency Markets Offer Promise and Risk' 10 *Emerging Markets Debt Report*, 3 February 1997; and The World Bank, *Global Development Finance 1998*, p. 25.
7. The World Bank, *Global Development Finance 1998*, p. 31. See also S. Sugisaki, 'Economic Crises in Asia' (Address delivered at the 1998 Harvard Asia Business Conference, Harvard Business School, 30 January 1998).

5.2.2.1 Excess Liquidity in the Developed World

Every one of the lending booms in Latin America was predicated upon excess liquidity in the northern hemisphere. The principal lending booms to Latin America were in the 1820s, the 1860s, the 1920s and the 1970s, all periods of surplus liquidity in the creditor nations.[8] And, in each case, these capital flows led to economic collapses – in 1828, 1873, 1930 and 1982, respectively. The pattern continued with Mexico's peso crisis in late 1994. The preceding two years, 1993 and 1994, had seen record capital flows into Mexico at a time of excess liquidity in the US in particular.[9]

The story was precisely the same in Asia. Western capital poured into East Asian countries in record quantities in the two years to June, 1997. East Asian stocks and bonds were being acquired by US and European investors scornful of the low interest rates on offer in their home countries and fearful that the US stock market had reached unsustainable heights. Liquidity was at a peak in the US and Europe and flowed into emerging markets nations.

The conventional view of international capital flows is that developed country investors rationally and continually evaluate emerging markets investment opportunities and when these opportunities, on a risk adjusted basis, offer returns in excess of those available domestically, capital flows into the emerging markets.[10] This can be described as an 'investment-pull' model. The analytical focus is on the emerging markets nation itself and the assumption is that *'growth prospects precede investment inflows'*.[11] This model assumes that capital flows across international borders to emerging markets nations on the same basis as it moves around within a developed economy. For this reason, it is an appealing model but it is contradicted by economic history.

The prospects for growth in Latin America in the 1970s weren't markedly superior to those in the 1960s. But in the 1970s the OPEC oil price rise led to excess liquidity and a lending boom to Latin America resulted. East Asia's growth prospects weren't better in the early to mid-1990s than in the 1980s, but there was far more liquidity in developed nations in the 1990s which depressed returns in those markets and led to massive capital flows to some East Asian countries.[12] The focus of this 'capital-push' model is on liquidity in the developed world and the

---

8. See generally, Dawson, *The First Latin American Debt Crisis: The City of London and the 1822–1825 Loan Bubble*, p. 244; Delamaide, *Debt Shock*, pp. 95, 96, 99 and 120; Marichal, *A Century of Debt Crises in Latin America*, pp. 95 and 212–213; Skiles, 'Latin American International Loan Defaults in the 1930s: Lessons for the 1980s?' pp. 1, 17; and Stallings, *Banker to the Third World: U.S. Portfolio Investment in Latin America, 1900 – 1986*, pp. 294–295.
9. C. Makin, 'Doesn't anybody remember risk?' *Institutional Investor*, April 1994, 41; and M. Tobin, 'Emerging Markets trading house – Chase delivers the goods', (1994) 1061 *IFR*.
10. Levinson, 'The International Financial System: A Flawed Architecture', 21; M. Pettis, *Can Financial Crises be Prevented?*, an unfinished paper, June 1998.
11. Pettis, *Can Financial Crises be Prevented?*, 1 (emphasis in original).
12. The World Bank, *Global Development Finance 1997*, p. 160; and The World Bank, *Global Development Finance 1998*, pp. 9, 31.

assumption is that *'capital inflow precedes and causes growth'*.[13] The magnitude of these capital flows relative to the size of the recipient markets leads to major investment-driven growth and any sharp decrease in flows is, because of their relative magnitude, inherently destabilizing.

The 'capital-push' model is less logically satisfying than the 'investment-pull' model because it suggests international financial markets aren't rational and scientific in their operation. It suggests that early in the cycle when little capital is flowing to the emerging markets, psychological factors such as the ease and security of investing at home tend to predominate, and later in the cycle when copious quantities of capital are flowing to the emerging markets and they are thus performing strongly, a generalized discounting of risk and bandwagon effect come strongly into play. 'Capital-push' is the only model that accords with economic history.

5.2.2.2 The Central Role of Crossover Investors

Crossover investors is the term for mainstream institutional investors that add emerging market bonds to their portfolios for higher yield. They include multinational corporations, pension funds, insurance companies, high-yield (junk bond) funds, high-grade bond funds and hedge funds. These funds control such vast amounts of capital that their typical five% allocation to the emerging markets far exceeds the capitalization of specialist emerging markets funds. In times of high inflows to capital markets, fixed income yields in the developed countries shrivel. Institutional investors then typically begin to cross over into non-traditional markets in search of higher yields.[14]

In 1996 and early 1997, with their high credit ratings, East Asian issuers appealed in particular to crossover investors. The flow of capital allowed yields to decline so dramatically that Indonesia was able to issue USD 400 million of ten-year Yankee bonds at only one percentage point over US Treasuries – emerging markets investors were severely underestimating the country risk.[15]

The crossover phenomenon is, in essence, the story of a broad array of money managers becoming comfortable with higher risk investments and learning to leaven their portfolio with some higher risk assets in the quest for a higher overall return.[16]

From 1995 to early 1997, the crossover investors thus drove the traditional emerging markets money from the established markets so that it, in turn, supported

---

13. Pettis, *Can Financial Crises be Prevented?*, 2 (emphasis in original).
14. P. Eavis, 'The crossover factor' (1997) 4 *Emerging Markets Investor*, 17; and 'Emerging Markets Trends' 1167 *IFR*, 25 January 1997; and 'Crossing the line' 1151 *IFR*, 21 September 1996.
15. 'Sovereign bond deal of the year' (1997) 8 *AsiaMoney*, 38. For instance, the Czech Export Bank was able to obtain a three-year USD 150 million revolving credit (syndicated loan) priced at a mere 12.5 basis points over Libor: 'Eastern Europe: Tidal wave of foreign finance' 1151 *IFR*, 21 September 1996.
16. K. Mullin, 'Yield: the opium of global investors', 1200 *IFR*, 12 September 1997.

the sharp growth in issuance of local market short-term bonds. Without the crossover phenomenon, the total indebtedness of East Asia would have been significantly less by mid-1997 – a fact not appreciated in most analyses of the crisis.

5.2.3　　　Financial Sector Weaknesses

This cause of the crisis has two facets:

(i) the inability of local financial sectors to intermediate increased capital flows efficiently; and
(ii) the premature liberalization of local financial markets.

5.2.3.1　　Failure to Intermediate Capital Flows Effectively

One of the few traits shared among the five principal nations of the Asian economic crisis was an inadequately sophisticated and supervised local financial sector. The local financial systems were unable to efficiently intermediate capital and allocate it to productive uses. The capital inflows often went into property and stock market investments, driving up the price of those assets in speculative bubbles.[17]

Disclosure and regulatory standards were inadequate across the region.[18] Faced with a steep yield curve,[19] local banks succumbed to the dangerous temptation to borrow short and lend long and did so, in the main, without hedging their foreign exchange exposures. This lack of adequate prudential regulation was compounded by the moral hazard engendered by the crony capitalism prevalent in many countries in the region. Local banks were often owned and controlled by people with strong connections to the ruling political party and their frequent choice of highly risky, highly lucrative funding strategies was doubtless influenced by the prospect of a local bail-out should the risks result in losses.

Indiscriminate international borrowing and domestic lending had been common throughout the region, and when the bubble burst domestic banks were in crisis in many countries, particularly Indonesia, Korea and Thailand.[20] The productive capacity of the region had far outstripped the sophistication and regulation of its financial sectors.

Indeed, it is suggested that a useful indicator of whether capital flows to an emerging market nation are excessive is the destination of the funds. When the great majority of incoming foreign capital is being used to increase the productive capacity of a nation, local regulators should be able to be reasonably comfortable.

---

17. Sugisaki, 'Economic Crises in Asia'.
18. The World Bank, *Global Development Finance 1998*, p. 4.
19. A yield curve is a graph which plots yield of fixed interest securities against their time to maturity. A steep yield curve means yields on longer term securities are much higher than on shorter term securities.
20. R. Dornbusch, 'A Bail-out Won't Do the Trick in Korea', *Business Week*, 8 December 1997, 26; and R. Garran, 'Korea Crisis', *The Australian*, 19 November 1997, 36.

When the majority of incoming foreign capital is funding a boom in the local stock and/or real estate markets it is time for local regulators to adopt measures to make their nation a less attractive destination for foreign capital.

5.2.3.2 The Premature Liberalization of Local Financial Markets

In Thailand's case, foreign money had flooded into the economy:

(i) directly as institutional investors invested in stocks and bonds, particularly short-term local market bonds; and
(ii) indirectly as Thai banks borrowed heavily from their foreign counterparts through the Bangkok International Banking Facility established in 1993.[21]

With the benefit of hindsight, the Bangkok International Banking Facility was established too early, before effective prudential controls and supervision were in place and functioning well. As the IMF has identified, 'a robust financial system underpinned by effective regulation and supervision of financial institutions'[22] is the overriding precondition to a nation liberalizing its capital controls. Thailand, Indonesia and Korea, in particular, had opened their economies to international capital flows without reinforcing the stability of their domestic banking sector in these ways.[23]

The dangers of premature liberalization of local financial markets are well made by the minimal effect of the Asian economic crisis on the Republic of China. Taiwan's local financial sector is closed to foreign banks and its financial markets are largely closed to foreign speculators through a system of strict limits on inflows and outflows of portfolio investment. Taiwan's heavily controlled financial markets and huge foreign exchange reserves served it exceedingly well. Taiwan is highly unusual in its capacity to fund its dramatic growth internally and the author is not recommending a path of financial isolation. However, Taiwan's experience underlines that appropriate regulation and supervision must precede financial market liberalization to gain the benefits of greater access to international capital without the destabilizing effects of massive capital flows.

5.2.4 FIXED EXCHANGE RATES

Fixed exchange rates offer lower costs of credit than floating rates because under a fixed exchange rate regime banks will typically seek to fund themselves in foreign currency (at rates invariably lower than local currency rates) and simply trust the peg of the local currency to the foreign currency to hold.[24] Fixed and undervalued

---

21. H. Chow, 'Crawling from the wreckage' 4 *Emerging Markets Investor*, July/August 1997, 15.
22. International Monetary Fund, *World Economic Outlook*, May 1998, at p. 9.
23. International Monetary Fund, *World Economic Outlook*, May 1998, at p. 6.
24. I. Viscio, 'The recent experience with capital flows to emerging market economies', 65 *OECD Economy Outlook*, 1 June 1998; and Bustelo, Garcia and Olivie, 'Global and Domestic Factors of Financial Crisis in Emerging Economies: Lessons from the East Asian Episodes', 78.

exchange rates also promote exports and deter imports. For all these reasons, Indonesia, Thailand, Malaysia and other East Asian nations in the early and mid-1990s had their currencies fixed to the US dollar. The dollar was appreciating and hence so were the local currencies.

The depreciation of the yen from mid-1995 onwards provided a further twist. As the 1990s progressed, East Asian economies began moving increasingly into high-tech exports in which they were competing with Japan. However while their exchange rates were pegged to the US dollar and thus appreciating, from mid-1995 onwards, their principal competitor enjoyed a depreciating currency,[25] and this was another ingredient in the recipe for a crisis.

5.2.5   REGION-WIDE LOSS OF CONFIDENCE

The severity of the Asian economic crisis exceeded the combined effect of its various causes[26] and can only be explained as the result of a region-wide loss of confidence. In Alan Greenspan's words, the workings of the international capital markets in the Asian crisis were based on a 'visceral engulfing fear'.[27] This was the common factor that turned quite different economic troubles in five countries into a regional crisis. The loss of confidence led to an outflow of capital – both domestic capital flight and a halt in external re-financing. This led to currency depreciation which uncovered massive, unhedged, foreign exchange exposures and severely damaged the balance sheets of local corporations.[28]

That the investment markets should have treated the whole of East Asia as one region might appear at first glance to be remarkably unsophisticated. The economies of Korea, Thailand and Indonesia have quite different strengths and weaknesses. Indeed, these economies have little in common beyond inadequately regulated and supervised local financial sectors.

This inability to distinguish between countries is unsophisticated if the task of market participants is to predict the economic fundamentals of each economy in the future. However, the primary task of market participants is to estimate the value the market will put on the debt in the future, not some underlying fundamental value (whatever that may be). In the words of Keynes:

> the energies and skill of the professional investor and speculator are mainly occupied ... not with making superior long-term forecasts of the probable yield of an investment over its whole life, but with foreseeing changes in the conventional basis of valuation a short time ahead ... Moreover, this behavior is an inevitable result of an investment market ... For it is not sensible to pay 25 for an investment of which you believe the prospective

---

25. East Asia Analytical Unit, Department of Foreign Affairs and Trade, Commonwealth of Australia, *Asia's Financial Markets: Capitalising on Reform*, 22 (1999).
26. The World Bank, *Global Development Finance 1998*, p. 40.
27. Quoted in P. Kelly, 'IMF tightens the screws on Suharto', *The Australian*, 11 March 1998, 13.
28. The World Bank, *Global Development Finance 1998*, pp. 5, 30.

yield to justify a value of 30, if you also believe that the market will value it at 20 three months hence.[29]

As the principal investors in emerging markets invest across all of the countries in a region, a sharp decline in values in one nation's debts will prompt the sale of some of the debts of other nations to meet margin calls or cover losses arising from the price declines. Furthermore, the tendency to view the emerging markets as one entity was well established in the tequila effect of 1995 in which Mexico's peso crisis resulted in a sell-off across the entire emerging markets sector – in nations as diverse as Argentina, the Philippines, Hungary and Thailand.[30] Accordingly, from the perspective of each separate investor, a loss of confidence in the entire region, and thus an exodus from lending and investment to the region, was rational.

It is generally accepted that excessive inflows of foreign capital, particularly short-term capital, into East Asian economies from 1993 to early 1997 was one of the principal causes of the Asian economic crisis. However, these economies are capital exporters, with some of the highest savings rates in the world. Capital inflows as a crisis cause should have been surprising. All that had to be done for Korea, Malaysia or Thailand to have all the capital they needed to fund their own development was for impervious barriers to the outflow of capital to be erected around those countries or for impervious barriers to the entry of this capital to be erected around developed countries.[31] Yet this is a very difficult task – contemporary capital is too fluid – and even if it were achievable the side effects of permanent capital controls, in terms of higher costs of credit and less innovative financial markets, can be unpleasant.

5.3 CONCLUSION AND LESSONS

The Asian crisis and the debt crisis were, accordingly, quite different types of crisis. The Asian crisis was far more the result of private sector than public borrowing.[32] The Asian crisis was in part the result of misallocated investment, not over consumption as was the debt crisis. The Asian crisis, with the exception of Indonesia, was in large measure a crisis of confidence: as the other nations rapid recovery from it has attested. The debt crisis was the result of unsustainable debt levels, it was not principally a crisis of perceptions. Nonetheless, a comparison of

---

29. J.M. Keynes, *The General Theory of Employment Interest and Money* (London, MacMillan, 1967), pp. 154–155.
30. G. Platt, 'Mexican Virus Fells Emerging Markets But Prognosis Good Among Healthiest' *Journal of Commerce*, 4 May 1995, 2A; 'Tequila slammers' 1064 *IFR*, 14 January 1995; 'Tequila hangover – a year to forget', 1112 *IFR*, 16 December 1995.
31. M.A. Espinosa-Vega, B.D. Smith and C.K. Yip, 'Barriers to International Capital Flows: Who Should Erect Them and How Big Should They Be?' (Working Paper No 99–6, Federal Reserve Bank of Atlanta, July 1999).
32. J. Stiglitz, 'Statement to the Meeting of Finance Ministers of ASEAN plus 6 with the IMF and the World Bank' (Kuala Lumpur, Malaysia, 1 December 1997).

the causes of the two crises does suggest some common lessons. Perhaps, at least five:

(1) In the contemporary world, fixed exchange rates are a high risk strategy and some sort of floating rate is much to be preferred.
(2) The denomination of most of a nation's foreign debt in foreign currency is likewise risky.
(3) Much more of the debt needs of emerging markets need to be funded with long-term local currency denominated capital.
(4) Capital tends to flow recklessly to emerging markets in times of surplus liquidity in the developed world.
(5) It is time to reconfigure the allocation of responsibility for international lending and investment.

Each lesson will be considered.

5.3.1 THE BENEFITS OF FLOATING EXCHANGE RATES

Floating exchange rates provide an automatic adjustment mechanism. When a nation's export competitiveness is declining, floating exchange rates will tend downwards, promoting exports, limiting imports, and bring the current account back into balance. Fixed exchange rates can impose a useful fiscal and monetary discipline on a domestic government (because if a government wishes to preserve its exchange rate it simply cannot print money to fund its budgetary desires). Undervalued rates also promote exports. However, the management of fixed rates, and the ability to reduce them as rapidly as may be required in our world of globalized capital flows, poses a major governance challenge to any government. As we have explored elsewhere, on balance, many developing countries may well be best off leaving this challenge to the market.

5.3.2 THE HIGH RISKS OF FOREIGN CURRENCY BORROWING

The second lesson from the debt crisis and the Asian crisis is that borrowing in foreign currency imposes a tremendous currency risk on the borrowing nation. Hedging on such a scale is extremely expensive and rarely done. Denominating loans and bonds in foreign currency increases the amount of indebtedness as it encourages lenders to discount the currency risk. This is an illusion. As both the debt crisis and Asian crisis demonstrate, if the currency risk is with the borrower due to the denomination of the debt, in times of trouble it is transferred to the lender by the incapacity of the borrower to service the debt.

Denominating loans in foreign currency also encourages borrowing as it reduces the interest rate on the debt (because lenders are not factoring in the currency risk). The interest rates that best reflect the real risks of borrowing by such borrowers are those on their local currency indebtedness. The accepted custom of denominating loans and bonds for emerging market nations in foreign currency masks the real cost of funds and encourages excessive indebtedness.

5.3.3 THE NEED FOR LONG-TERM LOCAL CURRENCY CAPITAL

The third lesson is the pressing need for emerging market nations to raise long-term capital in their own currencies. The principal source of local currency capital to date has been short-term local market bonds. However, the short tenor of these instruments brings with it tremendous instability. Long-term local currency capital markets will allow emerging market debtors to raise capital with the currency risk on the investors. Returns to investors will be greater when times are good, as debtors will have to pay more to borrow in their currency, and less when times are bad, through the operation of the exchange rate and such a repayment profile is well adapted to avert the types of crises we saw in the 1980s and 1990s. International assistance, particularly in the form of market and regulatory expertise and funding for local regulation, is required to enable emerging markets nations to develop their local capital markets, particularly local sovereign bond markets.

5.3.4 INTERNATIONAL CAPITAL FLOWS AS A PRODUCT OF DEVELOPED WORLD LIQUIDITY

Every developing country financial crisis from 1828 to 1998 was preceded by a period of high liquidity in the developed world that funded large capital flows to the developing countries. At times of high liquidity in developed nations, bank regulators in both developed and emerging economies should be on the look out for excessive capital flows to emerging markets (excessive flows being those that fund local consumption or fuel local asset market bubbles rather than those that fund an expansion in a nation's productive capacity). The primary task of both local and international bank regulators – to maintain the safety and soundness of their domestic banking systems – requires vigilance and control over the amount the international banks and institutional investors are lending to and investing in emerging markets nations.

5.3.5 THE URGENT NEED FOR A NEW PERSPECTIVE ON RESPONSIBILITY IN INTERNATIONAL LENDING AND INVESTMENT

It is time for a new framework for allocating responsibility in international lending and investment. Creditors and investors who make poor lending or investment decisions in the domestic context suffer the consequences. The ultimate sanction of bankruptcy provides a way out from under crippling debt for the debtor and typically results in substantial losses for creditors of, and investors in, the debtor. However, there is no equivalent to bankruptcy protection for sovereign debtors.

Indeed, it is almost as if the protection of bankruptcy has been replaced in the international context by a presumption that bad loans and bad investments are entirely the debtors' fault.[33] This is a convenient fiction for international banks and investors, nothing more. However, it is a fiction with severe consequences.

In the debt crisis, this fiction meant the 1980s became the lost decade for Latin America and sub-Saharan Africa – a decade in which the absence of debt relief meant more people in abject poverty and further decay of vital infrastructure each year. The view that the responsibility for the debt crisis lay principally on the debtors justified the creditors in their strong opposition to debt relief. In the end it was the mounting risk to democracy in Latin America that prompted the US Treasury to embrace the very limited amount of debt relief inherent in the Brady Plan and to 'persuade' banks to that point of view.[34] Appalling human suffering resulted from the resistance to debt relief, and thus from the fiction that bad international debts are purely the debtors fault.

In the Asian crisis, this fiction meant the IMF bail-outs of the Asian debtors could be, and were, made available for the purpose of fully repaying short-term bank debt – the very debt that, through its instability, had triggered the crisis and the very debt that through high interest rates the banks had been well rewarded for holding. Such bail-outs were highly counterproductive. They rewarded creditors for investing in the most destabilizing form of debt and did nothing for those creditors who had extended long-term debt: precisely the type of debt that should be encouraged. A default on such short-term debt would have avoided the severe moral hazard occasioned by this use of the bail out funds (which, incidentally, contributed directly to the market extending excessive credit to Russia in late 1997 and early 1998 and thus to Russia's crisis in August 1998).[35]

The IMF made the wrong call on the use of bail out funds for the Asian debtors because it was viewing the situation from the wrong perspective and analyzing it in terms of the wrong framework of responsibility. It is time, now, to reconfigure the framework for allocating responsibility for international loans and investments so as to recognize that international lending and borrowing is a joint endeavour for which each party is responsible.

5.4 THE ROLE AND IMPACT OF THE IMF IN THE ASIAN CRISIS

There are five principal criticisms of the IMF's response to the Asian Crisis:

(1) The IMF initially completely misdiagnosed the nature of the crisis.
(2) The IMF imposed excessive conditions upon the countries, and the timing of the reforms mandated by the conditions was inappropriate.

---

33. Levinson, *The International Financial System: A Flawed Architecture*, pp. 36–37.
34. Buckley, 'The Facilitation of the Brady Plan: Emerging Markets Debt Trading from 1989 to 1993' 21 *Fordham International Law Journal*, pp. 1803–1818.
35. Buckley, 'A Force for Globalisation: Emerging Markets Debt Trading from 1994 to 1999', (2007) Vol 30 No 2 *Fordham International Law Journal* 185.

(3) The IMF's principal focus was to protect the international financial system and foreign creditors.
(4) The IMF ignored the social costs of its policies.
(5) The IMF mishandled market expectations.

5.4.1 Misdiagnosis

The IMF has been criticized for initially treating the wrong type of crisis in the Asian crisis countries.[36] The IMF's initial policy prescriptions of fiscal austerity were designed to address a crisis of over-consumption, such as that which had gripped Latin America and Africa throughout the 1980s and into the 1990s. The Asian economic crisis was a completely different sort of crisis.

The IMF's initial response to the Asian crisis involved tight credit, increased interest rates and fiscal tightening. These policies caused domestic deflation in IMF program countries, worsened the crisis by causing widespread bankruptcies, and in most cases did not improve confidence but rather increased uncertainty. At the time Buira rightly observed that 'the Fund's strategy discourages investment, compounds the recessionary impact of the reversal in capital flows, and generally exacerbates the difficulties faced by firms, banks, and public finances'.[37]

Another of the failed IMF crisis responses was the attempt to induce a small depreciation in the exchange rate of crisis countries so as to promote exports, whilst tightening fiscal policy, in order to restore confidence. Unexpectedly the currencies in the IMF program currencies fell rapidly – the Thai baht fell by 50%; the Indonesian rupiah fell by 75% and the Korean won fell by 40%.[38] This in turn caused a downturn because the falling exchange rate increased the indebtedness of companies, leaving them unable to finance investment.

The IMF's assessment of Thailand's problems provides a good example of its failure to diagnose the crisis properly. The IMF initially thought that Thailand had 'a conventional demand-management problem – excessively easy fiscal and monetary policy and a deteriorating current account – requiring a general policy tightening'.[39] Instead De Brouwer describes Thailand as having 'joint capital account and financial system crises' which required the opposite treatment to that which

---

36. R. Weissman, 'Twenty Questions on the IMF', in *Democratizing the Global Economy*, K. Danaher (ed.), (Common Courage Press, 2001), p. 91; G. De Brouwer, *The IMF and East Asia: A Changing Regional Financial Architecture*, in *The IMF and Its Critics*, C. Gilbert and D. Vines (eds) (Cambridge, Cambridge University Press, 2003), p. 2.
37. A. Buira, *An Alternative Approach to Financial Crises*, (Princeton, Princeton University, 1999), p. 20. See also M. Corden, *The Asian Crisis: Is There a Way Out?*, (Singapore, Institute of Southeast Asian Studies, 1999), p. 34; and G. Corsetti, P. Pesenti and N. Roubini, *What Caused the Asian Currency and Financial Crisis? Part II: The Policy Debate*, NBER Working Paper No. W6834. Available at <ssrn.com/abstract=227609>, p. 16.
38. G. Irwin and D. Vines, 'International Policy Advice in the East Asian Crisis. A Critical Review of the Debate', in *Capital Flows Without Crisis? Reconciling Capital Mobility and Economic Stability*, D. Dasgupta, M. Uzan and D. Wilson (eds) (London, Routledge, 2001), p. 61.
39. De Brouwer, *The IMF and East Asia: A Changing Regional Financial Architecture*, p. 3.

they were prescribed – supportive, not tight, fiscal policy.[40] The IMF's focus on fiscal contraction was counter intuitive because the affected countries all had long histories of good fiscal policy.[41]

Exploring this misdiagnosis, Eichengreen discusses the problems with the IMF's requirements for fiscal austerity during the crisis:

> It failed to anticipate the severity of the Asian downturn or see that the restrictive fiscal policies it recommended would themselves make that downturn worse... the Fund's fiscal targets were too tight and... larger deficits should have been encouraged.[42]

These policies made the problems of banks and companies worse by making it harder to get credit, which in turn led to an increase in bad loans because loans could not be rolled over.[43]

5.4.2   Excessive Conditionality

Crisis countries that had IMF programs in place received IMF funds to support their recovery. This money always came with significant conditions attached. The IMF's initial conditions reflected the fund's policy that a prolonged crisis could be averted by increasing investor confidence in the crisis economies by undertaking major economic and financial sector reforms and reducing government spending to improve their balance of payments position.

The number and scope of conditions placed on IMF crisis funding is one of the major problems with the fund's approach to crises. Whilst most crises are caused by underlying problems with a country's economic fundamentals, the time to deal with these issues is not whilst the crisis is at its worst.[44] Crisis countries should have been allowed to focus on policies that would reduce the damage done by the crisis, rather than on long term policies aimed at preventing a crisis occurring again in the future. Corden also concludes that there were too many conditions on IMF relief, and that whilst the reforms were desirable it was not the time to implement them.[45]

---

40. *Ibid.*
41. Corden, *The Asian Crisis: Is There a Way Out?*, p. 14; and L.H. Meyer, 'Lessons from the Asian Crisis: A Central Banker's Perspective' (Working Paper No. 276, Levy Economics Institute, 1999).
42. B. Eichengreen, *Toward a New Financial Architecture: A Practical Post-Asia Agenda*, (Washington, DC, Institute of International Economics, 1999), p. 110.
43. Corsetti, Pesenti and Roubini, *What Caused the Asian Currency and Financial Crisis?*, p. 10.
44. De Brouwer, *The IMF and East Asia: A Changing Regional Financial Architecture*, p. 3. H.K. Pyo, 'The Financial Crisis in Korea and its Aftermath: A Political Economic Perspective', in *Capital Flows Without Crisis? Reconciling Capital Mobility and Economic Stability*, D. Dasgupta, M. Uzan and D. Wilson (eds) (London, Routledge, 2001), p. 243.
45. Corden, *The Asian Crisis: Is There a Way Out?*, p. 45.

Not only the timing, but also the types of conditions imposed by the IMF on a number of crisis countries were inappropriate. Some of these conditions involved countries further opening their economies. Given that the crisis itself may have been caused by over reliance on short-term international financing, recommending a further opening of the economy to international financing at this particular point was unwise. In this way, the IMF's policies simply gave program countries more of what had initially caused them problems.

The conditions imposed on Korea provide a good example of the wrongheadedness of IMF policies at the beginning of the crisis. The following conditions on Korea's IMF loan appear to have increased rather than decreased Korea's vulnerability to the vagaries of international capital flows. Korea was required to:

- review all remaining restrictions on corporate foreign borrowing, including short term borrowing;
- abolish restrictions on foreign ownership of land and real estate;
- permit equity investment in non-listed companies; and
- eliminate the aggregate ceiling on foreign investment in Korean equities.

5.4.3 PROTECTION OF THE SYSTEM AND OF CREDITORS

The IMF bail-outs of Indonesia, Korea and Thailand were extended upon the basis that the funds advanced would be used to repay debt then due, i.e. debt lent by short-term creditors. Foreign creditors were thus the main recipients of the money loaned to crisis countries. Critics have argued that IMF funds should have been used 'not for rescuing foreign creditors – nor for financing capital flight – but for financing compensating fiscal expansion'.[46] If the debtor nations, or at least the local banks and corporations in the debtor nations, had defaulted on their loans, this would have avoided the severe moral hazard occasioned by this use of the bail out funds which, incidentally, contributed directly to the market extending excessive credit to Russia in late 1997 and early 1998 and thus to Russia's crisis in August 1998. Allowing a default on this debt would also have freed these funds to be used to recapitalize the local banks, improve the local financial systems and stimulate the local economies.[47] To use these funds to, in effect, bail out the international banks rather than the debtors is only defensible in a framework of moral responsibility that holds the creditors blameless. Yet bad loans nearly always involve errors of judgment by both parties and the consequences of those errors should be shared. This is especially so as the burdens on the debtors usually fall on those least able to bear them – the poor and disadvantaged.

The IMF solutions in Asian countries were unjust because they allowed investors to avoid the consequences of their actions, which creates moral hazard and places the burden of the consequences of those actions on people who had no power to control them. Vasquez puts this criticism succinctly – 'Just as profits should not

---

46. *Ibid.*, p. 59.
47. Wellons, *Passing The Buck – Banks, Governments And Third World Debt*, p. 243.

be socialized when times are good, neither should losses be socialized during difficult times'.[48]

This highlights the central hypocrisy of IMF policies. Whilst the Fund insists that the market is the best mechanism to allocate money and resources during good times, in bad times it refuses to leave the market to apportion losses.

Many of the policies mandated by the IMF in crisis countries put the international banking system before those countries' citizens. As Soros put it:

> The net effect of this approach was to place the burden of adjustment mainly on the borrowing countries. They were required to service their debts to the limits of their capacity. The lenders did not get off scot-free, but their losses were much smaller than they would have been absent IMF intervention.[49]

If the IMF had not intervened to protect the creditors through bail-outs, it is likely the countries and their creditors would have negotiated other solutions. Creditors would have had enough incentive to accept a renegotiation of the debt, because otherwise they would have lost their entire loans.[50] This would have been preferable because it would have reduced the burden on crisis countries and forced financiers to accept responsibility for their bad investment decisions.

5.4.4 MISHANDLING OF MARKET EXPECTATIONS

Another criticism of the IMF's behaviour was that the Fund made matters worse in crisis countries by overemphasizing the supposed structural causes of the crisis.[51] Contrary to the Fund's intentions, this emphasis did not support confidence and recovery.[52] Cordon sensibly suggests that it would have been 'better to try to calm markets by emphasizing the positive features of these economies...' instead of highlighting all the flaws.[53] The IMF policy of encouraging bank closures in crisis countries caused 'a bank panic that helped set off financial market declines in much of Asia'.[54]

5.4.5 SOCIAL COSTS OF IMF POLICIES

One of the most damning criticisms of the IMF is that it ignored the social consequences of its policies during the crisis. The IMF seems to have ignored the

---

48. I. Vasquez, 'Why the IMF Should Not Intervene', <www.cato.org/speeches/sp-iv22598.html>, 4 December 2007; and R.P. Buckley, 'The Fatal Flaw in International Finance: The Rich Borrow and the Poor Repay' (2002) XIX No. 4 *World Policy Journal*, Winter 2002/2003, 59.
49. G. Soros, *Open Society: Reforming Global Capitalism*, (London, Little, Brown & Company, 2000), p. 269.
50. Vasquez, 'Why the IMF Should Not Intervene'.
51. Corden, *The Asian Crisis: Is There a Way Out?*, p. 48.
52. De Brouwer, *The IMF and East Asia: A Changing Regional Financial Architecture*, p. 2.
53. Corden, *The Asian Crisis: Is There a Way Out?*, p. 48.
54. D.E. Sanger, 'IMF Reports Plan Backfired, Worsening Indonesia Woes', *New York Times*, 14 January 1998.

burdensome impact of its policies on the poor. The recession that occurred in IMF program countries affected the poor the worst. The very people who had not benefited from the preceding 'miracle' in Asian countries bore the brunt of reduced public spending when things turned bad.[55] An example is seen in the aftermath of the financial crisis in Korea where there was an increase in the ratio of absolute poverty and greater inequality of income and wealth after the crisis. Pyo notes that in Korea 'the labour and capital income of the highest 10% in 1998 increased by 8%, while that of the other 90% of income earners decreased sharply'.[56]

5.5 CONCLUSIONS ON THE IMF'S ROLE IN THE ASIAN CRISIS

The IMF displayed little expertise in dealing with East Asia's problems in the late 1990s. Malaysia's economic policies during the Asian crisis, on balance, delivered slightly better economic results than those in countries under IMF programs and did so while better protecting the poor and enhancing local economic sovereignty.

Any consideration of international financial history since 1982 suggests that the IMF fails to meet the threshold test for claiming economic sovereignty over developing countries: that it can do the job better than the countries themselves. There are a number of reasons for this, including:

- The domestic Treasury and Ministry of Finance are more likely to understand their own economy. Policies crafted without a deep understanding of the culture and local institutions are less likely to succeed.
- Home-grown policies are more likely to be implemented and enforced rigorously than those imposed by the Fund. IMF programs are often hampered by ineffective implementation and enforcement. Policies developed abroad are rarely likely to be adopted and enforced with the enthusiasm and rigor of those developed at home. This is a simple fact of human nature. We all do more willingly what we choose to do, rather than what we are told to do.
- The model under which a strong IMF directs and guides the debtor nation's economy does not necessarily promote the development of the skills and confidence needed in the local finance ministry. Self-confidence in economic policy setting should be nurtured within developing country governments.
- The developing nation as policy maker has a narrower responsibility than does the IMF. The national government's job is to do the best for its people. The IMF strives to implement policies aimed at developing a healthy and stable international financial system. The IMF is subject to the direction and instruction of its member governments, particularly the larger OECD

---

55. Vasquez, 'Why the IMF Should Not Intervene'.
56. Pyo, 'The Financial Crisis in Korea and its Aftermath: A Political Economic Perspective', p. 248.

nations. It is wrong to think of the IMF as an autonomous, supra-national institution. The Fund is governed by a Board of Governors upon which voting rights are directly proportional to their special drawing rights (broadly their GDP).[57] Accordingly the direction of the IMF is set, overwhelmingly, by the rich countries. As one IMF staffer once said to me, 'When the leading industrial nations tell the Fund to jump, we ask how high'.[58]

If economic mismanagement is one reason a nation needs IMF assistance, it is understandable the Fund wishes to reshape the economic policies of that nation. However the IMF is very heavy-handed in how it wrests control from the Finance Ministry and Treasury of its client nations. On the basis of its performance, the IMF is not justified in assuming the economic sovereignty of its client nations.

It is worth noting that there are a number of changes the IMF could implement which would, in time, improve significantly the quality of its policies, and their appropriateness for specific developing countries. These changes to the Fund's policies and culture include:

(1) The Fund needs to study the lessons of institutional economics and the school of economists of which Douglass C North is perhaps the pre-eminent member.[59] The biggest problem with the Fund's policy prescriptions is that they give far too little weight to the institutional environment of the recipient country. The Fund needs to pay much more attention to the strength of the rule of law, and of other economic institutions in the countries for which it is setting economic policies. For instance, it is arguable that privatization of state-owned assets offers considerable efficiencies in the use of those assets, and may serve to enhance the economy of the nation that owns the assets. However, this can *only* be true if the institutional framework of that nation includes a strong rule of law, a free and active media, and a sophisticated financial and professional infrastructure able to price such assets accurately. In most developing nations, the range of potential purchasers is not wide and if these factors are missing it is virtually impossible to realize appropriate prices for the privatization of major assets. In the absence of these important economic institutions, a policy that may be welfare enhancing in the US, Britain or Australia will

---

57. SDR's are allocated as a result of a member's Quota, which is broadly determined by its economic position relative to other members. Various factors are considered in determining the quota, including GDP, current account balances, and official reserves. See International Monetary Fund, 'IMF Quotas: A Fact Sheet 2004', <www.imf.org/external/np/exr/facts/quotas.htm>, 4 December 2007.
58. This anecdotal evidence has been supported by recent research into the extent to which IMF and World Bank lending patterns support the interests of the major OECD countries. See R. Faini and E. Grilli, 'Who runs the IFIs?' CEPR Discussion Paper No. 4666, available from <ssrn.com/abstract=631010>.
59. D.C. North, *Institutions, Institutional Change and Economic Performance*, (Cambridge, Cambridge University Press, 1990).

only lead to knock-down prices for well-connected purchasers, as was seen in Russia in the early to mid-1990s. Thus, a potentially good policy in one institutional environment will *always* be the wrong policy in the environment prevailing in most developing countries.
(2) The Fund's officers need to approach in-country assignments with the attitude that local economists within the Ministry of Finance or Treasury Department and beyond are the best sources of advice on the local economy and such officers need to have far more training in the realities of the local economy than is today the case. Too often today Fund officers arrive with a 'we-know-best' attitude. This has to change. It alienates the local people with whom they will be working, and it denies the Fund's staff the very knowledge they need to craft policies that will have a good chance of working. The Fund needs to undergo a cultural and attitudinal change.
(3) Finally, and most importantly, the entire Washington Consensus needs to be reconsidered and revised, radically. The Washington Consensus, ironically given its name, does not reflect the policies formulated in Washington DC for the US economy. It is far more laissez-faire and admits of far less government involvement in an economy than the US government has in its own. Indeed, I know of no rich country government that applies such rigorous policies to its own economy. The arguments for government intervention in poor countries are stronger than they are in rich ones. The IMF's Board of Governors impose policies on poor countries they will not tolerate in their own countries. This has to change.

Chapter 6
Let's All Cry for Argentina

6.1   THE ARGENTINE EXPERIENCE

The 1980s were a lost decade in Latin America in general and Argentina in particular. The debt crisis of 1982 cast its long shadow over the decade: Latin American countries were net capital exporters as they repaid more than they were able to borrow, living standards plummeted, and infrastructure crumbled.[1]

The years from 1991 to 1998, in contrast, were a prosperous time in Argentina as the resolution from the creditor's perspective of the debt crisis through the Brady Plan encouraged the resumption of net capital flows into the country. Argentina's economy performed particularly strongly with GDP per capita increasing an exceptional 44% between 1991 and 1998. Argentina enjoyed its highest rates of growth since the 1920s and inflation was completely under control. Argentina has a strong base for an economy: a literacy rate of 96.2%, the best educational system in Latin America and rich natural resources.[2]

---

1. See Statement of Per Pinstrup-Andersen, *Food Security and Structural Adjustment* (Statement delivered before the House Committee on Banking, Finance and Urban Affairs hearings on the *International Economic Issues and Their Impact on the U.S. Financial System*, 101st Congress First Session, 4 January 1989), 165, 181; and Testimony of Dr Richard Jolly, Deputy Executive Director for Programmes, United Nations Children's Fund (Statement delivered before the House Committee on Banking, Finance and Urban Affairs hearings on the *International Economic Issues and Their Impact on the U.S. Financial System*, 101st Congress First Session, 4 January 1989), 14.
2. M. Kiguel, 'Structural Reforms in Argentina: Success or Failure?' (2002) XLIV(2) *Comparative Economic Studies*, pp. 83, 84 (44% increase calculated from Figure 1); and S. Arie, 'Rich Argentina tastes hunger', *The Observer* (United Kingdom), 19 May 2002. In the 1930s, on the back of strong beef and grain exports, per capita income in Argentina was on a par with that in France.

In these years, Argentina significantly improved its banking system, more than doubled its exports, increased infrastructure investment through privatizations and otherwise privatized a broad range of industries, experienced significant growth in oil and mineral production and achieved record levels of agricultural and industrial output. (This is not to suggest that many of the privatizations were not deeply problematic. It is a profound challenge to realize appropriate prices for the privatization of major businesses and assets in emerging markets nations for the range of potential purchasers is not wide and scrupulous and rigorous public accountability procedures are rarely present. There is much to suggest that many of the privatizations of the 1990s in Argentina were at a deep undervalue.) Nonetheless, Argentina was a darling of the IMF and the financial markets and was toasted as 'the best case of "responsible leadership" in the developing world'.[3]

Nonetheless at the end of 1998 Argentina entered a severe recession. The timing was dictated in part by external factors, in particular the 1997 Asian economic crisis and the August 1998 Russian crisis which together severely limited capital flows to emerging markets economies. Argentina accordingly had very limited access to new capital to finance budget deficits and service its debt. However, while these external factors influenced the timing of the crisis, they did not cause it. The causes will be considered in the next section.

The recession deepened into a severe crisis in late 2001 when the IMF refused to extend further credit to the nation, believing its economic programs to be unsustainable. As commercial lenders followed this lead, Argentina was denied access to capital and defaulted on its external debt of some USD 132 billion.

The government was forced to float the peso, which more than halved in value overnight, and still the crisis deepened. Eventually, on 19 April 2002 the government ordered the indefinite closure of all banks in Argentina.[4]

Today Argentina has regained its feet economically but UNICEF Argentina remains concerned that stunted growth and reduced mental capacities will be the long-term consequence of this economic crisis for millions of the nation's children.[5]

Notwithstanding eight years of prodigious growth in the 1990s, Argentina then underwent the worst economic crisis in its history and possibly the worst peacetime economic crisis in world history.[6] On one estimate total domestic financial

---

3. 'Chaos in Argentina', *The Nation* (New York), 21 January 2002, 3. See also 'Argentina: A Poster Child for the Failure of Liberalized Policies? Interview with Lance Taylor', *Challenge*, November/December 2001, 28.
4. D. Teather, 'Argentina orders banks to close', *The Guardian* (United Kingdom), 20 April 2002; M. Tran, 'Argentina scrambles to avoid financial collapse', *Guardian Unlimited* (United Kingdom), 22 April 2002.
5. Arie, 'Rich Argentina tastes hunger'.
6. M. Crutsinger, 'IMF Grants Argentina Debt Extension', *Associated Press Online* (New York), 9 May 2002; and D. Green, 'Let Latin America find its own path', *The Guardian* (United Kingdom), 5 August 2002.

assets shrunk from USD 126.8 bn in March 2001 to USD 41.5 bn in March 2002,[7] an utterly extraordinary destruction of wealth. How did this happen?

6.2   CAUSES OF THE ARGENTINE CRISIS

The principal causes of the crisis were the one to one peg of the peso to the US dollar, the massive inflows of foreign capital that were facilitated by the almost complete liberalization of Argentina's capital account[8] and Argentina's endemic corruption. The first two causes were promoted or supported by the IMF. The contribution of each cause, and of IMF policies, will be considered.

6.2.1   THE PESO-DOLLAR PEG

The peg was an effective means of stabilizing inflation, which was critical in promoting local economic activity and in rendering Argentina an attractive destination for foreign capital. However by making one peso equal to one US dollar, Argentina gave up the principal means by which a nation's balance of payments remains in balance and its exports remain competitive: adjustments in its exchange rate.

Compare Argentina's situation with that of Mexico and Brazil. When, in the wake of the East Asian and Russian crises in 1997 and 1998 capital flows to Mexico declined sharply, its currency decreased in value, thereby improving the competitiveness of its exports. Similarly when these and other factors affected Brazil, its government was able successfully (if a little shakily) to devalue the real 40% in January 1999 and thus neatly sidestep an incipient crisis in that country.[9] No such exchange rate flexibility was available to Argentina.

The Brazilian devaluation was particularly problematic for Argentina. Brazil is Argentina's major trading partner and overnight Argentine products became more expensive in Brazil, and Brazilian products cheaper in Argentina.

In summary, pegging the peso to the US dollar was always going to be highly problematic over the medium and long term.[10] Over time, unless the external

---

7. See *Economic Outlook, Argentina Quarterly Forecast Report*, (London, Business Monitor International, 2002).
8. M. Feldstein, 'Argentina's Fall' (2002) 81 *Foreign Affairs*, 8; and 'Argentina: A Poster Child for the Failure of Liberalized Policies? Interview with Lance Taylor', 28.
9. W. Gruben and S. Kiser, 'Why Brazil Devalued the Real', Federal Reserve Bank of Dallas, <www.dallasfed.org/eyi/global/9907real.html>; E. Amann and W. Baer, 'Anchors Away: The Costs and Benefits of Brazil's Devaluation' (Working Paper, University of Illinois at Urbana-Champaign College of Business, 2002), <www.business.uiuc.edu/Working_Papers/papers/02-0122.pdf>.
10. Under this law, to be able to guarantee convertibility the government had to back each peso in circulation with a dollar or similar hard currency at the central bank: Feldstein, 'Argentina's Fall', 8.

competitiveness of the Argentine economy exceeded that of the US economy, the tied exchange rate would inevitably lead to an overvaluation of the peso relative to the dollar. The only ways Argentine exports could have remained competitive was for productivity growth in Argentina to at least match the relative appreciation of the US dollar, or for private and public sector wages to decrease in Argentina, and such productivity growth in Argentina was all but impossible for the value of the US dollar is supported by the strength of its home economy and by the massive capital inflows from Europe and Asia and by the use of the US dollar as a de facto global reserve currency.

Likewise, reductions in nominal wages are a virtual political impossibility in any country. People will strenuously resist cuts in their nominal wages, while typically not even noticing reductions in the value of their wages when measured in a stronger, appreciating, foreign currency.[11]

The Argentine tragedy is that if, once hyperinflation was defeated in 1994, the peso had been allowed to gradually decline in value, growth in the nation's exports and economy might have been strong and sustainable[12] – much as the steady erosion in value of the Australian dollar in the mid-to-late 1990s empowered that economy and allowed it to continue to grow throughout the Asian crisis.

6.2.2   EXCESSIVE INDEBTEDNESS

The second cause of the crisis was the reliance by Argentina throughout the 1990s on international capital to finance budget and current account deficits. Throughout the boom from 1991 to 1997, Argentina was living, and thriving, on borrowed money. In this the Argentines were in step with their continent's history. Latin American nations have traditionally been unwilling to live within their means whenever debt has been available ever since they gained their independence in the 1820s.[13]

Borrowing to finance budget deficits is particularly problematic because this use of the funds will not generate the foreign exchange to service or repay the debt. The removal of capital controls permitted strong flows of foreign capital into the nation in these years. As I have argued elsewhere in this book, stringent prudential regulation must precede the liberalization of a nation's capital account.

---

11. Anne Krueger, the First Deputy Managing Director of the IMF, puts this economic truth gently: 'under a firmly fixed exchange rate, you need other sources of adjustment to maintain competitiveness'. See A. Krueger, 'Crisis Prevention and Resolution: Lessons from Argentina' (Paper presented at the NBER Conference on 'The Argentina Crisis', Cambridge, 17 July 2002), <www.imf.org/external/np.speeches/2002/071702.htm>.
12. J. Sachs, 'A Crash Foretold: Argentina must revamp its society and economy for a high-tech world' 159 *Time International*, 14 January 2002, 17.
13. Kiguel, 'Structural Reforms in Argentina: Success or Failure?', 101; L. Rojas-Suarez, 'Toward a Sustainable FTAA: Does Latin America Meet the Necessary Financial Preconditions?', unpublished paper, 10; R.P. Buckley, *Emerging Markets Debt: An Analysis of the Secondary Market* (London, Kluwer Law International, 1999), pp. 7–8.

In the early-to-mid 1990s the IMF encouraged the contemporaneous development of a nation's prudential regulation and the liberalization of its capital account. Increasing the quality and extent of prudential regulation is slow, hard work calling for considerable resources which, particularly in human terms, are often in desperately short supply in developing countries. Liberalizing capital controls can be achieved relatively swiftly and easily through legislation. For the IMF to promote the simultaneous, rather than sequential, adoption of these measures proved to be a recipe for disaster first in Indonesia, Korea, and Thailand and then in Argentina. A recent audit by the Independent Evaluation Office of the IMF into the Fund's role in Argentina in the 1990s agrees. It found that the Fund's 'surveillance underestimated the vulnerability that could arise from the steady increase in public debt, when much of it was dollar-denominated and externally held.'[14] In short, the IMF's own audit has found that Argentina borrowed too much, and the IMF acquiesced in this error.[15]

Argentina in the 1990s stands as strong evidence of a truism that international capital markets are extraordinarily slow to grasp: strong capital inflows generate strong growth that attracts further inflows. Basically, if global capital flows strongly into a relatively small economy like Argentina's or Thailand's, it will boom. The boom in turn makes it attractive to more capital, which in turn furthers the boom.

The resulting boom is unconnected to economic fundamentals and thus typically not sustainable. Foreign capital refuses to face this fact, for it profits in boom times, and without some form of sovereign bankruptcy regime its losses in hard times are limited. In addition, the careers and bonuses of individual bankers are greatly enhanced by the boom-time profits, and when hard times come, the individuals are rarely still in roles in which responsibility for losses can be sheeted home to them in any meaningful way. Much global movement of capital can be attributed to internal reward structures within banks that reward the volume of loans made, not their quality.

6.2.3   CORRUPTION

As always in Latin American financial crises, corruption played its insidious role. It contributed in three ways:

- Systemic corruption renders any economy profoundly inefficient as it increases transaction costs in many transactions. Corruption thus limited the returns derivable from the foreign capital in the Argentine economy.
- Through corruption, portions of the capital flows were diverted from their intended destination into the private accounts of politicians, senior civil

---

14. *Watchdog faults Argentina, but also IMF*, IMF Survey (Washington, DC, International Monetary Fund, 2004), 229, 230.
15. See Independent Evaluation Office (IEO) of the IMF, *Report on the Evaluation of the Role of the IMF in Argentina: 1991–2001*, <www.imf.org/External/NP/ieo/2004/arg/eng/index.htm>.

servants and leaders of industry.[16] When a significant proportion of the capital never even reaches the account of the debtor, repayment of the full amount will always be problematic.
- The corruption of the political process in Argentina means that capital was often borrowed to serve the interests of the elite and of the politicians themselves, rather than in the best interests of the nation.

Both the IMF and the Argentine government made egregious policy errors in Argentina. Nonetheless, without the rejection of corruption in all its forms by the Argentine people their economy will never function efficiently and their governments will continue to govern in ways that serve the interests of the Argentine elite and international capital, and not the interests of the common Argentine people. In the words of Professor Luiz Carlos Bresser Pereira when testifying before a US Congressional Committee:

> But, in spite of the growing evidence of the impossibility of paying the entire debt, a significant portion of the elites in the debtor countries remains willing to try to pay it. We can think of a number of explanations for that attitude – fear of retaliations by the banks, cultural subordination to the First World, willingness to be part of it, identification of the interests of the creditor countries with the interests of the banks, lack of information about the debates among the elites of the creditor countries about the debt, inability to size up the internal economic crisis in their own countries, identification of firm positions for debt reduction to radical or nationalist political attitudes – but I want in this testimony to underline only one explanation: the elites in general in the debtor countries are certainly not the ones that suffer most from the debt crisis; on the contrary, part of them is taking advantage from the debt.[17]

6.2.4 IMF POLICIES

Throughout the 1990s Argentina was, in many respects, a model IMF pupil.[18] It exhibited a degree of compliance with IMF-mandated policies that is rare among developing countries.

In liberalizing its capital account by relaxing capital controls Argentina was implementing IMF policy, and the pegging of the peso to the US dollar was supported by the Fund.[19]

---

16. P.W. Rasche, 'Argentina: test case for a new approach to insolvency?', *Studien von Zeitfragen*, 5 January 2002; E. Sweeney, 'Argentina: the Current Crisis in Perspective' (2002) 186 *America* 19; and N. Klein, 'Revolt of the wronged', *The Guardian* (United Kingdom), 28 March 2002.
17. Statement of Professor Luiz Carlos Bresser Pereira, *Solving the Debt Crisis: Debt Relief and Adjustment*, 330, 339.
18. Klein, *Revolt of the wronged*; C. Denny, 'Firefighters turn on tap again', *The Guardian* (United Kingdom), 12 August 2002.
19. Feldstein, 'Argentina's Fall', 8.

Throughout the 1990s the Argentine government enacted IMF economic policies. In May 2000, Charles Calomiris and Andrew Powell gave Argentina high marks for its reforms of its banking sector, saying:

> the Argentine experience in the 1990s with bank regulatory reform... has been one of the most determined efforts, among emerging market countries, to inject credible market discipline into the relationship between banks and depositors, and into the regulatory and supervisory process.... Argentina successfully implemented a system of bank regulation that achieved credible market discipline over banks.[20]

Even with a change of government during the severe recession, this record of compliance continued. Upon becoming president in late 1999, Fernando de la Rua raised taxes and made massive cuts in government expenditure, including a 13% cut in state workers' wages and deep cuts to education and pensions.[21] Mr de la Rua's policies were so unpopular that he was forced out of office one-half of the way through his term after violent street protests claimed 31 lives in late 2001.[22]

Fiscal contraction is bad policy in any recession yet it was the IMF's first policy prescription for the East Asian crisis in 1997, and the Fund repeated its error in Argentina in 1999. It is imperative that the IMF begins to put the maintenance of functional economies and the human rights of the peoples of debtor nations above the short-term capacities of those nations to service their foreign debts fully.

An increasing number of economists believe that Argentina's troubles stem directly from its implementation of IMF policies[23] and certainly the IMF's policies have contributed substantially to the crisis.

The lesson from the Argentine experience is that following IMF policies closely provides no insurance against ruinous crises. The IMF lauded Argentina's policy settings throughout the 1990s, and yet in late 2001 its economy still imploded. Argentina stands as testament to the fact that the IMF can get the policy settings very wrong.

6.3   THE RESTRUCTURING OF ARGENTINA'S INDEBTEDNESS

Argentina's initial workout offer to creditors in September 2003 was unprecedentedly aggressive. It called upon creditors to forgive 75% of the USD 94.3 billion in

---

20. C.W. Calomiris and A. Powell, *Can Emerging Market Bank Regulators Establish Credible Discipline? The Case of Argentina, 1992–1999*, NBER Working Paper No. 7715 (2000), <www.nber.org/papers/w7715>.
21. S. Jeffery, 'Crisis in Argentina', *Guardian Unlimited* (United Kingdom), 4 January 2002.
22. U. Goni, 'Argentina collapses into chaos', *The Guardian* (United Kingdom), 21 December 2001; and M. Healey and E. Seman, 'Down, Argentine Way', (2002) 13 *The American Prospect*, 12.
23. L. Rohter, 'Giving Argentina the Cinderella Treatment', *The New York Times* (New York), 11 August 2002, 14.

bonds and other debt and all the interest that had accumulated since Argentina's default in December, 2001.

Wiping out the accumulated interest meant the net present value of Argentina's offer was only 10% of total outstanding indebtedness.[24] The response of creditors was predictable: improve the offer or be frozen out of a capital markets for a very long time.

Argentina's initial offer was to exchange the 152 different bond issues held by its 500,000 bondholders in six different currencies into a mix of three bonds: par bonds with no reduction in principal but deeply reduced interest rates, discount bonds with a 63% cut in face value and lowish interest rates for the first ten years, rising to 8.51% thereafter, and a limited amount of peso-denominated, inflation-adjusted quasi-par bonds. GDP-linked payments were also attached to all bonds so that, if in any year, Argentina's GDP growth exceeds 3%, then 5% of the growth above 3% will be used to pay extra dividends on the bonds in pesos.[25]

President Nestor Kirchner described this offer as 'unmovable'[26] and Argentina refused to amend it for many months. Nonetheless, on 1 June 2004 an enhanced offer was made to recognize past due interest, but without reducing the size of the reduction in principal demanded.[27]

In late 2004 Argentina again improved the offer so that nearly USD 82 billion of bonds would be eligible for conversion into nearly USD 42 billion in new bonds with lower interest rates and much longer maturities. While this looked like an offer to honour about 50% of outstanding debt, there was no provision to honour the USD 23 billion in past due interest, so Argentina's offer represented more than a 60% discount – a 'haircut' of unprecedented proportions for lenders to a middle-income country.

The following ten reasons have supported Argentina's strong and aggressive approach to its debt negotiations:[28]

(1) Argentina has few assets abroad, so there is little that plaintiffs can do but be patient; i.e., judgments from lawsuits will be largely unenforceable.
(2) Having defaulted, Argentina has no standing to preserve in the capital markets and nothing more to lose. Prior to default most sovereigns will go to great lengths to preserve their standing in the financial markets and preserve their access to reasonably priced capital, however, once a sovereign borrower has defaulted, it no longer has standing to seek to preserve. It has nothing to lose.
(3) While shut off from global capital, Argentina's economy powered forward – growing at over 8% in 2003 and 2004. In the short term at

---

24. 'The end of the affair?' *The Economist*, February 20 2004; and J.F. Hornbeck, *Argentina's Sovereign Debt Restructuring* (CRS Report for Congress, 19 October 2004).
25. 'Argentina Details Plan to Swap Debt', *World Bank Press Review*, 2 November 2004.
26. 'The end of the Affair', *The Economist*, 20 February 2004.
27. Hornbeck, *Argentina's Sovereign Debt Restructuring*.
28. These reasons are principally drawn from Hornbeck, *Argentina's Sovereign Debt Restructuring*.

least, no longer having to service foreign borrowing proved more a blessing than a curse.
(4) If Argentina can sustain its strong economic growth of 2003 and 2004, it may well be able to attract home some or much of the estimated USD 100 billion of flight capital that Argentines hold abroad.
(5) Throughout the 1990s Argentina was the IMF's poster child. It can legitimately claim that its crisis in 2001 arose from following policies either suggested or endorsed by the IMF.
(6) The IMF has admitted it erred in guiding Argentina in the 1990s in the recent audit by the Independent Evaluation Office of the IMF.
(7) Argentina, for a sustained period, stuck to its commitment to use no more than 3% of its primary budget surplus to finance long-term debt restructuring – and has managed to gain the implicit approval of the IMF as 'official arbiter' to this approach.[29] It may have been assisted in attaining IMF support for this stance because some 15% of the Fund's total lending is to Argentina,[30] an extraordinary concentration of risk that banking regulators would never accept for a commercial bank and that puts the Fund in a position of conflict of interest. As the Fund's loans are immune from the reduction in principal, the debt relief improves their recoverability.
(8) Argentina owed USD 195.5 billion in bonds and loans, a staggering amount by any measure. It has 'made a reasoned case that its debt is simply too big to repay'.[31]
(9) Argentina's poverty rate, 27% in 1999, had doubled by 2003 to 54.7%; per capita GDP, USD 7,800 in 1999, had fallen by more than half to USD 3,800 by 2004, and debt that represented 47.4% of GDP in 1999, was 140% of GDP in 2004.[32] These statistics supported President Kirchner's contention that he would not service the debt from the 'suffering and hunger of the people'.[33]
(10) Finally, and perhaps most importantly, standing up to the IMF served to make President Kirchner extraordinarily popular at home.[34]

Argentina's debt negotiations dealt with roughly USD 104 billion of debt: USD 81 billion of principal, and USD 23 billion of past due interest. The balance was some USD 6.7 billion of official debt owed to Paris club creditors, USD 32.7 billion owed to the International Financial Institutions (IFIs) such as the IMF and World Bank, and some USD 52 billion owed to Argentine investors and

---

29. Hornbeck, *Argentina's Sovereign Debt Restructuring*; and M. Casey, 'The Economy: IMF Chief Presses Argentina on Spending, Debt', *The Asian Wall Street Journal*, 2 September 2004, A8.
30. 'Argentina and the IMF: Which is the victim?', *The Economist*, 6 March 2004, 63.
31. Hornbeck, *Argentina's Sovereign Debt Restructuring*.
32. *Ibid.*
33. 'Argentina and the IMF: Which is the victim?', *The Economist*, 6 March 2004, 63.
34. 'An Amber Light', *The Economist*, 31 January 2004, 34.

banks that was reduced in 2001 and then further devalued when 'pesofied' in 2002. The Argentine government, quite reasonably, argued that default to the IFIs was not an option, and that the holders of the debt that had been 'pesofied' had already contributed enormously to the resolution of this crisis, to their severe economic detriment.[35] This left the debt owed to other countries (Paris Club debt) and the debt held by foreign investors that had not been pesofied to bear the pain of restructuring.

In March 2005, 76% of Argentina's creditors accepted its offer to exchange its debt for bonds at the unprecedented discount of some 66% on a net present value basis. In the words *The Financial Times*, 'Argentina gambled, and the gamble paid off'.[36] Argentina emerged from its period as a defaulting debtor on the most advantageous terms ever secured by a middle-income country in a debt restructuring in history. On the basis of Argentina's experience a nation defaulting on its debt as a strategy to secure superior terms on the debt's restructuring, is a card worth playing, and playing forcefully, as shall be considered in more detail in Chapter Eight.

Nonetheless, so massive had Argentina's debt overhang become that Kenneth Rogoff, former Chief Economist of the IMF, has concluded that a sustainable debt level for a nation like Argentina would be about 30% of GDP, or one-third of Argentina's debt levels at the time its offer was accepted.[37]

---

35. Hornbeck, *Argentina's Sovereign Debt Restructuring*.
36. 'Argentina sets a dangerous precedent: The IMF should set tough conditions for further lending', *The Financial Times*, 7 March 2005, 20.
37. C. Reinhardt, K. Rogoff and M. Savastano, 'Debt Intolerance', (NBER Working Paper No. 9908, 2003) <www.nber.org/papers/w9908>.

Chapter 7

Debt Relief for Poor Countries and for Iraq

7.1   DEBT RELIEF

In 1996 under the leadership of the new President, James Wolfensohn, the World Bank put together the Highly Indebted Poor Country initiative, HIPC, which proposed debt relief for the world's most indebted poor countries. Under the HIPC initiative, poor countries can qualify for assistance after meeting all of the eligibility criteria set out by the IMF, including having an unsustainable debt burden. They then must implementing various World Bank mandated policies and meet certain economic targets before qualifying for relief.[1]

In Cologne in 1999 the world's rich countries, in response to the extraordinary grass-roots campaign coordinated by Jubilee 2000, promised to cancel over USD 100 billion of poor country debt. This promise found its expression in the Enhanced HIPC initiative. In the words of Jim Wolfensohn:

> This initiative is a breakthrough . . . It deals with debt in a comprehensive way to give countries the possibility of exiting from unsustainable debt. It is very good news for the poor of the world.[2]

In Tanzania, for instance, debt relief as a result of the enhanced HIPC initiative, plus an increase in British aid, resulted in 1,925 primary schools being built, in

---

1. International Monetary Fund, 'The HIPC Initiative: Delivering Debt Relief to Poor Countries' <www.imf.org/external/np/hipc/art0299.pdf>, 4 December 2007, 2; and The World Bank Group, 'HIPC – Debt Relief for Sustainable Development' <www.worldbank.org/hipc/about/hipcbr/hipcbr.htm>, 15 February 2005.
2. J.D. Wolfensohn, President, World Bank, in The World Bank Group, 'HIPC – Debt Relief for Sustainable Development'.

37,261 new teachers being employed, and to a near doubling in the number of children at primary school.[3]

Yet today not even one-half of that promised debt relief has been extended and the IMF and World Bank have acknowledged that the HIPC program has failed to reduce poor countries' debts to sustainable levels even when they are graduating from the program. HIPC has foundered on the complexity and conditionality of its process, the length of time it has taken countries to progress through it, and the inadequate debt relief that it has provided to countries that have completed the process. The HIPC initiative has only been applied to some 27 countries of the 38 countries that potentially qualify for HIPC assistance. Furthermore, there are many countries that do not qualify for the HIPC initiative and yet for which the requirements of debt service severely compromise their capacity to provide basic education and healthcare, such as Indonesia.[4]

As a response to the problems of poor country debt, debt relief granted under HIPC has been far too niggardly; far too limited in the countries to which it applies; and predicated upon far too many conditions that have often not served the debtor countries and have made qualifying the relief far too difficult.

Throughout this HIPC process the US argued strongly and consistently against generous debt relief for poor countries. It has argued that such debt relief was against the debtor nation's interests as it would undermine their access to global capital.[5]

HIPC was better than nothing, but achieved far, far less than it could have done, at least until the US was faced with clearing up the mess created by its invasion of Iraq.

7.2 THE US APPROACH TO IRAQI DEBT

Iraq's total sovereign indebtedness was about USD 120 billion, nominal value, at year-end 2004.[6] This does not include some USD 200 billion in reparations

---

3. J. Hari, 'Aid and debt relief a waste of money? Try telling that to the people of Tanzania' *The Independent*, 15 June 2005, 27.
4. International Monetary Fund and International Development Association, 'Heavily Indebted Poor Countries (HIPC) Initiative – Status of Implementation (2003)', <http://siteresources.worldbank.org/INTDEBTDEPT/ProgressReports/20253192/StatusImplementationSept2003.pdf>, 4 December 17 February 2005, 4; and INFID (International NGO Forum on Indonesian Development) 'Indonesia's Foreign Debt: Imprisoning the people of Indonesia' (2000), <www.odiousdebts.org/odiousdebts/index.cfm?DSP=content&ContentID=2385#_ftnref9>, 18 February 2005.
5. R. Dodd, 'Sovereign Debt Restructuring' (2002) 14 (1–4) *The Financier* <www.financialpolicy.org/dscsovdebt.pdf>, 6 April 2005, 3; J.P. Thomas, 'Bankruptcy Proceedings for Sovereign State Insolvency', United Nations University World Institute for Development Economics Research, Discussion Paper 2002/109 <www.wider.unu.edu/publications/dps/dps2002/dp2002-109.pdf>, 7 April 2005.
6. Paris Club, 'The Paris Club and the Republic of Iraq Agree on Debt Relief' (Press Release, 21 November 2004).

nominally owed to Kuwait and Saudi Arabia as a result of the first Gulf War. The amount of USD 120 billion, included accrued interest and penalty fees, and was roughly comprised of the following:[7]

Arab nations (primarily Kuwait and Saudi Arabia)	USD 60 billion
Japan	USD 7 billion
Russia	USD 6 billion
France	USD 5 billion
Germany	USD 4.5 billion
United States	USD 3.5 billion
Italy	USD 2.5 billion

The balance was debt owed under unpaid contracts, most of it owed to military contractors.[8]

In late 2004 the Paris Club, the standing group of 19 governments with large claims on other governments, agreed to write off 80% of the debts owed to them by Iraq. This quite extraordinary degree of debt relief has to be understood in the context that the most desperately poor nations on the planet, such as Ethiopia and Burundi, typically had received debt relief from the Paris Club in the 50% to 67% range. Yet, gross national income per capita in Ethiopia and Burundi in 2002 was USD 100 per annum whereas gross national income per capita in Iraq was estimated by the World Bank to be in the range of USD 736 to USD 2,935 per annum.[9]

By global standards Iraq is not even poor. So why was it granted such an exceptional degree of debt relief?

Throughout 2004, the US had James A. Baker travelling the world seeking to drum up support among rich nation creditors for the total cancellation of Iraq's debts. To the best of my knowledge this is the first time the US has ever argued strongly for the total cancellation of a nation's sovereign debt. This is most curious, because, as we have seen, on the basis of poverty Iraq is not a strong candidate for

---

7. The amounts of debt owed to the respective creditors include principal and accrued interest. Virtually all sources agree that Iraq's total sovereign indebtedness is of the order of USD 120 billion although reports diverge on the amounts owed to individual creditor countries. See 'U.S. forgives $4.1 Billion in Iraq Debt: Snow Urges Other Countries to Follow Suit' *The Associated Press*, 18 December 2004; N. Onishi, 'Japan Open to Forgiving Iraqi Debt – If Others Do So' *New York Times*, 29 December 2003, <www.benadorassociates.com/article/866>, 16 February 2005.
8. 'Iraq Debt Write-off Wins Approval' *BBC News*, 21 November 2004 <news.bbc.co.uk/2/hi/business/4029905.stm>, 19 November 2005. See also E. Mekay, 'Debt Relief Weighted Down by IMF Burden' (2004) *Global Policy Forum* <www.globalpolicy.org/socecon/develop/debt/2004/1123imfiraq.htm>, 18 February 2005.
9. Paris Club, 'Paris Club Agrees to Reduce Burundi's Debt by 67% in Net Present Value' (Press Release, 4 March 2004); and World Bank, *2004 World Development Indicators* (World Bank, 2004), pp. 14–16.

debt relief. Once its oil wells are again operating at close to capacity, Iraq should be able to service its debts quite comfortably. After all, it does have the world's second largest recorded oil reserves, (10.8%), behind those of Saudi Arabia (25.2%).[10]

The challenge is to restore a functional economy to Iraq and rebuild its infrastructure so that it can again enjoy the benefits nature has bestowed upon it. To this end, Iraq is a very strong candidate for aid. Developed countries recognized the economic and political imperatives to rebuild Iraq's shattered infrastructure and put a new government there on a firm footing. They also tended to recognize the moral imperative of redressing the devastation inflicted in the Iraq war. No debt relief at all would hamper Iraq's long-term growth, but it was striking that the US was seeking such a high degree of relief for Iraq when far poorer countries had only received relief from 35% to 65% of their debts.[11] Furthermore, in the short-term, debt relief only saves Iraq the interest it would otherwise have had to pay. If debt relief today has to come at the cost of aid equal to one-half or even one-third of the amount of debt to be forgiven, Iraq would be far better off with the aid for the immediate impact of the aid would be far greater, and Iraq's needs were immediate.

Debt relief would be part of any sensible plan to rebuild Iraq, but if one was to create an assistance package for Iraq from scratch and with no other agendas, it would comprise far less debt relief than the US has sought, and secured, and far more aid than has been granted and proposed. Much like Europe in the aftermath of World War II, Iraq needs to be rebuilt and once it has been rebuilt its long-term economic capacity should not be in doubt.

Nonetheless, in November, 2004 the Paris Club of wealthy creditor nations agreed to cancel 80% of the USD 39 billion in debt owed to them by the Republic of Iraq. This relief was staged over three phases:

– 30% of outstanding debt as at 1 January 2005 (USD 11.6 billion) to be cancelled immediately;
– a further 30% to be cancelled upon agreement of a standard International Monetary Fund programme, with all the conditionalities this implies; and
– a further 20% of the initial stock to be cancelled upon completion of the last IMF board review of three years of implementation of the standard IMF programme.

The remaining 20% of the initial debt stock was rescheduled over a period of 23 years including a grace period of 6 years.

According to the Paris Club, this plan represents 'a comprehensive debt treatment of the public external debt owed to them' and reduces the total debt

---

10. C. Tarnoff, *Iraq: Recent Developments in Reconstruction Assistance* (CRS Report for Congress, 20 December 2004), 6; and Centre for Strategic and International Studies, *The Changing Geopolitics of Energy – Part IV: Regional Developments in the Gulf, and Energy Issues Affecting Iran, Iraq, and Libya* (Washington, CSIS, 1998) at 6.
11. IMF and IDA, 'Heavily Indebted Poor Countries (HIPC) Initiative) – Statistical Update (2004)' <www.imf.org/external/np/hipc/2004/033104.htm>, 17 February 2005.

stock owed to the Paris Club from USD 38.9 billion to USD 7.8 billion. However Jubilee Iraq has pointed out that Iraq will still be:

> shackled with over USD 25billion of debt, not to mention new loans being peddled by the IMF and World Bank, and the USD 31 billion in reparations awarded so far. Furthermore, IMF conditions – such as privatization and ending food rations – could further exacerbate the poverty and instability in Iraq.[12]

The track record of IMF imposed economic policies in invigorating poor countries' economies in the past two decades has been poor, so it is a real concern to note the extent to which this debt relief will impose extensive policy constraints upon the new Iraqi government.[13]

When a nation accepts IMF policy constraints it typically has to accept IMF advisers sitting in the offices of its Finance Ministry and Central Bank giving advice, and effectively dictating policy. In particular, the IMF is highly likely to require privatization of state-owned assets. As was seen dramatically in Russia, privatization in an environment that lacks a strong rule of law and strong institutions to monitor the process is highly likely to result in state assets being sold at a gross undervalue and a small group of entrepreneurs benefiting disproportionately.[14]

So while this debt relief will be a great benefit to Iraq, it is not likely to be an unalloyed benefit.

Since the Paris Club decision the US has gone one step further and cancelled all the debt that Iraq owes to it.

Interestingly, to the best of my knowledge, no developed country government has mentioned the 'odious' word in relation to Iraq's debt, preferring instead to term it unsustainable. Yet the real argument for debt relief for Iraq, certainly on this massive scale, is that the debts are odious. The Doctrine of Odious Debt arose out of the US-Spanish War of 1898. The idea is that certain sovereign debt is illegitimate and should not have to be repaid if:

(1) it is incurred for a purpose does not benefit the people of the debtor nation; and
(2) it is incurred without the consent of the people.[15]

---

12. 'Problems with the Paris Club Deal', *Jubilee Iraq*, 24 November 2004, <www.jubileeiraq.org/files/Paris%20Club%20problems%20article.htm>, 19 February 2005.
13. J. Woodroffe and M. Ellis-Jones, 'States of Unrest: Resistance to IMF Policies in Poor Countries' <www.globalpolicy.org/socecon/bwi-wto/imf/2000/protest.htm>, 19 February 2005.
14. E. Toussaint, 'The Odious Debt of Russia, The new Oligarchs, and the Bretton Woods Institutions' <www.cadtm.org/spip.php?article536>, 4 December 2007; see also J. Stiglitz, *Globalisation and Its Discontents* (London, Penguin, 2002), pp. 136–151.
15. P. Adams, 'Iraq's Odious Debts' (Cato Institute Policy Analysis No. 526, 2004), 2; M. Kremer and S. Jayachandran, 'IMF Seminar: Odious Debt' <www.imf.org/external/np/res/seminars/2002/poverty/mksj.pdf>, 17 February 2005, 3–5.

In the words of Adams, 'If a despotic power incurs a debt not for the needs or in the interest of the state, but to strengthen its despotic regime or to repress the population that fights against it .. this debt is odious for the population of all of the state.'[16] In such a case, many commentators believe that such debt ought not to have to be repaid by the people through higher taxes or lower government expenditures on health, education and other social services. The reasoning is that 'This debt is not an obligation for the nation; it is a regime's debt, a personal debt of the power that has incurred it, and consequently it falls with the fall of this power.'[17]

Most definitions of odious debt require both limbs for debt to be considered odious, i.e., it must be incurred without the people's consent, and not be used for their benefit. The concept is that it is appropriate for a people to have to repay loans incurred by a dictator without their consent if the loans were used to build hospitals or public infrastructure.[18]

Much, if not most, of Iraq's debt represents loans made to the regime of Saddam Hussein, principally to enable it to buy weapons from the creditor nations. As then Interim Prime Minister, Iyad Allawi wrote in an opinion piece: 'The vast majority is odious debt, used to build up the war machine of the ousted regime, largely through arms purchases supported by the lending countries.'[19]

The rich nations have avoided justifying this debt relief by labelling the debts as odious for fear of setting a potentially expensive precedent. Indeed, Germany's Finance Minister, Hans Eichel, said, 'by doing this we see a special situation for Iraq. This does not create a precedent for any other case.'[20] Presumably, Germany's Finance Minister was seeking to avoid creating a precedent for other nations with legitimate complaints of odious debt such as the Philippines and Nigeria.

The US argued vigorously for debt relief for Iraq on an unprecedented scale, for a country that doesn't need it on this scale.[21] So what is going on?

If you return to the earlier list of creditors of Iraq you'll notice that you have to look a long way down the list to find the US – it is owed only some USD 3 billion, or 2.5% of Iraq's total sovereign indebtedness. Pretty clearly, a major reason the US pushed for the total cancellation of Iraqi debt was that it was the cheapest way, for the US, to assist Iraq.

This doesn't explain why nations that were owed much more than America, such as Japan, France, Germany and Russia, agreed to cancel 80% of the debts Iraq

---

16. Adams, 'Iraq's Odious Debts', at 3.
17. Kremer and Jayachandran, 'IMF Seminar: Odious Debt', 5.
18. Adams, 'Iraq's Odious Debts', at 5; and R. Rajam 'Odious or just Malodorous?' (December 2004) *Finance and Development*, pp. 54–55.
19. I. Allawi, 'Economic and security problems must be solved, not just for us but for the world' *The Independent*, 20 September 2004, 5.
20. MaBiCo Finance Company, 'G20 Meeting: Eichel Confirms Paris Club agrees to 80 pct Iraq debt cancellation' <www.mabico.com/en/news/20041120/foreign_debt/article13452/>, 19 February 2005.
21. See L. Wroughton, 'IMF Approves Aid for Iraq, Pushes for Debt Relief' <www.globalpolicy.org/security/issues/iraq/contract/2004/0929imf.htm>, 18 February 2005.

owed to them. After all French, German and Russian companies were frozen out of bidding for reconstruction contracts in Iraq, yet they have accommodated US demands on debt relief, when debt relief costs them far more than it costs the US[22]

The reasons why creditor countries acceded to US demands for debt relief for Iraq undoubtedly vary among the countries. Russia appears to have been motivated by the desire for its oil companies to begin doing business again in Iraq, and promises appear to have been held out in this regard.[23] All of the developed nations feel they have an interest in promoting the spread of democracy in the Middle East and all feel the moral imperative to redress the devastation of the war. Furthermore, there is the practical issue that if a functional economy cannot be restored in Iraq these debts are unlikely to be serviced.

Yet in September 2004 these factors and US pressure were insufficient to make France and Germany, in particular, agree to this level of debt relief for Iraq. France and Germany's major objection was one of principle. It struck these nations as particularly unfair that the US was seeking this level of debt relief for Iraq when desperately poor countries were being offered far less debt relief under the Enhanced HIPC Initiative. And then the US dropped its long-held opposition to total debt relief for the poorest nations, and begun to advocate strongly for the cancellation of all the debts of the HIPC countries. It seems the total forgiveness of HIPC debt was a price the US was prepared to pay to win support for the cancellation of Iraq's debts.

For decades the US had taken a consistent hard line on the HIPC initiative and debt relief arguing against generous debt cancellation on the grounds that it was not in the interests of debtor nations or of the international financial system. Then, in the twinkling of an eye, in 2004 the US changed direction and started arguing for total debt relief for the HIPC nations and 95% relief for Iraq's debts – an extraordinary sea change by any measure.

This newly generous US approach to debt relief is important. The track record of developing countries applying money saved as a result of debt relief to good effect in development and anti-poverty efforts is good. Nonetheless, this US initiative attracted considerable criticism focused almost entirely upon its effect on the Bank and the Fund.

Most indebtedness of the poorest countries is owed to the World Bank and, to a much lesser extent, the IMF. The Bank and Fund feared that if mandated debt relief of this level had to be funded from their own resources it would compromise their discharging their other functions severely. In particular, the capacity of the World Bank to assist the many poor countries that don't qualify for HIPC relief may have been greatly curtailed. Virtually no one argues that total debt

---

22. D. Jehl, 'Pentagon Bars three Nations From Iraq Bids' *New York Times*, 10 December 2003; and 'U.S. forgives $4.1 Billion in Iraq Debt: Snow Urges Other Countries to Follow Suit' *The Associated Press*, 18 December 2004.
23. C. Marquis 'Russia Sees Iraqi Debt Relief as Link to Oil, US Aides Say' *New York Times*, 17 January 2004.

cancellation for the HIPCs will not improve their plight significantly and is not worth doing provided the impacts on the Bank and Fund can be managed.

The British government responded to these concerns by strongly urging that the rich nations cover the cost of forgiving World Bank loans for the next decade and by arguing for the IMF to fund this debt relief internally. Britain pressed for the IMF to progressively sell down its gold reserves so as to be able to write-off the loans it has made to the poorest nations.[24] The IMF holds 103.4 million ounces (3,217 metric tons) of gold, a holding valued on its balance sheet at about USD 9 billion. As of 28 February 2005, the market value of the holding was about USD 45 billion. The IMF itself believes that if rich donor countries are not going to fund more debt relief for the poorest countries, the next best alternative would be carefully planned sales of a small portion of the IMF's gold and the IMF's analysis shows that, managed well, such gold sales need not disrupt the market, cause volatility or injure gold producing countries.[25]

In June, 2005 the G-8 nations agreed to write off more than USD 40 billion of debt owed by 18 of the poorest nations to the World Bank, African Development Bank and the IMF. These are the nations that have already reached completion point in the HIPC process. As further countries meet the programs targets for good governance and economic reform then they too will qualify for this degree of debt relief. The G-8 nations agreed to provide additional funds to the World Bank and African Development Bank to compensate them for the lost income from the servicing of this debt for the initial group of 18 countries. This funding was announced with great fanfare, but in practice the assurance of funding only lasts for the initial three-year funding period.

The intention is for the G-8 nations to make good the shortfall to the World Bank and African Development Bank for the life of the loans, but this is not guaranteed, as once we are into the next three-year funding round for the International Development Agency (the World Bank's concessional lending arm) it will be impossible to know if the funds earmarked for this debt relief are additional to what otherwise would have been provided, or not.[26]

Furthermore, this debt cancellation applies only to 18 of the 38 HIPCs. As stated above, in time it may well be extended to more of the HIPCs but on the track record to date extension to further countries will be very slow, and highly indebted nations such as Indonesia are not within the framework, or eligible for assistance. Most debt campaigners believe at least 40 further nations, in addition to the 18 post-completion point HIPCs, need this degree of debt relief.

Nonetheless, the desire of the US to provide assistance to Iraq in the cheapest possible way for the US, i.e., by cancelling Iraq's debts, appears to have benefited the poorest of the world's poor nations by leading to the complete cancellation of their debt. When push came to shove, not even the US Administration of President

---

24. UK Treasury, Executive Summary: Debt Relief Beyond HIPC (2005).
25. IMF, 'Factsheet: Gold in the IMF' <www.imf.org/external/np/exr/facts/gold.htm>, 5 April 2005.
26. C. Giles and F. Tiesenhausen Cave, 'International Economy' *Financial Times*, 13 June 2005, 8.

Debt Relief for Poor Countries and for Iraq

George W Bush could withstand the arguments of France and Germany that it was obscene to argue for the total cancellation of Iraq's debts without affording the same treatment to nations many, many times poorer than Iraq.

There is another, more creative, alternative to simple debt cancellation for highly indebted countries. An alternative that gives the creditor nations more control over how the cancelled funds are spent, and an alternative to which we now turn.

7.3 DEBT-FOR-DEVELOPMENT EXCHANGES

Many countries like Indonesia and the Philippines, with regions of extreme poverty, fall short of qualifying as a HIPC, and have therefore not benefited at all from the debt relief initiatives considered above. Nonetheless, the debt burden on the Philippines is severe. Just how severe can be seen from government expenditure in 2006: over 32% of government spending went to servicing interest on debt alone, compared to less than 14% on education, less than 5% on defense and only 1.3% on health.[27] When one factors in principal repayments as well, the situation becomes utterly intolerable, with total debt service in 2005 consuming almost 60% of total government expenditures, a proportion projected to rise to 68.5% in 2006. In 2006, therefore, over two-thirds of every peso spent by the Philippines government was spent on paying interest or repaying principal on its debts. In the words of Habito and Beja, '[u]ltimately the debt penalty compromises the country's long term human development and economic growth.'[28]

Because it does not qualify as a HIPC, the Philippines has had to rely for debt relief on the initiatives of individual developed countries. In general terms, debt relief can take many forms. These include partial or complete debt cancellation, debt buybacks and debt-swap agreements.

A debt buyback refers to the purchase of debt by the debtor country from its creditors or through the secondary market. Debt buyback schemes raise moral hazard issues because the purchase price of the debt on the secondary market is influenced by the actions of the debtor country. For example, Brazil defaulted on its interest payments from 1989 to 1991 which deflated the price of its debt substantially and liberated the funds to purchase it, which Brazil duly did.[29]

Debt-swap agreements began to come to prominence in the late 1980s. The name debt-swap is a misnomer because no swap or exchange actually takes place. Put simply, under a debt-for-development swap, for example, instead of repaying

---

27. C.F. Habito and E.L. Beja Jr, 'Beating the Odds?: The Continuing Saga of a Crisis-Prone Economy', part of the *Civil Society Monitoring of the Medium Term Philippine Development Plan (MTPDP)* (2006), 11.
28. Ibid, 10.
29. L.C. Buchheit, 'Moral Hazards and Other Delights', (April 1991) *International Financial Law Review* 10, note 130 at 10–11; G. Anayiotos and J. de Piniés, 'The Secondary Market and the International Debt Problem' (1990) 18 *World Development* 1655; and Buckley, 'Debt Exchanges Revisited: Lessons from Latin America for Eastern Europe', 675–683.

the creditor nation, the debtor country uses the money that it owes the creditor nation, or an agreed proportion thereof, in development projects in its own territory agreed upon by the two countries.

Debt-swaps can benefit the international financial community, the governments that are party to the agreement, and the communities affected by the agreement. For the international financial community debt-swaps can reduce debt levels and increase debt prices in the secondary market. For creditor governments debt swaps allow control over the uses to which the funds liberated by debt they cancel are put. For debtor governments debt swaps can promote development, protect the environment, and reduce debt.[30] For local communities, swaps can substantially reduce poverty levels and support much needed local projects. Debt-swaps can be used to achieve many different objectives depending on their specific terms.

Debt-equity swaps were the initial form of debt swap but of late have lost favour to debt-for-development and debt-for-environment swaps. Debt-equity agreements involve the sale by an investor of external debt to the debtor government in return for a discounted amount of local currency which must then be invested locally in shares in a local company or otherwise.[31] Debt-equity swaps offer investors a preferential exchange rate for their investments. The discount rate at which the debt will be converted into equity is set by agreement between the investor and the debtor government or at an auction at which potential investors bid. Debt-equity schemes can increase investment and permit debtor nations to recapture part of the secondary market discount in the value of their loans. However, their potential disadvantages, more often than not, have out-weighed their advantages. With the exception of Chile's quite extraordinary experience, debt-equity schemes have typically resulted in strong inflationary pressures, a loss of foreign currency, substantial budgetary burdens, and a misallocation of resources. To use Professor Rudy Dornbusch's word, the advocacy of debt-equity schemes by the IMF, World Bank and US Treasury was 'obscene'.[32]

Debt-equity swaps have had a chequered past. However, the fact that debt-for-development swaps grew out of debt-equity swaps, should not prejudice the assessment of what debt-for-development has to offer. Debt-for-development exchanges or debt-for-investment projects, as they are also known, benefit both donor and recipient countries on several different levels. These can encompass a

---

30. J. Bergsman and W. Edisis, 'Debt-Equity Swaps and Foreign Direct Investment in Latin America' (Discussion Paper No 2, International Financial Corporation, 1989), 2.
31. Paris Club, 'Debt Swap Reporting: Rules and Principles' (2006) <www.clubdeparis.org/en/public_debt.html>, 20 April 2006; Buckley, 'Debt Exchanges Revisited: Lessons from Latin America for Eastern Europe'.
32. The full quotation is: 'Washington has been obscene in advocating debt-equity swaps and in insisting that they be part of the debt strategy. The US Treasury has made this dogma, and the IMF and the World Bank, against their staff's professional advice and judgment, have simply caved in': R. Dornbusch, 'Panel Discussion on Latin American Adjustment: The Record and Next Steps' in *Latin American Adjustment: How Much Has Happened*, John Williamson (ed.) (Washington, DC, Institute for International Economics, 1990), pp. 312, 324.

range of projects, including debt-for-development and debt-for-nature or debt-for-environment agreements.

Debt-for-development projects are preferable to debt-equity swaps because they are not inflationary and promote poverty relief and sustainable economic development. Debt-for-development projects on even a small scale can offer substantial benefits to the economy and environment of the debtor country. For example, while Costa Rica's debt-for-nature agreement reduced its total external debt by less than one%, it was described by the Costa Rican Minister of Natural Resources, Energy and Mines as 'absolutely essential.... [because otherwise] [t]here would have been no money to purchase land bridges between parks, to start tree nurseries for farmers, or even fight forest fires'.[33] Debt-for-development projects have also been implemented successfully in the Philippines, the Dominican Republic, Madagascar, Mexico, Poland, Indonesia, Uganda and Zambia.

Germany and Indonesia have conducted several successful debt-for-development projects. The first was a debt-for-education swap in December 2000 under which, in return for the cancellation of some 25.6 million euros of debt, Indonesia agreed to spend the equivalent of 12.8 million euros to build and equip 511 learning resource centers in 17 provinces to enhance the quality of teacher training in the basic sciences. In the second agreement, in October 2002, some 23 million euros of debt was cancelled in return for Indonesia's undertaking to put the equivalent of 11.5 million euros into building 100 new schools. In 2004 Germany and Indonesia entered into a debt for-environment agreement under which some USD 29.25 million of debt was cancelled.[34]

The Philippines and the United States signed a debt for-development agreement in September 2002 in which the US agreed to cancel USD 5.5million of the Philippines' debt to it. In return the Philippine Government agreed to fund tropical forest conservation activities through local NGOs in the Philippines. The Philippines agreed to apply in local currency to conservation activities the amount it would save in debt service repayments over the next 14 years.[35]

Two small, successful debt-for-development projects were implemented recently between Egypt and Italy, and Egypt and Switzerland. These two projects combined amounted to only 1.6% of Egypt's total external debt but the benefits received were significant. Despite the fact that Egypt is a middle-income country, the Egyptian experience is a valuable reference point for debt-for-development projects elsewhere. Egypt's experience shows the benefit of debt-for-development

---

33. L.C. Wee, 'Debt-for-Nature Swaps, A Reassessment of Their Significance in International Environmental Law' (1994) 6 *Journal of Environmental Law*, 57, 63; See also Buckley, 'Debt Exchanges Revisited: Lessons from Latin America for Eastern Europe'.
34. T. Hotland, 'RI, Germany Agree US$29.25m Debt Swap Deal', *The Jakarta Post*, 15 May 2004, 13 ; 'Indonesia, Germany to Sign US$60m Debt Swap Deal', *The Jakarta Post*, 8 November 2004; Embassy of the Republic of Indonesia, 'Indonesian – German Bilateral Relations' <www.indonesian-embassy.de/en/about_indonesia/bilateral_relations.htm>, 3 June 2006.
35. US Department of the Treasury Office of Public Affairs, 'Factsheet: US-Philippines Debt-Reduction Agreement Under the Tropical Forest Conservation Act (TFCA)' (TFCA Debt Swap Signing Ceremony with Philippines, 19 September 2002).

swaps focusing on projects that yield immediate returns to communities. In Egypt, information and communications technology projects were chosen because of the impact of such technology in enhancing human resources and global competitiveness. The goals included making the technology available to every segment of the population and providing the training and education required to use it. Egypt's projects created new economic and social opportunities for underprivileged groups such as women, rural communities, and low waged and low skilled workers.[36]

In summary, debt-for-development projects are not new. It is a technique that has been applied by numerous developed countries in numerous developing countries and has consistently served the interests of both. They are techniques that deserve broader and more frequent use than they have received to date, to further the interests of both creditor and debtor nations.

---

36. S. Kamel and E. Tooma, 'Exchanging Debt for Development: Lessons from the Egyptian Debt-for-Development Swap Experience' (Economic Research Forum and Ministry for Communication and Information Technology (MCIT), Egypt, September 2005), 15.

Chapter 8
Measures Available to Debtor Nations

There are a number of measures available to debtor countries to improve their interaction with global capital. The principal measures include:

(1) rigorous and effective local prudential regulation;
(2) appropriate debt policies;
(3) appropriate exchange rate policies;
(4) the development of local capital markets;
(5) the timely and appropriate use of capital controls; and
(6) being more willing to play the default card.

Each measure will be considered.

8.1   RIGOROUS LOCAL PRUDENTIAL REGULATION

The clearest example of the perils of seeking to liberalize and regulate financial sectors simultaneously is to be seen in the experience of East Asia in the 1990s. Most nations affected by the Asian economic crisis shared unsophisticated and poorly supervised financial sectors. For this reason, the increased capital inflows of 1995 and 1996 ended up principally in property and stock market investments, driving up the price of those assets in speculative bubbles. Such investments cannot generate the foreign currency needed to repay foreign currency debt. This is not rocket science. If a nation is borrowing abroad in foreign currency, it had better be investing the borrowed funds in activities that will generate the foreign exchange with which to service, and eventually repay, the loans.

In East Asia, the local finance sectors were insufficiently sophisticated to intermediate the increased flow of capital efficiently and disclosure and regulatory standards were inadequate across the region.[1] Local banks borrowed short, lent

---

1. World Bank, *Global Development Finance 1998*, p. 4.

long, and did not hedge their massive foreign currency exposures. Proper prudential regulation would have identified and required the minimization of these massive risks. However the East Asian nations didn't have proper prudential regulation because the IMF had encouraged the simultaneous liberalization and regulation of their financial sectors in the early 1990s.

Foreign money had flooded into Thailand because the Bangkok International Banking Facility had been established too early, before effective prudential controls and supervision were in place and functioning well. Indonesia and Korea, in particular, had likewise opened their economies to international capital before reinforcing the stability of their domestic banking sectors.

The regulation of globalized capital flows will, in all probability, continue to fall to nation states aided, as is proper and appropriate, by the standard setting activities of international bodies such as the Basle Committee of the Bank for International Settlements. This is achievable and there is no evidence to date that national regulation of capital flows, handled properly, is inadequate for the task (although there is much evidence of poor national prudential regulation coupled to some poorly considered interventions by supranational agencies such as the IMF).[2] The challenge before the international community is to assist national regulators to discharge their duties effectively. The international community is doing much good work in this regard in terms of the preparation of appropriate international standards and otherwise making available expertise and information.[3] However regulation is labour intensive and expensive. This is particularly so in developing countries in which skilled capital markets professionals are rare. And it is on this front – resources – that the international community's contribution is far from adequate.

It was striking that the IMF identified poor local prudential regulation and underdeveloped local capital markets as two of the principal contributing causes to the crisis and yet the IMF-orchestrated bailouts contained not one dollar to improve prudential regulation or develop local capital markets. Tremendous efforts have gone into generating international standards designed for adoption by national regulators to improve the entire international financial system. It is time now for rich countries to put money in behind these good ideas so as to fund their implementation in developing countries. In financial regulation the rule of law operates principally at the national level and this is the level at which the world's efforts and resources should be directed.

Liberalized local financial markets offer real benefits, but only if they follow stringent regulation that is both on the statute books and effectively enforced. The tatters to which the domestic financial sectors of Indonesia and Thailand were reduced in the late 1990s are testament to the imperative for such regulation of

---

2. See for instance the IMF-orchestrated bailouts of East Asian nations in 1997 in Buckley 'An Oft-Ignored Perspective on the Asian Economic Crisis: The Role of Creditors and Investors', pp. 453–54.
3. See Doug Arner's excellent book generally for soft law developments in the past decade, D.W. Arner, *Financial Stability, Economic Growth, and the Role of Law* (Cambridge, Cambridge University Press, 2007).

incoming capital flows. International capital flows have the capacity to artificially inflate emerging market economies not prepared to control them. The resulting adjustment when the capital stops flowing, as history says at some point it will, can be exceedingly painful.

8.2 DEBT POLICY

Three clear lessons of debt policy emerge from the Mexican peso crisis, the Asian economic crisis, the Russian collapse and Argentina's implosion. The first is to borrow less in foreign currency. The second is to issue less short-term debt. The third flows from the first two, and is to issue more long-term local currency denominated debt.

8.2.1 BORROW LESS FOREIGN CURRENCY DEBT

There is substantial evidence that high levels of external indebtedness render an economy far more vulnerable to currency and financial crises.[4] Extensive borrowing in foreign currency poses three problems.

The first is when the foreign currency borrowing is coupled to a fixed exchange rate as it was in Mexico, Thailand, Indonesia and Argentina. This poses an enormous temptation to local bankers and businesspeople to borrow in foreign currency and onlend the proceeds in local currency, or invest the proceeds in local assets. In either case, the differential between returns on local currency loans or stocks and the cost of the foreign currency borrowings amounts to a licence to print money. For as long as the fixed exchange rate peg holds, the potential profits are enormous (and accrue to the local banks and businesses). Of course, the differential exists because the foreign currency is more stable and less likely to depreciate than the local currency. Thai baht and Indonesian rupiah fell over 50% in value in late 1997. Banks and businesses that had borrowed in US dollars and onlent or invested in local currency suddenly saw an effective doubling of their foreign debt. The losses were catastrophic and did not only affect the banks and businesses that had profited earlier. The ensuing crises in Mexico, Thailand, Indonesia, Korea and Russia affected the nutritional status, infant mortality rates, healthcare and educational levels of the common people of these countries.

The second problem with excessive foreign currency borrowing is that foreign capital inflows in excess of those needed for productive development tends to fuel speculative and unsustainable bubbles in the local real estate and stock markets.

The third problem with excessive foreign currency borrowing is that it masks the real currency risks. It doesn't remove the risks – it simply ensures they are with

---

4. R.S. Rajan, 'The Southeast Asian Currency and Financial Crisis: Review of Experiences and Implications for IMF Policy', (Working Paper No. 1, The Institute of Policy Studies, Singapore, 1998).

the party least able to absorb them, the borrower. Borrowing in local currency incorporates the currency risk and will thus be at a higher rate. If Asian and Argentine banks and businesses had had to borrow in local currency in the mid-1990s, they would have borrowed less and when a downturn came the currency risk would have been on the international lenders.

8.2.2 ISSUE LESS SHORT-TERM DEBT

Short-term debt brings with it tremendous volatility. This debt is mostly sovereign bonds of between 30 and 180 days duration and often denominated in local currency. The short tenor means that investors can always refuse to roll over the debt when storm clouds gather. Its denomination in local currency means that any darkening on the economic horizon will almost ensure a stampede out of these instruments because any devaluation in the local currency will represent a direct capital loss on the investment for foreign investors. An over reliance on, and preponderance of, such debt instruments was one of the major precipitating factors behind Mexico's crisis in late 1994, Korea's in 1997 (even with a floating exchange rate for the won),[5] the other Asian countries in 1997 and Russia's in 1998.

8.2.3 ISSUE MORE LONG-TERM LOCAL CURRENCY DENOMINATED DEBT

On the other hand, long-term local currency denominated debt, debt with maturities of three years and upwards, brings with it a repayment profile well suited to the needs of developing nations. Indeed, much like a floating exchange rate, such debt serves as something of an automatic self-regulating device. When nations borrow in their own currency and their economy is healthy, the real cost of such borrowing tends to be high, as interest rates are generally higher on local currency debt. When their economy is going badly the real cost of the borrowing tends to be low due to a deteriorating exchange rate. Thus debtors pay heavily when they can afford to, and less when they cannot. Such a repayment profile is well adapted to avert the types of crises we have seen of late, and that are so damaging to debtors and investors alike. Accordingly, debtors should be anxious to pay the higher premia required to raise long-term, local currency denominated capital.

Although issuers cannot move much ahead of the investor base in these matters, remarkably, debtors positively sought short term and foreign currency denominated debt in the periods preceding the Asian and Russian crises.[6] In the words of Robert Rubin, 'One of the striking elements of the recent crisis was the

---

5. F. Caramazza and J. Aziz, 'Fixed or Flexible? Getting the Exchange Rate Right in the 1990s', <www.imf.org/external/pubs/ft/issues13/Issue13.pdf>, 17 March 2000).
6. R.E. Rubin, 'Treasury Secretary Robert E. Rubin Remarks on Reform of the International Financial Architecture to the School of Advance International Studies' (Press Release, 21 April 1999).

extent to which countries actually reached for short-term capital, and thereby greatly increased their vulnerability to crises down the road'. Debtors strove for the lowest cost of funds and were not willing to pay for more appropriate tenors and currencies for their debt. Debtors need to support the lead of the supranational institutions, on the rare occasions when they seek to establish a market in a local currency by raising some of their own capital by issuing bonds in that currency. Ratings agencies need to reflect the lower real risks of default in their ratings of local currency bond issues. The multilateral development banks and the Paris Club of official OECD nation creditors could all do far more to support the development of deep and liquid markets in local currency denominated debt by redenominating restructured borrowings into local currency – an idea explored in more depth towards the end of the next chapter.

If the day arrives when the great majority of emerging markets sovereign borrowing is long-term and denominated in the currency of the debtor, the international financial system will be inherently far more stable and the risks of international debt raising will be apportioned far more equitably between creditors and debtors than has been the case to date.

8.3 EXCHANGE RATE POLICIES

A floating exchange rate is a major avenue of economic adjustment for an economy. For instance, if Thailand's economy is strong, the demand for capital within Thailand, and hence Thai interest rates, will increase. At the same time, direct and portfolio investment in Thailand will become more attractive to foreigners who will buy baht with which to invest directly or will buy Thai stocks and bonds. The increase in demand for baht, plus the higher Thai interest rates, will each tend to strengthen the currency. The higher currency will, in turn, tend to reduce Thai exports, as they become relatively more expensive, and increase correspondingly cheaper imports, thus moving the economy towards an equilibrium state. Likewise, when the Thai economy turns down, its lower priced currency will tend to promote exports and reduce imports. A floating exchange rate regime thus tends to move an economy towards equilibrium.

Fixed exchange rates appeal to developing countries in particular because they offer lower costs of credit and lower rates of inflation and provide discipline against monetary or fiscal excesses by government.[7] Fixed exchange rates have proven critical in breaking wage-price-currency spirals that had led to ruinous inflation in nations such as Argentina and in promoting exports (through undervalued exchange rates) and a stable external environment in times of export-led growth in Asia, most notably in Japan and, more recently, China.[8]

---

7. M. Feldstein, 'A Self-Help Guide for Emerging Markets', *Foreign Affairs*, March-April 1999, 93.
8. I. Viscio, 'The Recent Experience with Capital Flows to Emerging Market Economies' 65 *OECD Economic Outlook*, 1 June 1998, 177.

The cost of credit is lowered under a fixed exchange rate regime as borrowers will typically trust to the peg and borrow in foreign currency (at rates invariably lower than local currency rates). As the Asian crisis demonstrated conclusively, this behaviour is highly risky and masks the real cost of borrowing in a foreign currency: the currency risk doesn't go away merely because one's domestic currency is pegged to the foreign currency. As a lax monetary policy that permits inflation will also erode the value of the currency, a government committed to a fixed exchange rate is forced to eschew the politically attractive option of increasing the money supply to meet the demands of domestic pressure groups and thus the fixed rate imposes a most useful discipline on the government.

However, fixed exchange rates pose their own political and economic problems. When the economy of a nation with a fixed exchange rate is performing less strongly than that of the nation(s) to whose currency its currency is fixed, the peg requires adjustment or the fixed currency will become overvalued. Choosing to devalue the nation's currency is often difficult for politicians as it risks inflation and may well be seen domestically as evidence of a failure in economic leadership. It is no coincidence that there was a national election in Mexico in August 1994 and a peso crisis four months later: a government about to face the electorate declined to make the tough but necessary decisions and preferred, very humanly, to hope that a change in economic conditions might intervene to avert a crisis.

In short, it is very easy, with a fixed rate regime, for a nation's currency to become overvalued. It happened in Mexico in 1993 and 1994, in Thailand and Indonesia in 1996–97, in Russia in 1997–98 and in Argentina in the late 1990s. Furthermore, smaller economies lack the resources to defend the value of their currency against speculative attack and so the system gives their central banks relatively little room within which to manoeuvre.

(To understand speculative attacks on currencies, it is necessary to understand that speculators can sell currency they do not own. If you or I try that with a car or boat the local constabulary will soon be a calling. However, investors can simply borrow a currency such as baht or rupiah, sell it for a hard currency, such as US dollars, and then trust to a fall in the value of the baht or rupiah before they have to repurchase it to repay the borrowing or, more simply, enter into a forward contract to sell the currency and only intend to purchase the currency to fulfil the contract at the date for settlement of the forward contract. Accordingly, there can, in the short term, be waves of currency sales that are not preceded by currency purchases which tends to depress the price of the currency and enhance the likely profitability of the speculative attacks. Having said this, while speculative attacks may hasten the onset of a crisis, they are never, in themselves, its cause because for such attacks to be profitable, the currency must already be under considerable pressure.)

The other problem with fixed exchange rates is that they encourage excessive borrowing in foreign currency. Borrowers tend to take the lower interest rates that are usually on offer abroad and trust to the fixed exchange rate to deal with the currency risk.

Under a fixed exchange rate in difficult times, economic contraction will be greater and labour markets are likely to adjust to the contraction through quantity (fewer jobs) rather than price (lower real wages). Poverty is inversely correlated with economic growth, and unemployment is a major source of poverty.[9] Accordingly, for both of these reasons, a fixed exchange rate regime is only justifiable, from the perspective of the poor, if it lessens the likelihood of economic crisis. However, this has not been established. Indeed, the converse appears true.

An overvalued fixed exchange rate was at the heart of each of the Mexican peso crisis of late 1994, the Asian crisis of 1997, the Russian collapse of 1998, Brazil's devaluation of early 1999 and Argentina's implosion shortly thereafter. While a floating exchange rate is no insurance against a currency crisis (as Korea learned in 1997) the overwhelming policy lesson is that flexible exchange rates provide some protection against such crises and the accompanying economic problems. A pure floating exchange rate may not be strictly necessary, a managed flexible rate, provided it is managed in a sensible and market responsive manner, may be enough.[10] However a fixed rate, in the contemporary world of massive capital flows, is an invitation to trouble. And as the impact of financial crises falls disproportionately upon the poor through increases in unemployment and decreases in government services, a flexible exchange rate regime offers a degree of insurance for the poor.

Utterly fixed, inflexible exchange rates are highly dangerous[11] and are only apt to work if the external competitiveness of the economy that has fixed its rate continues over time to match or exceed that of the nation to the currency of which its rate has been fixed. In Argentina's case making the peso convertible into dollars resolved the inflationary spiral. Within three years the peg had defeated the hyperinflation of up to 5,000% per year that had long dogged this nation. With the benefit of hindsight, the opportunities to revoke the peg were in 1994 once inflation had been defeated, or in 1996–97 when the economy was recovering in the wake of Mexico's Tequila crisis.

However, given Argentina's appetite for foreign debt, at no time would breaking the peg have been easy. This is one of the principal difficulties with fixed exchange rates: devaluation is often extremely difficult as it hurts vested interests and can appear politically as an admission of defeat. As so much of the individual and corporate debt in Argentina was denominated in US dollars, a devaluation at

---

9. A. de Janvry and E. Sadoulet, 'Growth, Poverty and Inequality in Latin America: A Causal Analysis, 1970–1994', Inter-American Development Bank Conference on Social Protection and Poverty, February 1999, 5; G.S. Fields, *Growth and Income Distribution*, in *Essays on Poverty, Equity and Growth* (G. Psacharopolous ed.) (Oxford, Pergamon Press, 1991); and N. Lustig, 'Crises and the Poor: Socially Responsible Macroeconomics' (Presidential Address to the Fourth Annual Meeting of the Latin American and Caribbean Economic Association, Santiago, Chile, 22 October 22 1999), <www.lacea.org/Conferences_files/presidential.pdf>, 4 December 2007.
10. Such management of exchange rates, however, has proven a difficult task: Meyer, 'Lessons from the Asian Crisis: A Central Banker's Perspective'.
11. Feldstein, 'Argentina's Fall'.

any stage would have caused considerable economic dislocation and some corporate and personal insolvencies.[12]

The attractiveness of fixed exchange rates, with their capacity to keep a cap on inflation, impose fiscal and monetary discipline on the domestic government and provide stability for exporters, is understandable. However for many developing countries their disadvantages may well outweigh these advantages. Fixed rates often tend over time towards becoming overvalued, as the economies of most emerging markets nations don't perform as strongly as the economies of the currencies to which their currency is tied; and when exchange rates become overvalued, devaluation can be very difficult politically. Devaluation will always impose severe costs on those who have unhedged foreign currency exposures, and the banks and major corporations most likely to have such exposures are often politically very influential. Furthermore, devaluation can appear to be an admission by a government of defeat as an economic manager, especially as citizens often tend to conflate the value of their nation's exchange rate and their nation.

Yet if a nation's exchange rate is becoming overvalued urgent action is needed because overvalued rates lead to declines in exports, burgeoning current account deficits, capital flight and, ultimately, to a currency crisis. The costs of these crises, as seen in the 1990s, are massive. Floating exchange rates provide a substantial degree of insurance against crises.

8.4   CAPITAL CONTROLS

Four things must be kept in mind, and are often overlooked, in discussions of capital controls.

> (1) Free capital mobility is a relatively recent phenomenon. Capital controls were only abandoned by most developed nations in the early 1980s having previously been in place throughout the Bretton Woods era since World War II.[13] Indeed, global economic growth has been lower since the general abandonment of capital controls by developed nations than it was during the Bretton Woods era. While there are many potential explanations for this, it makes it difficult to argue that capital controls unduly restrain economic growth.[14]
>
> (2) The US developed its productive capacity behind heavy trade barriers in the 19th century. At the time the United Kingdom sung the praises of free

---

12. *Ibid.*
13. The US and Canada had traditionally operated fairly liberal capita accounts. The UK removed its controls in 1979, Japan in 1980, Germany in 1981, Australia in 1983 and New Zealand in 1984: B. Eichengreen and M. Mussa, 'Capital Account Liberalization: Theoretical and Practical Aspects', (Occassional Paper No. 172, IMF, 1998), pp. 35–36; and F.Block, 'Controlling Global Finance', (1996) *World Policy Journal*, pp. 24, 30.
14. R. Wade, 'The coming fight over capital controls', 113 *Foreign Affairs*, 22 December 1998, 41.

trade, as such a policy enhanced its strong position and suited its interests. There were few free marketeers in the then emerging market known as the United States.[15] Of course this all changed as the 20th century, and US economic strength, progressed. Capital has replaced goods in significance in the movement of resources between nations. The interests of many emerging economies may best be served by barriers to the free movement of capital, just as the interests of the US were perhaps best served in the 19th century by barriers to the free movement of goods.

(3) Free trade served Britain's interests last century when it was the largest producer of manufactured goods. The US requires access to foreign savings to finance its high-consuming, low-saving way of life and its high levels of investment because the US household savings rate is the lowest of any major industrial economy.[16] The hard line Washington consensus in favour of unfettered international capital mobility reflects US strategic interests. Asian nations, in the main, enjoy high savings rates and can finance much of their economic development internally. Indeed, if the citizens of these countries could be forced to keep their savings at home, the nations would have little need for foreign capital.[17] For instance, at the end of 1997 Asian investors outside Japan held almost USD 165 billion in US Treasury securities at the end of 1997 – almost the entire combined GDP of Malaysia and the Philippines[18] – funding the US needed to sustain its living standards.

(4) Capital controls, in conjunction with some of the other policies recommended here, can give countries a real measure of control over their economy. In the aftermath of the Asian crisis, it was critical that China maintain the value of its currency as the increase in the competitiveness of China's exports in the wake of a devaluation would have devastated other teetering economies in the region. As Peter Fisher, Executive Vice President of the Federal Reserve Bank of New York, said in 1998, 'I sleep sounder knowing the People's Republic of China has capital controls and they are working to improve them. I think that's a plus for the world economy'.[19] Capital controls, and China's massive foreign exchange reserves, enabled it to hold the line tightly on its currency.

Viewed from the vantage point provided by these four factors, capital controls appear a sensible policy option for developing countries – just as they were for all countries between 1945 and the 1970s. Of course, the world has changed in the

---

15. J.K. Galbraith, *The Culture of* Contentment (Boston, Houghton Mifflin, 1992), p. 46.
16. R. Wade and F. Veneroso, 'The Gathering World Slump and the Battle Over Capital Controls' (1998) 231 *New Left Review*, 41.
17. Such a restriction is, of course, extremely difficult, if not impossible, to implement. See consideration of outflow controls in text above.
18. The combined GDP's of Malaysia and the Philippines in 1997 were some USD 180 billion.
19. IMF Economic Forum, 'Financial Markets: Coping with Turbulence' <www.imf.org/external/np/tr/1998/TR981201.htm>, 5 October 1999.

interim, and in a more globalized world which offers cheaper credit and a much higher degree of financial innovation in capital and credit markets, the costs to a nation of turning its back on globalized capital is correspondingly higher than it once was. Nonetheless, it is an interesting aspect of the power of ideas that controls that were common in developed countries in the early 1970s could be treated as utter economic heresy when introduced by Malaysia in the late 1990s.

Dr Mahathir's imposition of controls over outflows of capital from Malaysia in September 1998 attracted widespread condemnation from the international financial community. This was unsurprising. However, in the months leading up to this decision, some economic heavyweights had challenged the conventional wisdom and suggested that restrictions on capital flows were no bad thing. Paul Krugman argued in September, 1998 that outflow controls may well be necessary to retain capital in an economy while its government implemented the policies of fiscal expansion that he, and many others, saw as necessary in Asia.[20] Without such controls, upon the implementation of such policies capital would typically flee an emerging market. Dani Rodrik, of Harvard, took an even bigger bite arguing there was little evidence linking capital market liberalization to higher economic growth and positive proof of the risks of such liberalization.[21] The Washington consensus on free market economics had been promoted and pursued with a remarkable consistency notwithstanding the serious challenges made to it in the wake of the debt crisis in the 1980s. Fascinatingly, however, for the first time in over fifteen years the consensus began to disintegrate quite quickly on the issue of the desirability of the unfettered movement of capital. By 1 December 1998 at a seminar organized by the IMF, the three of the four participants who spoke of capital controls were supportive of Chilean-style inflow controls (which we will consider shortly).[22] The participants were speaking in their personal capacities but were senior employees of the IMF, the Federal Reserve Bank of New York and Salomon Smith Barney, the large investment bank; and so reflect a quite remarkable turnaround in sentiment.

Thus far I have taken the traditional approach in discussing capital controls which is to do so without defining the term or distinguishing between the various types of controls. Let's remedy that.

In broad terms, capital controls can be either restraints on foreign exchange transactions or on capital account transactions and, if the latter, can be placed on capital inflows or capital outflows. These restraints can, in their turn, take the form of taxes or quantitative restrictions.[23] A detailed analysis of the full gamut of available capital controls is beyond the scope of this work, and has been well done elsewhere. We will focus on capital account controls, and, in particular on

---

20. P. Krugman, 'Saving Asia: it's time to get Radical', *Fortune*, 7 September 1998, 75.
21. Dani Rodrik, 'Development Strategies for the Next Century', 2000 available at <http://siteresources.worldbank.org/INTABCDEWASHINGTON2000/Resources/rodrik_japan.pdf>.
22. IMF Economic Forum, 'Financial Markets: Coping with Turbulence'.
23. Rajan, 'The Southeast Asian Currency and Financial Crisis: Review of Experiences and Implications for IMF Policy'.

the capital inflow controls imposed by Chile from 1991 to 1998 and the capital outflow controls imposed by Malaysia in 1998.[24]

8.4.1 CHILE'S CONTROLS

Chile's capital account surplus reached 10% of its GDP in 1990 and short-term flows represented one-third of this amount. Fearing a reversal in capital flows as in 1982 Chile introduced its capital controls in 1991, modified them twice during the decade, and suspended them in 1998, as the downturn in international capital flows rendered controls unnecessary.[25]

Chile's capital controls had five elements:[26]

- All portfolio flows including foreign loans and bond issues were subject to the requirement that an amount equal to a set proportion of the flow had to be put on interest-free deposit with the Central Bank for one year irrespective of the duration of the capital inflow. The proportion was initially set at 20%, in May 1992 it was increased to 30%, and then in June, 1996 reduced to 10%.
- Credit lines for trade finance were subject to the same reserve requirements.
- Bonds issued abroad by local companies had to have an average minimum maturity of four years.
- Shares issuance abroad by local companies was limited to companies with relatively high credit ratings and in a minimum amount of at least USD 10 million.
- Initial investment capital (but not profits) in foreign direct investment could not be repatriated for one year.

The first four restrictions are inflow controls, the last is an outflow control. Most international attention has focused on the first restriction, the unremunerated reserve requirement. The second restriction, on trade finance credit, is undesirable in that it tends to reduce a nation's international trade but necessary as otherwise the first restriction would be too readily circumvented.

---

24. Numerous other countries have, of course, used capital controls. The experiences of Brazil (1993–97), Colombia (1993–98) and the Czech Republic are analysed in C.M. Reinhart and R.T. Smith, 'Temporary Controls on Capital Inflows' (Working Paper No. 8422, NBER, August 2001); the experience of Chile with its earlier inflow controls imposed from 1978 to 1982 is analysed in Edwards 'How Effective Are Capital Controls?', 11; and the experiences with inflow controls of Brazil (1993–97), Chile (1991–98), Malaysia (1994), and Thailand (1995–97) and with outflow controls of Spain in 1992 and Thailand (1997–98) are analysed in Ariyoshi, Habermeier, et al, 'Country Experiences with the Use and Liberalization of Capital Controls', IMF Paper, January 2000 <www.imf.org/external/pubs/ft/capcon/index.htm>, 29 February 2000.
25. Reinhart and Smith, 'Temporary Controls on Capital Inflows'.
26. Rajan, 'The Southeast Asian Currency and Financial Crisis: Review of Experiences and Implications for IMF Policy', Table 3.

The general consensus is that Chile's controls served to lengthen the average maturity of the capital it received.[27] Views are more divided over whether they also served to reduce the volume of capital inflows. Certainly there was a strong initial effect: the capital account surplus fell from 10% of GDP in 1990 to 2.4% in 1991 and short-term debt inflows were virtually eliminated. When capital inflows surged again in 1992, the proportion of the non-renumerated reserve requirement was increased, again successfully. Foreign direct investment appears to have been relatively unaffected by the controls.[28]

However, the controls increased the cost of credit within Chile considerably, particularly for small and medium size businesses that found evasion of the controls most difficult. This is a substantial price for any economy to pay. In addition, there is a wide range of factors to which the good performance of Chile's economy under these controls can be attributed. In summary, Chilean style capital controls may prove a very useful policy option for some countries for limited periods before sophisticated evasive techniques can be developed, but are certainly no universal panacea, nor are they cost free.[29]

8.4.2 Malaysia's Controls

Malaysia had itself implemented inflow controls in 1994, but it is best known for its outflow controls implemented on 1 September 1998.[30] In summary, these controls included:[31]

- Restriction of trading in Malaysian stocks to the Malaysian Stock Exchange.
- Foreign exchange controls prohibiting unofficial trading and import and export of the ringgit.

---

27. Ariyoshi, Habermeier, et al, 'Country Experiences with the Use and Liberalization of Capital Controls', 23; Edwards 'How Effective Are Capital Controls?'; Eichengreen and Mussa, 'Capital Account Liberalization: Theoretical and Practical Aspects', pp. 49–52 (and the sources there cited); Feldstein, 'Argentina's Fall', 7; Reinhart and Smith, 'Temporary Controls on Capital Inflows', 8.
28. Eichengreen and Mussa, 'Capital Account Liberalization: Theoretical and Practical Aspects', pp. 49–52 (and the sources there cited); Reinhart and Smith, 'Temporary Controls on Capital Inflows', 8; Rajan, 'The Southeast Asian Currency and Financial Crisis: Review of Experiences and Implications for IMF Policy'; Reinhart and Smith, 'Temporary Controls on Capital Inflows'; Edwards 'How Effective Are Capital Controls?', 25.
29. Edwards 'How Effective Are Capital Controls?', 25. The conclusion of Ariyoshi, Habermeier, et al, ('Country Experiences with the Use and Liberalization of Capital Controls', 23) is that inflow controls were partly effective in reducing the level and increasing the maturity of inflows in Malaysia and Thailand, and in affecting the composition of the inflows in Colombia and possibly in Chile but were largely ineffective in Brazil.
30. Malaysia's inflow controls included, among other things, a ceiling on non-trade and non-investment external liabilities of banks and a prohibition on sales of short-term bonds to non-residents and non-trade related swaps and forward transactions on the bid side with foreigners (Rajan, 'The Southeast Asian Currency and Financial Crisis: Review of Experiences and Implications for IMF Policy').
31. S.H. Poon, 'Malaysia and the Asian Financial Crisis – A View from the Finance Perspective', *African Finance Journal*, Special Issue (1999).

- Restrictions on investment abroad by Malay residents.
- Punitive taxes if capital was withdrawn from the country in under one year.

The controls resulted in the elimination of the offshore market in ringgit and, in effect, withdrew the ringgit from the international currency trading system as they resulted in all ringgit trading occurring through the Central Bank.

In February 1999 these controls were replaced by a graduated exit tax on capital outflows such that capital already within the country that was repatriated within seven months of its entry into Malaysia was taxed at 30%, capital repatriated between seven and nine months was taxed at 20%, between nine and twelve months at 10% and thereafter not at all. Profits on capital already in the country were free of taxes upon exit. Capital brought into Malaysia after February 1999 was free of taxes upon repatriation, but all profits therefrom were subject to a 30% tax if withdrawn within twelve months of being made and a 10% tax thereafter.[32]

One of the common criticisms of capital controls, particularly outflow controls, is that they disrupt everyday commerce. Malaysia's experience suggests the everyday difficulties are not as large as often suggested. Furthermore, the absence of capital flight when Malaysia's controls were relaxed suggests outflow controls can be successfully imposed as, and held out to be, a temporary measure.[33]

The IMF's assessment was that the controls were effective in curtailing speculative pressures on the ringgit, and were enhanced by the country's relatively good economic fundamentals, the authorities' efforts to make the controls transparent and their efforts to strengthen Malaysia's financial sector.[34]

The initial vociferous criticism of Malaysia's outflow controls has proven to be utterly misplaced. The controls have done little harm and some good in providing a period of stability and, in the words of the IMF study, affording 'the Malaysian authorities some breathing space to address the macroeconomic imbalances and implement banking system reforms'.[35]

8.4.3   THE USES OF INFLOW CONTROLS

Developing nations are better served by direct investment than portfolio investment and by long-term debt rather than short-term debt.[36] Capital inflow controls, used sensibly, can go some small way to achieving those goals.

---

32. R. Gengatharen, 'Destabilising Financial Flows: Are Capital Controls the Solution' (1999) *LAWASIA Journal*, 20–22; and Wade and Veneroso, 'The Gathering World Slump and the Battle Over Capital Controls', 21.
33. P. Krugman, 'Analytical Afterthoughts on the Asian Crisis', <web.mit.edu/krugman/www/MINICRIS.htm>, 4 December 2007.
34. Ariyoshi, Habermeier, et al, 'Country Experiences with the Use and Liberalization of Capital Controls', 36.
35. Ariyoshi, Habermeier, et al, 'Country Experiences with the Use and Liberalization of Capital Controls', 37. See also, to the same general effect: Edwards 'How Effective Are Capital Controls?', 23; and Gengatharen, 'Destabilising Financial Flows: Are Capital Controls the Solution', 12–13.
36. Eichengreen and Mussa, 'Capital Account Liberalization: Theoretical and Practical Aspects', 22.

The potential need for some regulation of inflows can be seen from the experience of the five Asian economies most affected by the 1997 crisis: Indonesia, Malaysia, the Philippines, South Korea and Thailand. They received USD 93 billion of private capital inflows in 1996 which changed to USD 12 billion in private capital outflows in 1997. The reversal in one year of USD 105 billion represented some 11% of their combined GDP and was comprised of a USD 77 billion turnaround in commercial bank lending, a USD 24 billion turnaround in portfolio equity and USD 5 billion reversal in non-bank lending. Foreign direct investment remained constant at about USD 7 billion.[37]

The clearest lesson from the crises in Mexico, Asia and Russia was the danger of excessive short-term indebtedness and other forms of short-term capital inflows. There is strong evidence that the ratio of short-term debt to foreign currency reserves is a powerful predictor of financial crises, and that higher short-term debt levels are associated with more severe crises. Short-term financing is simply not suitable, in the main, for the needs of developing countries. There is accordingly a strong argument for capital controls along Chilean lines that fall most heavily on short-term inflows.[38]

8.4.4 THE USES OF OUTFLOW CONTROLS

Capital outflow controls may well be required to provide a fence behind which emerging markets nations can build strong monetary and financial systems and sophisticated and well-resourced prudential regulators. Capital markets impose different disciplines upon the US, on the one hand, and emerging markets nations, on the other. The US government can stimulate its economy through deficit spending without prompting a retreat of international investors for these investors trust the US Federal Reserve to keep a tight rein on the money supply and thus on inflation. However, the same deficit spending approach by an emerging market nation would prompt a hasty withdrawal of capital for fear of inflation and currency depreciation. Given this is how markets work, capital controls may well be necessary to erect a fence behind which an emerging market government can reflate its economy after a crisis. It is bad policy to toss out 'the single greatest discovery of the Keynesian revolution, namely the importance of fiscal stablizers'.[39] Even the IMF has effectively admitted that its initial policy prescription of fiscal contraction served only to deepen the Asian crisis; and the nations of the region made a tremendous recovery from the crisis once they pursued expansionist fiscal policies. Outflow controls may well be necessary if policies of fiscal expansion are to be pursued.

---

37. J.J. Norton, ' "Are Latin America and East Asia an Ocean Apart?" The Connecting Currents of Asian Financial Crises' (1998) 4 *NAFTA Law and Business Review of the Americas*, 93.
38. D. Rodrik and A. Velasco, 'Short-term Capital Flows' (Working Paper No. W7364, NBER, September 1999); and B. Eichengreen, 'Bailing in the Private Sector: Burden Sharing in International Financial Crisis Management' (1999) 23 *The Fletcher Forum of World Affairs*, 60.
39. B. Eichengreen, 'Capital Controls: Capital Idea or Capital Folly?', <www.econ.berkeley.edu/~eichengr/policy/capcontrols.pdf>, 4 December 2007.

8.4.5 Inflow and Outflow Controls Compared

The empirical research suggests that inflow controls are more effective than outflow controls.[40] Outflow controls are best used as a temporary counter-crisis measure. Outflow controls lose their effectiveness more quickly and completely over time than do inflow controls. The incentive to avoid outflow controls is much stronger than for inflow controls and much easier: under-invoicing or over-invoicing is easy to effect and extremely difficult to police. Nonetheless, the effectiveness of inflow controls also declines over time as markets exploit the potential to channel restricted flows through exempted channels. For this reason, enduring inflow controls need to be particularly comprehensive in coverage and rigorously enforced.[41]

Inflow controls by their nature are up-front and transparent. Foreign investors know of them upon investing. The risk of outflow controls being unilaterally imposed part way through an investment's life may well be a significant disincentive to investment and this is a potential cost of such controls. The critical thing with all controls is that they be administered and enforced cleanly and transparently, which may be a challenge for some countries.

8.4.6 Inflow Controls in Developed Countries

Interestingly, there is quite a strong case that capital controls might best be imposed by developed countries. Recent fascinating research suggests that barriers to the free movement of capital into developed countries can increase capital stocks, and GDP, in both developed and developing nations. Like much economics, the proof of this relies on so many assumptions that it is not at all clear whether it can serve as a policy guideline for the real world. However, in a world in which so much capital flows from developing to developed countries, it makes intuitive sense.[42] The net effect of international financial flows is to transfer capital from high-saving to low-saving countries. For the past two decades, this has largely meant from poorer countries to the US and, to a much lesser extent, the UK and some other European countries. Capital inflow controls in developed countries would, paradoxically,

---

40. D. Mathieson and L. Rojas-Suarez, 'Liberalization of the Capital Account: Experiences and Issues', (Occasional Paper No. 103, IMF, March 1993); and Reinhart and Smith, 'Temporary Controls on Capital Inflows'.
41. J. Cuddington, 'Capital Flight, Estimates, Issues and Explanations', Princeton Essays in International Finance No. 58; Edwards 'How Effective Are Capital Controls?', 7; S. Edwards, *Real Exchange Rates, Devaluation and Adjustment* (Cambridge, The MIT Press, 1989); Viscio, 'The recent experience with capital flows to emerging market economies', 177; Wade and Veneroso, 'The Gathering World Slump and the Battle Over Capital Controls', 30; Eichengreen and Mussa, 'Capital Account Liberalization: Theoretical and Practical Aspects', 11; and Ariyoshi, Habermeier, et al, 'Country Experiences with the Use and Liberalization of Capital Controls', 26.
42. See M.A. Espinosa-Vega, B.D. Smith and C.K. Yip, 'Barriers to International Capital Flows: Who Should Erect Them and How Big Should They Be?'.

result in more capital, and capital in the most appropriate currency, where it is needed most, in developing countries.

8.4.7 CONCLUSION ON CAPITAL CONTROLS

In conclusion, for as long as a developing nation has a thin financial market, unsophisticated private sector risk management techniques and an unsophisticated and under-resourced capital market regulator, there are good arguments for controls, from time to time, on capital inflows, as the US Council on Foreign Relations has recommended.[43] This is particularly so in Asia, where high local savings rates diminish significantly the need for completely open capital markets. As an economy's own capital markets deepen, and its regulatory systems mature, then it can safely liberalize its capital account. Many developing nations are many years away from being in that position.

In the interim, of course, the admonition against free lunches generally holds. Capital controls have costs. Controls restrict access to foreign capital for investment, increase real interest rates, require expensive public administration and may reduce the pressure for domestic policy reform.[44] In particular, capital controls require considerable administration, and just as with trade barriers, capital controls can reduce the pressure for, and thus delay, needed policy adjustments.[45] Policy reform and the development of efficient regulatory institutions must be continued apace by developing nations even when controls are in place. Inflow controls can play a real role in stabilizing an economy during periods of high and increasing inflows of global capital. Controls are a policy option that developing nations should be ready to implement, when needed.

8.5 BE MORE WILLING TO PLAY THE DEFAULT CARD

The party with the most power in any negotiation is the party that needs the negotiated result the least.[46] To display this power, a party must be willing to

---

43. Council on Foreign Relations, *The Future of the International Financial Architecture; A Council on Foreign Relations Task Force* (1999) Foreign Affairs (New York), 169; and see Bustelo, Garcia and Olivie, 'Global and Domestic Factors of Financial Crises in Emerging Economies: Lessons from the East Asian Episodes', 78.
44. 'The perils of global capital', *The Economist* (USA), 22 August 1998, 52. And, of course, capital flows are not the only mechanism for the transmission of contagion. Even a completely closed capital account will not insulate an economy from trade-related contagion ('Emerging-market measles', *The Economist* (US) August 1998, 52) as Taiwan experienced in the wake of the Asian crisis. See also R. Wade and F. Veneroso, 'The Gathering World Slump and the Battle over Capital Controls' (1998) 231 *New Left Review*, 40.
45. Ariyoshi, Habermeier, 'Country Experiences with the Use and Liberalization of Capital Controls'.
46. Fisher and Ury, *Getting to Yes* (Boston, Houghton Mifflin, 1991), pp. 19–40; H. Astor and C. Chinkin *Dispute Resolution in Australia* (Butterworths, 2nd ed., 2002); H. Brown and A. Marriott, *ADR Principles and Practice*, (Sweet & Maxwell, 2nd ed., 1999), pp. 104, 113.

walk away from the negotiating table. As the House of Lords has found, each party 'is entitled, if he thinks appropriate, to threaten to withdraw...or to withdraw in fact, in the hope that the opposite party may seek to reopen the negotiations by offering him improved terms'.[47]

Yet since 1982 developing nation debtors have been consistently reluctant to stop servicing their debt, to default, and have thus largely forsaken this source of power in negotiations over the restructuring of their indebtedness. Why might this be so? And has this been a productive approach to debt renegotiation? This section seeks to answer these two questions.

Before doing so, a threshold point needs to be made. We are considering the reluctance of debtors to cease servicing their debts. Under most bonds and loan agreements, non-payment of interest or principal is a ground upon which a creditor can declare a debtor in default, but default is not an automatic event. Being in default under one financing agreement will typically trigger cross-defaults under other agreements, and so the capacity to declare a borrower in default is something creditors reserve to themselves.[48] 'Default' is not used here in this technical sense, but rather in the lay sense, of simply failing to honour one's obligations.

In the overwhelming majority of sovereign debt crises, from the sixteenth century to the mid-twentieth century, sovereign debtors defaulted on their debts.

Defaulting on the debt is a less radical suggestion than it might, on the surface, appear. The moral legitimacy of the loans, often pushed onto nations by over-enthusiastic bankers, and often accompanied by bribes of debtor nation officials, is often questionable. The human suffering entailed by putting debt service before the nutrition and health of a nation's people is often appalling; and Jeffrey Sachs, at least, advocates it. Sachs is one of America's most distinguished macro-economists and special advisor to the UN Secretary-General on the millennium development goals project. He is hardly a radical. Yet recently, in addressing an African leaders gathering he said, 'If they won't cancel the debt – and I'm stretching here – I would suggest that you do it yourselves.'[49]

Nonetheless, default, of late, has been relatively rare.

In the protracted aftermath of the 1982 debt crisis most debtors never stopped servicing their debt. They typically did so throughout the 1980s with money advanced specifically for this purpose by the creditors (in effect capitalizing interest payments by borrowing new money to make them). This has been the case for the debt crisis debt of almost all Latin American debtors except, to my knowledge, of Peru and Brazil.

In 1985, Alan Garcia came to power in Peru as its new President and promptly announced that Peru would limit its debt service payments on medium and long-term debt to 10% of exports. Bankers protested vehemently. They saw this as a

---

47. *Walford v Miles* 2 AC 128, 138 [1992].
48. See K.M.H. Wallman, 'The Politics of Default: Politically Motivated Sovereign Debt Default and Repudiation' (1985) 20 *Texas International Law Journal*, 477.
49. D. Eviatar, 'Spend $150 Billion Per Year to Cure World Poverty', *The New York Times*, 7 November 2004.

dangerous precedent and strove to isolate the nation and brand it a pariah.[50] Other debtors declined to follow Peru's lead.

On 20 February 1987 Brazil announced that it was temporarily suspending interest payments on about USD 67 billion of private foreign debt and effectively freezing about USD 15 billion of short-term credits and money-market deposits by foreign banks. The Brazilian finance minister noted that since 1983 Brazil had paid USD 45 billion in interest and received only USD 11 billion in fresh funds.[51]

The international banking community was shocked. Brazil's GDP had risen 5.7%, 8.3% and 8.2% in 1984, 1985 and 1986[52] and it appeared to be leading the region into recovery. Brazil stressed the moratorium was temporary, and, as it turned out, interest repayments were resumed in early 1988 and arrears repaid in late 1988.[53] Nonetheless, Brazil used this payment interruption wisely and very quietly bought back significant amounts of its debt on the secondary market at prices that were severely reduced by this moratorium.[54]

Since the debt crisis was partially resolved by the Brady Plan in the early 1990s, there have been ten major national debt crises. In late 1994 Mexico's peso crisis erupted, in late 1997 Indonesia, Korea and Thailand were swept up in the East Asian economic crisis and from 1998 to 2001, Argentina, Ecuador, Turkey, Pakistan, Ukraine and Russia all endured their own crises.

Of these nine nations, only three defaulted on their debts: Argentina, Ecuador and Russia. Mexico again serviced all of its debt, this time using money advanced to it by the US from the US Exchange Stabilization Fund. The other six all restructured their indebtedness and managed to avoid defaulting.

In the East Asian economic crisis that erupted in July 1997 each sovereign debtor met all of its obligations and many of the obligations of its corporate sector. Under the terms of the IMF-organized bail-outs, sovereigns typically brought all short-term debt, including that of corporate borrowers, under their sovereign guarantee. The former short-term debt of the country and its private sector corporations became long-term sovereign debt owed to the international financial institutions and other official creditors.

In Ecuador's case, a banking crisis in 1998 led to a run on the banks in early 1999. In September 1999 the government decided to default on its Brady bonds and eurobonds and to restructure its domestic debt. After about a year a debt exchange

---

50. P. Montagnon, 'An Impasse that is difficult to resolve', *Financial Times* (Peru), 26 September 1986, special supplement.
51. 'Brazil calls the Shots' 662 *IFR*, 28 February 1986, 677; C.F. McCoy and P. Truell, 'Lending Imbroglio: Worries Deepen Again On Third World Debt As Brazil Stops Paying', *Wall Street Journal*, 3 March 1987; and Pastor, 'The Debt Crisis: A Financial or a Development Problem?', p. 14.
52. Morgan Guaranty Trust, *World Financial Markets* (June/July 1987), 4.
53. P.T. Sudo, 'Chase Announces Plan to Fortify LDC Reserve', *The American Banker*, 24 January 1989, 3; and P. Truell, 'Big Banks See Bonanza in Fourth Quarter – Brazil's Catch-Up on Interest Payments is Main Reason', *The Wall Street Journal*, 26 October 1988.
54. Buckley, 'Debt Exchanges Revisited: Lessons from Latin America for Eastern Europe'.

using exit consents was implemented for all the Brady bonds and eurobonds and debt service was resumed.

In August 1998 the Russian government imposed a three-month moratorium on private sector payments on external debt, extensive capital and exchange controls and a freeze on some bank deposits.

Argentina's default is the largest sovereign debt default in history. Argentina's aggressive approach is instructive, and will be considered in some detail. Before doing so, however, it is worth noting that the Ukraine, Pakistan and Turkey were able to manage their way through their crises using various combinations of capital and exchange controls, bond exchange offers, floating of exchange rates, and debt restructurings.[55]

At the height of its economic implosion, Argentina was virtually ungovernable, with a succession of presidents in two weeks. However, it emerged from this period with a government firmly resolved to stand up to the international financial community in general and the IMF in particular.

Argentina's initial workout offer to creditors in September 2003 was unprecedentedly aggressive. And in the succeeding 18 months of negotiation and stand-off the Argentine government displayed unprecedented resolve for a developing country. The eventual resolution of the crisis, as was seen in Chapter Six, by way of a debt 'haircut' of some 66% was unprecedented, and, in this author's view, entirely appropriate. The lesson from the Argentine experience is that when the ethics and morals of the situation are on the debtor nation's side (eg. in Argentina's case, the IMF had agreed with the policies that had led to this impasse, and its resolution any other way would have imposed unacceptable suffering on the Argentine people) debtor nations need to be more willing to play the default card, and to play it more forcefully, than they have in the past quarter century.

Before 1982 most sovereign debt crises led to default. After 1982 less than a quarter of nations in crisis have defaulted on their debt. Why might there have been this reversal of a well-established historical trend?

The immediately obvious answer would appear to be the effective repeal by the US and England of the sovereign immunity of sovereign borrowers. Between 1976 and 1978, the United States and the United Kingdom enacted legislation that introduced a new restricted version of sovereign immunity under which sovereigns engaged in commercial activities could waive their immunity expressly or impliedly.[56] This is relevant as virtually all sovereign loan agreements and bonds

---

55. For an analysis of the crises in Ecuador, Russia, Pakistan and Ukraine, and their resolutions, see International Monetary Fund, 'Sovereign Debt Restructurings and the Domestic Economy Experience in Four Recent Cases' <www.imf.org/external/NP/pdr/sdrm/2002/022102.pdf>, 4 December 2007.
56. In the US, the legislation was the Foreign Sovereign Immunities Act of 1976 28 USC ss 1330, 1332(a)(2)–(a)(4), 1391(f), 1441(d), 1602–1611 (1994); and in the UK, the State Immunity Act of 1978. See also J.W. Dellapenna, *Suing Foreign Governments and their Corporations* (New York, Transnational Publishers, 1988), pp. 3–8; and G.R. Delaume, 'The Foreign Sovereign Immunities Act and the Public Debt Litigation: Some Fifteen Years Later' (1994)

are governed by English or New York law. A United Nations study in the 1980s found that over 80% of the total value of emerging market loans were governed by agreements which incorporated an express waiver of immunity[57] and under the new legislation most of the other borrowings would have amounted to an implied waiver of immunity.[58]

Accordingly, certainly since 1982, legal action against recalcitrant sovereign debtors has been an option. However, it has never been one likely to yield a reasonable return for few sovereign debtors have substantial assets abroad over which attachment can be levied.

The conventional view is that nations have only two reasons to service their debts: the preservation of their reputation and potential access to capital markets, and the threat of sanctions.

Creditors routinely threaten lawsuits when faced with a potential default, but, in truth, sovereigns typically have few assets outside their own jurisdiction that are liable to seizure in the event of default. I agree with Jerome Sgard when he says,

> States, in fact, have only one single reason to respect their contractual liabilities: they have a long term interest in protecting their good reputation so as to be able to re-access capital markets in the future, at a reasonable interest rate.[59]

Sanctions are far more of a threat in theory than in practice. Law suits have arisen from Argentina's default, however while these may have been worthwhile for individual creditor plaintiffs, as a whole Argentina simply has far too few assets abroad for it to make any real difference to the nation, or its creditors as a whole, if execution was levied over all of them, and this is the situation with virtually all sovereign borrowers.

As with the threat of sanctions, the benefits of continued access to global capital markets can also be overstated. There are two reasons for this.

The first reason, as Argentina's experience has demonstrated, is that the avoidance of the need to service current debt can often more than offset the benefits of new indebtedness. Certainly, from 1982 to 1990 Latin America repaid far more

---

88 *American Journal of International Law*, 257. See also G.W. Larson, 'Default on Foreign Sovereign Debt: A Question for the Courts?' (1985) 18 *Indiana Law Review*, 965.

57. ECLAC/CTC, *Transnational Bank Behaviour and the International Debt Crisis*, 12–13.
58. Under the US legislation, an implied waiver of immunity arises when a sovereign engages in (i) commercial activity in the US, (ii) an act in the US in connection with commercial activity outside the US, or (iii) an act outside the US in connection with commercial activity outside the US which act has a direct effect in the US. See 28 USC s 1605(a)(2) (1994); *Republic of Argentina v Weltover, Inc.* 504 US 607 (1992) and P.J. Power, 'Sovereign Debt: The Rise of the Secondary Market and Its Implications for Future Restructurings' (1996) 64 *Fordham Law Review*, 2727–2732.
59. J. Sgard, 'The Renegotiation of Sovereign Debts and the Future of Financial Multilateralism', paper presented at the Fifth Pan-European Conference of the Standing Group on International Relations (The Hague, 9–11 September 2004), 4. This was the finding of Eaton and Gersovitz, in their seminal research into reputational models, in 'Debt with Potential Repudiation: theoretical and Empirical Analysis', (1984) 48(2) *Review of Economic Studies*, 289.

than it received in new credits[60] and from 2001 to 2005 Argentina was in the same net cash flow position from having no access to new money and not servicing its debts. No new money would have been advanced beyond that required to keep payments on Argentina's debt current so all that would have happened in those four years, had Argentina not defaulted, is that its total debt stock would have increased, substantially, as its interest payments in effect were capitalized.

The second reason is that capital tends to flow again into regions when potential returns justify it and not otherwise. Financial markets make their decisions on the prospective return from an investment. A nation's payment history is but one factor to stir into the mix of issues likely to determine how profitable a new investment will be; and as Auerback has noted, the 'apparent indifference of "new money" creditors to a sovereign debtor's default history is not a recent phenomenon.'[61]

In the resolution of the debt crisis, countries which serviced their debt continually, such as Mexico, were among the first to receive their Brady restructurings, while less co-operative debtors such as Argentina and Brazil had to wait two and four years, respectively. But international capital in the form of equity investment and eurobond purchases was flooding into both Argentina and Brazil long before their restructurings were implemented. And Peru, which did not service its debt fully for nearly a decade, eventually received a Brady-style restructure on better terms than more compliant nations because its debt-service record indicated less capacity to pay. In short, history contradicts the finance community's constant claim that continued debt service is always in the debtors' interests.

Furthermore, much international finance remains available irrespective of the outcome of debt renegotiations. Trade finance, project finance, suppliers' credits and official loans from the International Financial Institutions (World Bank, IMF, regional development banks, etc) are always likely to remain available irrespective of a default. In the words of Norman Bailey in analyzing the debt crisis in the 1980s, 'debtor states will . . . be able to do business if they are called into default. Such action will largely affect direct lending operations, but trade will continue'.[62]

So, if lawsuits are unlikely to be a real deterrent to default, and continued access to global capital, while important, is not as important as creditors assert, why has there been this marked trend away from default – at least as a device to extract better terms from creditors in the inevitable renegotiation of the debt?

There is, of course, no definitive answer to this question. However a number of observations can be made. Firstly, the fact that history and analysis do not support the claim of the international financial community that full debt service is always in the debtor nation's interests does not mean the claim has not been made at every

---

60. Sachs, *Developing Country Debt and the World Economy*, p. 10.
61. R.M. Auerback, 'Sovereign Debt: Default and Restructuring of Debts Owed to Private Creditor', (2003) 18 *Journal of International Banking Law and Regulation*, 442.
62. Norman Bailey's comments in *Comity, Act of State, and the International Debt Crisis: Is There an Emerging Legal Equivalent of Bankruptcy Protection for Nations*, Proceedings, Seventy-Ninth Annual Meeting, The American Society of International Law, 130.

opportunity and has not been persuasive, particularly as it has often been reinforced by political pressure brought to bear by the US and other foreign governments.

Secondly, and even more significantly, the answer to this question has more to do with the personal perspectives, economic interests, and standing on the world stage of the elites of the debtor countries and the members of their governments and technocracies than it does with what would ultimately be in the best interests of the majority of their common people.[63]

All of these factors remain potent in influencing nations' choices. In particular, I would stress the influence on the individual decision makers of their own background and their own economic interests.

The educational qualifications and backgrounds of Finance Ministers and the senior technocrats in Finance Ministries in most developing countries, certainly in middle income ones, include a preponderance of doctoral qualifications from US universities. These people have typically spent anywhere between three and ten years in higher education in North America and this exposure usually influences their perspectives on matters financial. As Professor Bresser Pereira, former Finance Minister of Brazil, has identified, 'the elites in general in the debtor countries are certainly not the ones that suffer most from the debt crisis; on the contrary, part of them is taking advantage from the debt'.[64] When the capital flows in those holding assets profit as local stocks and real estate increase in value. Before the capital-inflow induced boom peaks, the economic elites typically begin to invest their money abroad. They know their own economy better than outsiders. They know when to bail out. And their doing so is one of the triggers for the end of the boom. When the boom ends, and the capital flows out, almost routinely the debt is socialized and transferred onto the sovereign, which services it by decreasing services and increasing taxes on the common people.

The loans of the 1970s brought 'massive returns to the rich'[65] in Latin America just as the loans of the 1990s did for the rich in Argentina. The share of income of the richest 10% of the population in the Latin American countries increased as a result of the debt crisis, at times substantially. Strong capital inflows in developing countries invariably benefit those able to make use of them and holding the assets likely to increase in value as a consequence of the extra economic activity. The capital outflows, when they come, fall most heavily upon the common people as the debts are often socialized. Why would the elites in the debtor nations seek to stop the merry-go-round and get off? The ride is too lucrative.

This section set out to answer why in the sovereign debt game debtors have been so reluctant in recent decades to play the default card, and to assess whether this reluctance has served them?

---

63. See statement of Professor Luiz Carlos Bresser Pereira, *Solving the Debt Crisis: Debt Relief and Adjustment*. See also Sachs, *Developing Country Debt and the World Economy*, pp. 26–27; see also S. Griffith-Jones, 'A history of debt crisis management' in *Third World Debt – Managing the Consequences*, S. Griffith-Jones (ed.) (IFR, 1989), 16–17.
64. Pereira, *Solving the Debt Crisis*, 339.
65. 'A Survey of Latin America', *The Economist* (UK ed.), 13 November 1993.

Various reasons have been identified here for this reluctance and virtually all of which can be ascribed to two factors:

(i) the success of creditors in arguing that exclusion from global capital markets would be more wide-reaching, last for longer, and be more damaging to the debtor, than history attests it would; and
(ii) a democratic deficit in the debtor countries.

By a democratic deficit, I refer to the manner in which these nations are regularly governed in the interests of their elites, not their common people. Servicing foreign indebtedness is usually in the personal and economic interests of the elites in the debtor nations, but is often not in the interests of those who will typically have to be less healthy, less educated and less well nourished to enable the debt to be repaid.

History suggests this reluctance to default has not served the debtor nations. Having defaulted for a sustained period, Argentina received an unprecedented amount of debt relief. Peru received extra debt relief in its Brady restructuring as its default was seen to indicate a reduced capacity to service its debt, and the resolution of Ecuador's default in the late 1990s was highly favourable for the debtor. So, to date, history supports the basic negotiation theory with which this section commenced: that the willingness to walk away from a negotiation will, on average, improve the result of that party. Perhaps it is time for more debtor nations to follow Argentina's lead, and put the interests of their people ahead of those of the international financial community?

Chapter 9
Global Measures to Improve the System

The balance sheet structure of developing countries tends to render them crisis-prone and thus generates systemic volatility internationally. This chapter begins by considering this problem and analyzing what these nations and some of the multilateral institutions can do to redress this weakness in balance sheet structure. It then moves on to consider briefly a small tax on international currency transactions, the so-called Tobin tax, as a means both of improving the efficiency of international capital markets and dissuading speculative money flows. The chapter concludes by addressing the three essential elements in every national financial system that are entirely missing in the international system: a financial regulator, a lender of last resort, and a bankruptcy regime. None of these functions are provided by the supra-national institutions. This chapter analyses the impact of the absence of each of these critical elements on the international financial system, and what we might be able to do about it. It concludes that the most realizable reform is the establishment of a sovereign bankruptcy regime.

9.1   THE NATIONAL BALANCE SHEET PROBLEM[1]

The essential problem with the balance sheets of most nations is that they cannot borrow abroad in their own currencies. This inability of developing nations to borrow in their own currency leads to currency mismatches on their national

---

1. My sincere thanks to my good friend, and leading financial sector development expert, Peter Dirou, for his permission to reuse here parts of what we wrote and published as Buckley and Dirou, 'How to Strengthen the International Financial System by Improving Sovereign Balance Sheet Structures' (2006) 2 *Annals of Economics and Finance*, 257.

balance sheets. These mismatches render these economies vulnerable to external shocks and are a major source of damaging volatility for the entire international financial system.[2] This next section argues that these mismatches need to be remedied, and considers how the multilateral development banks and the Paris Club could take the lead in doing so in the interests of international financial stability.

While the structural flaws in national balance sheets are attracting more attention, this attention is yet to translate into international policy action, and developing countries face profound difficulties in overcoming this structural flaw in their balance sheets by themselves. One way of buying protection against these interest and exchange rate changes is through accumulating foreign exchange reserves. But this comes at a cost, in the form of the often substantial differential in the usually very small return on the invested reserves (typically US government securities, a major reserve asset for most countries), and the return that could have been generated by investing these funds at home. Governments could finance more of their development expenditures from their own reserves, with less recourse to foreign borrowing, if they did not need such large foreign exchange reserves to serve as insurance against the volatility built into their national balance sheets.

9.1.1 THE VOLATILITY MACHINE

The structural flaws in national balance sheets are a failure of the international financial system to adequately transfer risk to those best able to bear it. Professor Michael Pettis argues forcefully that international financial crises are caused primarily by unstable domestic financial structures, particularly the structure of sovereign balance sheets, rather than by weaknesses in the international financial architecture. In his words, 'The problem with the current architecture is not that global financial markets are too volatile or free capital markets too dangerous but that sovereign capital structures are not usually designed with this volatility in mind.'[3]

Pettis has likened capital structure to a 'volatility machine'. In his view, external shocks such as substantial changes in commodity prices or global liquidity are amplified by unstable capital structures. The capital structure 'determines whether an external shock becomes an irritant or a calamity.'[4] The instability in the balance sheet is caused by a reliance on short-term debt, floating rate debt, and foreign currency debt. This leads to mismatches between foreign currency assets and liabilities, such that adverse interest rate and exchange rate changes arising from an external shock increase both debt-servicing costs and debt stocks dramatically in local currency terms.

---

2. M. Pettis, *The Volatility Machine: Emerging Economies and the Threat of Financial Collapse* (Oxford University Press, 2001).
3. *Ibid.*, 199.
4. *Ibid.*, 127.

The nature and impact of short-term capital inflows, and the appropriate policy response, and the need for rigorous financial regulation, have attracted considerable attention in the years since the Asian crisis commenced in 1997. But it is only more recently that the place of foreign borrowing on sovereign balance sheets has attracted closer examination.

9.1.2 ORIGINAL SIN

Most developing countries have little alternative to borrowing in foreign currency. In the words of Hausmann and Rigobon, '[i]t is as if an emerging market suffers from an inherited burden, almost irrespective of the policies of their governments'.[5] This inherited burden of not being able to borrow externally in their own currencies has been labelled 'original sin' by Eichengreen and Hausmann.[6]

It would be easy to attribute 'original sin' to weak policies and institutions in the countries affected. Why should foreign investors invest in the currencies of countries with a track record of high inflation and loose fiscal policy? But even developing economies with sound fiscal and monetary policies suffer from this problem, Chile being the oft-quoted example. Research discloses a strong relationship between 'original sin' and a country's status as advanced or emerging and a weak relationship between 'original sin' and economic variables such as inflation and fiscal balances, and institutional factors such as the rule of law.[7]

Why are so many developing countries so reliant on external borrowing in a foreign currency? Or, more precisely, why do many developing countries have difficulty borrowing externally in their own currency? It is mainly the larger developed countries that can issue debt externally in their own currencies. Why might this be so? Part of the answer is to be found in portfolio theory, as Eichengreen, Hausmann and Panizza have stated:

> While each additional currency adds opportunities for diversification, it does so with decreasing marginal benefits. In a world with transactions costs (which increase with the number of currencies in which investors take positions), the optimal portfolio will therefore have a finite number of currencies.[8]

Original sin is a manifestation of incomplete financial markets.

---

5. R. Hausmann and R. Rigobon, 'IDA in UF: On the Benefits of changing the currency denomination of concessional lending to low-income countries' (Harvard University, 2003), <siteresources.worldbank.org/INTDEBTDEPT/RelatedPapers/20263430/IDA_UEF_Benefits-of-changing.pdf>, 4 December 2007.
6. B. Eichengreen and R. Hausmann, *Exchange Rates and Financial Fragility, in Federal Reserve Bank of Kansas City*, New Challenges for Monetary Policy (Symposium Proceedings, Jackson Hole, 26–28 August 1999), 329, 330.
7. International Monetary Fund, 'Does currency denomination of debt hold key to taming volatility?' (2004) 33 *IMF Survey*, 71; and B. Eichengreen, R. Hausmann and U. Panizza, 'Currency Mismatches, Debt Intolerance and Original Sin: Why They Are Not the Same and Why It Matters' (Working Paper 10036, National Bureau of Economic Research, 2003), 37.
8. Eichengreen, Hausmann and Panizza, 'Currency Mismatches, Debt Intolerance and Original Sin: Why They Are Not the Same and Why It Matters', 38.

Part of the answer to the question regarding the difficulty of borrowing in one's own currency is that domestic bond markets are underdeveloped, and the challenges of developing local bond markets are explored later in this chapter. Typically, in developing countries, there is no fixed-interest bond market or an active forward market in foreign exchange against the US dollar.[9] The lack of a forward market is a consequence of the inability to determine the interest rate differential between currencies and, hence, the forward premium. This incompleteness translates into currency and maturity mismatches, both of which promote financial instability.

9.1.3 CURRENCY MISMATCHES

The role played by unhedged aggregate dollar liabilities in the Latin American, Asian, Russian and Argentine crises is widely acknowledged. This inability to hedge is another manifestation of incomplete financial markets. If a country is borrowing in foreign currency because it cannot borrow in local currency, it will also not be able to hedge its exposure.[10]

Goldstein and Turner have taken a particular interest in currency mismatches. In their view these 'mismatches pose a serious threat to financial stability and sustainable economic growth in emerging economies'.[11] They have developed a measure of the mismatch – the Aggregate Effective Currency Mismatch (AECM) – that captures net foreign reserves, exports and imports of goods and services and the foreign currency share of total debt.

However, Goldstein & Turner attribute currency mismatches to weaknesses in policies and institutions, as opposed to the international financial system. They see as critical the lack of incentives to hedge against currency risk arising from fixed exchange rate regimes and poorly designed official safety nets. They have also identified as contributing factors: weak regulatory structures, lack of information on currency mismatches, poor credit assessment by banks, insufficient efforts to develop domestic bond markets and encourage the use of hedging instruments, and unsound public debt management policies that overemphasize foreign currency denominated debt rather than inflation-indexed debt. All of these factors do contribute to instability, but nonetheless, until developing countries can meet their capital raising needs in their own currencies, currency mismatches will remain a major source of damaging volatility.

A Report of the Independent Evaluation Office of the IMF has concluded that the IMF needs to more rigorously assess the balance sheet effects (the volatility

---

9. R. McKinnon and G. Schnabl, 'The East Asian Dollar Standard, Fear of Floating, and Original Sin' (Working Paper No.11, Hong Kong Institute for Monetary Research, 2003), 6.
10. Eichengreen and Hausmann, *Exchange Rates and Financial Fragility, in Federal Reserve Bank of Kansas City*, 330–331: 'Assuming that there will be someone on the other side of the market for foreign currency hedges is equivalent to assuming that the country can borrow abroad in its own currency'.
11. M. Goldstein and P. Turner, *Controlling Currency Mismatches in Emerging Markets* (Washington DC: Institute for International Economics, 2004), 2.

machine effects) of economic shocks in its Article IV consultations[12] and in September 2003, the G-7 finance ministers and central bank governors urged the Fund to 'identify currency mismatches in emerging economies as a key part of its efforts to improve the effectiveness and persuasiveness of Fund surveillance'.[13]

I agree with Goldstein and Turner's critique of fixed exchange rate regimes. A nation's choice, and management, of its exchange rate regime can contribute to mismatches.[14] Floating exchange rates can make it difficult to manage mismatches, but it does not follow that floating rates should be shunned. One of the lessons of the Asian financial crisis was that floating exchange rates improve the resilience of the international financial architecture.

For most developing countries, greater use of regional currencies such as the Euro would be preferable to a fixed exchange rate. It may even be that dollarization (adopting the US dollar as the national currency) is preferable to a fixed exchange rate. As Eichengreen and Hausmann explain:

> Once the dollar is adopted for all domestic payments, currency mismatches dissolve, since income streams are now denominated in the same unit as liabilities. Maturity mismatches are attenuated because it now becomes easier to issue long-term paper in dollars. The greater willingness of foreigners to lend at long maturities and of residents to leave their money at home deepens domestic financial markets, rendering them less fragile and crisis prone.[15]

However, dollarization brings its own problems, both economic and political, and is not a solution that, as yet, has appealed to many countries. Its principal economic problems are the loss of the economic adjustment capacity afforded by a floating exchange rate, which proved so devastating to Argentina, and the loss of seigniorage from issuing one's currency.

9.1.4 LOCAL CURRENCY BOND MARKETS

What is clear, is that if a sovereign borrower is to strengthen its balance sheet through less foreign currency exposure, it must develop local bond markets. In Pettis's words:

> [T]he development of and active use of a fixed-rate local currency market for funding government and corporate financing needs is probably the single

---

12. A.M. Mansor, et al, *The IMF and Recent Capital Account Crises: Indonesia, Korea, Brazil* (Independent Evaluation Office Report, International Monetary Fund, 2003), 52–53.
13. Goldstein and Turner, 'Controlling currency mismatches in emerging market economies: Alternative to the original sin hypothesis', 2. See also M. Pettis, 'Reengineering the Volatility Machine – How the IMF Can Help Prevent Financial Crises' (Fall, 2003) *World Policy Journal*, 57–58.
14. For an analysis of the weaknesses and risks inherent in fixed exchange rate regimes, see R.P. Buckley, 'A Tale of Two Crises: The Search for the Enduring Lessons of International Financial Reform' (2001) 6 *UCLA Journal of International Law and Foreign Affairs*, 1; and Buckley, *International Capital Flows, Economic Sovereignty and Developing Countries*.
15. Eichengreen and Hausmann, *Exchange Rates and Financial Fragility, in Federal Reserve Bank of Kansas City*, 331.

most important step an LDC can take in reducing its sensitivity to external shocks.[16]

Longer term local currency debt reduces refinancing risk and also acts as a type of insurance: an exchange rate weakening will increase inflation, which, in turn, reduces the real cost of servicing debt denominated in local currency.[17]

Local currency bond markets are an obvious, although only partial, remedy to the problem of 'original sin'. The development of these markets has attracted considerable interest, particularly since their absence was seen as a contributor to the Asian economic crisis. The reality, though, is that development of these markets is notoriously difficult.

Bond markets require sophisticated securities laws for their efficient operation, and in the aftermath of the Asian crisis of 1997 many East Asian nations have worked to enact such laws. But, as always, more is needed than simply laws on statute books. The operation of bond markets require sophisticated accounting, banking, trading and legal skills – all of which are in short supply in many developing countries. People with such skills can typically command high salaries in the private sector, which imposes an added burden on regulators in these countries – how to afford the people they need to regulate these markets? Macroeconomic policy settings have also worked to impede market development. Strong fiscal positions in Asia reduce government borrowing requirements and bond markets work best when there are well developed yield curves for sovereign debt, at a margin above which corporate bonds are then typically priced.

The importance of banks to bond market development is often underestimated. Banks fulfil many roles: as issuers, holders, underwriters, guarantors, trustees, custodians and registrars. Bond markets are not a substitute for credit markets. Each complement the other. Well-developed bond markets are unlikely to be found in countries with an underdeveloped or weak banking sector. As the Bank for International Settlements has noted, 'it is important to have healthy banks to have a sound bond market. And a bond market may improve the health of banks, by improving market discipline.'[18]

Domestic bond markets are important. Highly developed domestic bond markets will alleviate currency mismatches, and governments are right to work to develop these markets. However, it is essential to understand that building a market takes time as it requires the interaction of a range of factors including, among others, participants' skills, liquidity conditions, the regulatory framework, trading and settlement platforms, and the development of investor demand. Unfortunately, many countries have not had the luxury of time. Their foreign currency exposures have needed to be addressed with some urgency.

There is a top echelon of developing countries emerging with increasingly developed bond markets and associated hedging capabilities. These include

---

16. Pettis, *The Volatility Machine: Emerging Economies and the Threat of Financial Collapse*, p. 168.
17. *Ibid.*, pp. 168–169.
18. Goldstein and Turner, 'Controlling currency mismatches in emerging market economies: Alternative to the original sin hypothesis', 62.

Hong Kong, South Africa, Mexico, Korea and Poland, and there is a second tier that includes Brazil, the Czech Republic, Chile and Taiwan where good progress towards this end has been made.[19] However most developing countries, including those that are most vulnerable to financial volatility, simply lack the institutional and human capacities to develop their own bond markets at this time. The developing countries that most need local currency bond markets are decades away from having the prudential, human and institutional infrastructure in place to support them.

Domestic bond markets contribute to the reduction of currency risk. Less apparent, perhaps, is their contribution to the reduction of interest rate risk. Australia provides a case in point.

With consistent fiscal surpluses and ever lower levels of net debt the Commonwealth Government questioned whether it should continue to issue government bonds.[20] Its review into the issue considered a number of arguments for retaining the government bond market: the pricing and referencing of other financial products, managing financial risk, providing a long-term investment vehicle, implementing monetary policy, providing a safe haven in times of financial volatility, attracting foreign capital inflows, and promoting Australia as a global financial centre. The key conclusion of the review was that the cost of managing interest rate risk would rise in the absence of a government securities market, as Treasury bond futures market are more efficient at this task than interest rate swaps.[21] The loss in efficiency would translate to a higher cost of capital. Given this conclusion, it was decided to continue to issue government bonds and public debt management policy in Australia now seeks to contribute to financial sector efficiency and manage cost and risk in the government's debt portfolio.[22]

In sum, the development of local bond markets will reduce the currency mismatch problem on national balance sheets as it will allow sovereign to raise substantial amounts of their capital at home, but such development is difficult to achieve. Efficient bond markets require a highly developed rule of law, and complex supporting legal, institutional and human infrastructure. These factors take years and years to develop. Many developing countries are working towards this end. Most are decades away from achieving it. So what can the international financial community do to assist now?

9.1.5   AN INTERNATIONAL SOLUTION

There are potential remedies for sovereign balance sheet induced instability: re-regulating domestic financial markets, reimposing capital controls, adopting

---

19. *Ibid.*
20. Commonwealth of Australia Treasury Department, *Review of the Commonwealth Securities Market* (Discussion paper prepared for the Commonwealth Debt Management Review, 2002).
21. B. Comley and D. Turvey, 'Debt Management in a Low Debt Environment: The Australian Government's Debt Management Framework' (Working Paper 2005–02, Commonwealth of Australia Treasury Department, 2005), 48.
22. *Ibid.*, 48–49.

a common international currency, and adopting an international solution to the currency-mismatch problem.[23]

More controls over financial markets, in particular, barriers to international capital flows in the form of capital controls, would solve the problem but at quite a high cost as credit would be more expensive in developing countries and financial sector innovation much reduced.[24] Financial sector development, done well, enhances economic development. I have argued elsewhere in this book that national governments should implement rigorous financial sector regulation and should be willing to use capital controls for limited periods to achieve defined ends. But to seek to build one's economy behind permanent capital control barriers is both very difficult to do in this globalized era and expensive in terms of limited access to credit. Capital controls should be in every national government's bag of options – but they are rarely a permanent answer.

The adoption of an international currency is intuitively appealing as then there would be no currency mismatches. However, nations lose the adjustment effects to international competitiveness provided by exchange rate movements, and, anyway, it is not a practical option for the foreseeable future although the success of the Euro and the debate about an Asian currency unit do hold out the prospect of future international currency consolidation.

This leaves us, then, to enquire into the feasibility of the fourth option: an international solution to the currency mismatch problem.

Eichengreen is certain some form of international initiative is needed.[25] While countries remain burdened with currency mismatches, and domestic markets remain underdeveloped, extreme domestic volatility will remain. And such volatility will always threaten international financial instability. Debtor countries can only do so much by themselves to minimize this instability. Creditors need to assume more responsibility and international institutions are best placed to play the leading role. The IMF needs to go beyond improving its surveillance of balance sheet structures to developing initiatives to restructure those balance sheets.

This initiative could be developed globally under the umbrella of the United Nations' Millennium Development Goals. Goal 8 directs the international community to 'deal comprehensively with developing countries' debt problems through national and international measures to make debt sustainable in the long-term'.[26] This is in addition to enhanced debt relief for heavily indebted poor countries and the cancellation of official bilateral debt, which are separately mentioned under Goal 8.

---

23. B. Eichengreen, R. Hausmann, *Original Sin: The Road to Redemption* (USA: John F. Kennedy School of Government), pp. 21–34.
24. *Ibid.*, p. 23. Although I would argue these opportunity costs are not as high as the cost of crises facilitated by financial sector liberalization.
25. *Ibid.*, pp. 14–15.
26. United Nations, 'UN Millennium Development Goals (MDG)' <www.un.org/millenniumgoals/>, 4 December 2007.

Global Measures to Improve the System

There are several possibilities for more actively addressing currency mismatches: the multilateral development banks (MDBs), such as the World Bank and Asian Development Bank, could change their lending policies; emerging market borrowers could make greater use of local currency-indexed bonds; and creditor countries and MDBs could redenominate foreign currency loans in local currency in debt restructurings.[27] These options will each be considered.

9.1.5.1 Changing the Lending Policies of Multilateral Development Banks

MDBs usually lend in US dollars. In doing so, the MDB protects itself against currency risk but contributes to the currency mismatch problem facing its borrower and thus works against its own development mandate. Urgent change to the lending practices of the MDBs is required, particularly for the concessional finance windows of these institutions.

To illustrate, the World Bank lends through the International Bank for Reconstruction and Development (IBRD) and the International Development Association (IDA), its concessional finance arm. The IBRD operates in international markets and actively minimizes currency mismatches from its perspective; i.e., it seeks to avoid funding its lending in local currency by borrowing in other currencies. In the words of Hausmann and Rigobon 'missing markets on its liability side prevent the IBRD from lending in more appropriate forms'.[28] So, US dollar lending has become the standard. But there is an alternative in the form of a debt market in inflation-indexed emerging market currencies. If this market existed, the World Bank could borrow in a basket of these inflation-indexed currencies and lend to individual countries in their own inflation-indexed currency. In so doing, the World Bank would become part of the solution rather than part of the problem.[29]

It may be arguable that the IBRD should not be in the business of promoting solutions to currency mismatches at the expense, perhaps, of its own balance sheet. I argue, however, that this is precisely what the IBRD should be doing as its primary function is to alleviate poverty. Certainly there would seem to be few arguments against the IDA adopting this course. Its development mandate would be better fulfilled by a move away from US dollar lending and it is funded by grants from developed countries, not by its own borrowing, so lending in local currencies would not generate currency mismatches for it. The IDA could lend in inflation-indexed local currency at current interest rates and achieve the same level of IDA reflows.[30]

---

27. J. Williamson, *Curbing the Boom-Bust Cycle: Stabilising Capital Flows to Emerging Markets* (Washington, DC, Institute for International Economics, 2005).
28. Hausmann and Rigobon, 'IDA in UF: On the Benefits of changing the currency denomination of concessional lending to low-income countries', 13.
29. *Ibid.*, 6.
30. Eichengreen and Hausmann, *Original Sin: The Road to Redemption*, 12; and *ibid.*

This approach is a far superior mechanism for transferring and managing risk than leaving the currency risk with the debtors. The IDA could diversify its risk across member countries and borrowing countries could have a debt stock that remains constant in terms of domestic consumption, as opposed to being denominated in the relatively more volatile and counter-cyclical foreign currency. The indexing would also allow inter-temporal smoothing of the risk through debt service being relatively more in the years when the economy is performing better and relatively less when the economy is performing poorly.

Furthermore, this approach would underpin the adoption of a floating exchange rate. Countries could adopt a more flexible exchange rate because they would be less concerned about currency mismatches and the associated 'fear of floating', a fear that has led to inappropriate and ultimately unsustainable fixed exchange rates in many countries.[31]

9.1.5.2 Local Currency Solutions

To the extent it is difficult for borrowing countries to issue conventional 'vanilla' local currency debt there are index-linked solutions that would ameliorate the mismatch problem. Williamson advocates issuing GDP-linked bonds in international markets and inflation-indexed bonds in domestic markets. He would complement these instruments with a fiscal incentive that would encourage both borrowers and lenders in emerging markets to issue and hold local currency-denominated financial instruments with the objective of substantially reducing currency mismatches.[32]

Investor resistance to GDP-indexed bonds is potentially an issue, but the MDBs are in an ideal position to promote these instruments. The most obvious way is to incorporate these instruments into sovereign debt restructurings. This would provide an investor base, a deep and liquid market, and MDB 'blessing' for the instrument. The MDBs would have an ongoing role in promoting the instrument in their dialogue with member countries, gauging investor interest, and underpinning the quality of national statistical agencies: a necessity if the GDP statistics, and thus the GDP-indexed bond, are to be credible.

9.1.5.3 Re-orienting the Paris Club

The use of GDP-linked bonds in debt restructurings suggests a role for the Paris Club. The Paris Club has historically presented itself as a debt collector largely independent of international debt relief initiatives. Of late, however, there has been a gradual evolution towards debt relief. Since the Evian Approach of October 2003, the Paris Club has taken more account of ongoing debt sustainability and adopted

---

31. McKinnon and Schnabl, 'The East Asian Dollar Standard, Fear of Floating, and Original Sin'.
32. Williamson, *Curbing the Boom-Bust Cycle: Stabilising Capital Flows to Emerging Markets*, pp. 110–111.

a more flexible approach in deciding on the treatment to be adopted.[33] But financial distress is related not only to debt levels but also to the relationship between revenues and debt servicing costs.[34] The volatility machine can come into play for almost any debt level: the greater the mismatch, the greater the potential distress. Even a reduced debt stock denominated in foreign currency exposes a nation to potentially severe volatility.

Rather than merely reducing the total debt owed to its member nations, it would be preferable for the Paris Club to also re-denominate the re-negotiated debt in the local currency of the debtor. Some may argue this allows the debtor to inflate the debt and debt-servicing obligation away. This incentive is there, but that does not mean the borrower would be prepared to accept the wider economic costs of inflation to achieve this narrow end. In today's world, central banks are far less tolerant of inflation and inflation will raise the cost of issuing any new debt.

Clearly, the Paris Club redenominating debt into local currency transfers currency risk from the debtor to the creditors. But this is as it should be: the creditor is in the best position to assume the risk and the greater currency risk, to an extent, is offset for the creditors by the substantially reduced risk of default.

9.1.6   CONCLUSION ON NATIONAL BALANCE SHEET STRUCTURES

Foreign currency exposures of sovereign borrowers and of banks and corporates in emerging economies continue to pose a threat to the stability of the international financial system. Borrowing countries can do more to strengthen sovereign balance sheets through better public debt management practices but they are severely constrained by not being able to borrow internationally in their own currency. While the importance of developing domestic bond markets is well-recognized and initiatives are under way to assist in this development, it will take time to develop these markets, and, in any case, there will be limits on the number of currencies demanded in an internationally diversified portfolio.

The MDBs are far better placed than individual countries to support financial instruments that reduce currency risks. They could construct a synthetic instrument for their own operations that was based on a basket of emerging market currencies and they could promote the issuance of GDP-indexed bonds and inflation-indexed bonds by member countries. They could also incorporate GDP-indexed bonds in sovereign debt restructuring exercises.

But the most effective debt restructuring initiative, and the one that could be most easily implemented, provided there is sufficient political will, is for Paris Club reschedulings to be denominated in the currency of the debtor country. This would require creditor countries to bear the foreign exchange risk, but this is

---

33. Paris Club, 'The Evian Approach' <www.clubdeparis.org>, 4 December 2007.
34. Pettis, *The Volatility Machine: Emerging Economies and the Threat of Financial Collapse*, p. 103; and Buckley, 'A Tale of Two Crises: The Search for the Enduring Lessons of International Financial Reform', 1.

a risk worth taking given the risk of ongoing debt-servicing problems caused by exchange rate weakening in the borrowing country.

At the end of the day, all efforts to strengthen the international financial system will be liable to be undermined by foreign currency mismatches. The international community, through the MDBs and the Paris Club, are the instrument of international financial cooperation, and have been neglecting their duty by not taking the lead in addressing currency mismatch problems. The opportunity to substantially enhance international financial stability is there to be taken and needs to be taken soon.

Having considered the immediate systemic improvements available to the MDBs and Paris Club, we will now consider the currency transactions tax, before addressing the three missing institutions in the international financial architecture: a global financial regulator, a lender of last resort, and a sovereign bankruptcy regime.

9.2 A TAX ON INTERNATIONAL CURRENCY TRANSACTIONS

This proposal is for a minute tax to be levied on international currency transactions, in the order of 0.1% to 0.25%. Such a tax was the brainchild of the Nobel laureate in economics, James Tobin, and it is often referred to as a Tobin tax. He first proposed the idea in his 1972 Janeway Lecture at Princeton, and wrote about it some years later.[35] Tobin conceived of the tax not to raise revenue but to dissuade speculative short-term capital flows in particular and thus reduce volatility in such flows, i.e.,. to serve as sand in the cogs of international financial flows. In the 1970s Tobin's idea sank without trace, in the face of enthusiasm for the brave new world of floating exchange rates. However, as the 1980s and 1990s progressed, and the damaging effects of international financial volatility became ever more apparent, so did the benefits of a currency transactions tax.

A tax as low as James Tobin conceived, would raise considerable money, but probably do little to dissuade much speculative activity. A tax high enough to dissuade such activity would impair the operations of global capital markets and create liquidity problems. The answer to this problem was devised by Paul Bernd Spahn who proposed a two-tier tax, comprising a low tax for normal transactions (along the lines conceived of by Tobin) and a much higher tax on transactions when exchange rates moved outside pre-set bands, in other words a much higher tax on transactions deemed to be speculative attacks on currencies.[36]

The Mexican peso crisis of late 1994, the Asian economic crisis of 1997 and Russia's economic meltdown in 1998 established that short-term capital flows

---

35. J. Tobin, 'A Proposal for International Monetary Reform' (1978) 4 *Eastern Economic Journal*, 153–159.
36. P.B. Spahn, 'The Tobin Tax and Exchange Rate Stability' *Finance & Development*, June 1996, <www.worldbank.org/fandd/english/0696/articles/0130696.htm>, 4 December 2007.

are destabilizing and debtor countries are best served by minimizing the proportion of capital inflows that are short-term in duration. Accordingly, a Spahn tax would in all probability make a distinct contribution to the stability of the international financial system.

A currency transaction tax is a bit like the congestion tax London has imposed on cars entering its CBD and that has done so much to cut congestion and speed travel times in that city. The reason for the congestion tax is to improve the functioning of a system, the revenue from it is a pure bonus. The reason for a currency transactions tax is likewise to improve the functioning of a system, the international financial one, and the revenue it would generate is a pure bonus, and would be massive.

Anti-globalization protesters have seized on the potential revenues from such a tax, as a potent source to fund the financing for development required if we are to achieve the Millennium Development Goals.[37] The MDGs are the goals to which all nations committed in 2000 to halve global poverty and hunger and the number of people without access to safe water, achieve universal primary education and a three-quarter decline in maternal mortality, to halt and reverse the spread of HIV/AIDS and other human development goals, all by 2015. According to a United Nations study, all of these goals can be achieved with an increase in annual aid funding of USD 50 billion per annum[38] or less than 5% of global arms expenditure.

Other proponents of changes to the international financial architecture have focussed on such a tax as a means to fund their proposed changes, for instance, the proceeds of such a tax could fund an international lender of last resort. The proceeds have also been suggested as an autonomous source of revenue for the activities of the World Bank and IMF or of the United Nations. However the countries that principally fund these international organizations through their annual subscriptions (ie. the rich countries) are unwilling to forego the control that being the source of funding gives them. They simply do not trust these international organizations, or their governance mechanisms, to that point. This is particularly so for the largest financier of all, the United States of America.

Estimates of the revenue such a tax would raise vary widely, due to the different levels at which such a tax could be set, and the strongly dissuasive effect it is designed to have on the very transactions it is taxing. A likely revenue range, however, is between USD 75 billion and USD 150 billion per annum. To put this sum into context, at the time of writing the developed nations spend about USD 50 billion a year on aid to poor nations, and a doubling of this amount would achieve the Millenium Development Goals. In other words, even on the most conservative estimates, the revenues from a currency transactions tax would make a huge impact on global poverty and on mortality due to AIDS, malaria, and tuberculosis.

---

37. United Nations, 'UN Millennium Development Goals (MDG)' <www.un.org/millenniumgoals/>, 4 December 2007.
38. United Nations, Report of the High Level Panel on Financing for Development, available at <www.un.org/reports/financing/report_full.htm#appendix>

The billionaire financier, George Soros, supports such a tax, even though it would be against his personal interests, not on the grounds it would reduce volatility, as he suspects it may not, but on the grounds of fairness. He doesn't see why financial transactions should not be taxed when under the value-added tax regime most nations have, most other transactions are taxed. So he argues the concept of a currency transactions tax should be expanded into a tax on all financial transactions.[39]

Some nations have taken steps towards such a tax. The national parliament in Belgium has passed a law that will implement a Spahn tax once all countries in the Eurozone do so. The Canadian House of Commons in March 1999 resolved to enact such a tax 'in concert with the international community.' And such a tax, applied regionally, is an element of the initiative in late 2007 to establish a Bank of the South in Latin America. It is understandable that Belgium or Canada don't wish to disadvantage their own markets with a tax that, in the absence of universal coverage, will be so easily avoided by channeling transactions through other markets. The South American initiative is the only one that is scheduled to proceed without waiting for other nations to follow suit.

So if such a tax would in all probability improve the international financial markets, and reduce damaging volatility, while also raising desperately needed funds that could be applied to the fight against poverty and disease, why don't we have it?

The answer to this question has many parts. There are real difficulties in collecting the tax, as for the tax to be enforceable all jurisdictions would have to participate. There are questions of how to tax derivatives and synthetic instruments, because virtually all actual transactions can be replaced by a derivative or synthetic, so these would have equally to be taxed. But these problems could be overcome, if there were the political will to do so. Problems of similar orders of difficulty are being overcome with respect to limiting the financing for terrorism, for which there is the political will.

The sad truth, however, and this is a truth I find particularly galling, is that in a world in which over one billion have to survive on less than one US dollar per day, there is simply not the will in the rich nations to save millions of lives by addressing global poverty and disease if the price of doing so is to inconvenience their financial sectors and the operations of their major banks. A currency transactions tax is a cost-free source of funding with which to tackle the largest problems facing humanity. That the opportunity has not been seized suggests a moral emptiness at the core of our global system.

And so we come to the three elements that are essential to the stability of every national financial system that are entirely missing in the international system: a financial regulator, a lender of last resort, and a bankruptcy regime.

---

39. G. Soros, address to The Asia Society Hong Kong Center 11th Annual Dinner, Hong Kong, 19 September 2001, <www.asiasociety.org/speeches/soros.html>, 4 December 2007.

9.3 A GLOBAL FINANCIAL REGULATOR

Within national financial systems central banks often discharge a number of functions including those of financial regulator and lender of last resort.[40] This section deals with financial regulation. The next will deal with the lender of last resort function.

Global financial regulation is today handled by bodies such as the Basle Committee on Banking Supervision and the Financial Stability Forum, the implementation of which is left to national authorities. This flexible system of soft law provides guidance to national authorities that seek to implement effective regulation but is not a coherent system and the international 'regulators' have no authority to require national authorities to enact certain regulations.[41]

A truly global financial regulator would be able to supervise transnational capital flows extended by commercial banks, supranational institutions and developed country sovereigns. As capital flows are now global, and the operations of capital markets are global, financial regulation needs to be global. The problems of markets and capital flows being transnational while regulation remains national are obvious. However, no existing supranational institution has the credibility to be a plausible candidate for the role, and there is almost no appetite, particularly within the US, to create yet another supranational institution.[42] The decisions of such a regulator would have far reaching consequences for each nation's financial system as, almost inevitably, such decisions would have the effects of favoring one nation's financial system over another. Accordingly, the establishment of a global financial regulator with enforcement powers poses a massive challenge to the sovereignty of nations. As strong as the need is, for these reasons, the prospects of a global financial regulator with mandatory enforcement powers are extremely slight.

9.4 A LENDER OF LAST RESORT

Banking is an inherently unstable business as it typically involves banks holding illiquid assets (such as long-term mortgages) and highly liquid liabilities (such as short-term deposits). A lender of last resort (LoLR) provides stability to each national banking system by committing in advance to lend funds to banks freely

---

40. For a consideration of the role of central banks in ensuring financial stability, see G.J. Schinasi, 'Responsibility of Central Banks for Stability in Financial Markets' (Working Paper No. WP/03/121, IMF, June 2003).
41. D. Arner, *Financial Stability, Economic Growth, and the Role of Law*, Cambridge University Press, 2007, pp 5 & 195–226.
42. J. Stay, 'Reform of the International Financial architecture: What has been written?' in *International Financial Governance Under Stress Global Structure Vs National Imperatives*, Underhill and Zhang (eds) (Cambridge, 2003).

and quickly, on good security and at high interest rates in times of need (according to the classic 19th century prescription of Walter Bagehot).[43] The provision of large amounts of funds quickly and freely discourages runs on banks by depositors as they are assured the bank will have funds to meet their claims. The requirements of good security and high interest rates discourages banks from relying on the lender of last resort's services and avoids the moral hazard that would otherwise flow from the provision of such a service.

There is no LoLR in the international system notwithstanding that many commentators, some distinguished,[44] consider the IMF discharges this role.

The International Monetary Fund conditions its loans and the bailouts it orchestrates upon economic reform in the recipient countries so these commitments to lend do not have the unconditional nature required to quell the fears of creditors and investors.[45] Secondly, the IMF typically disburses these funds slowly over time as compliance with the required reforms is proven by the recipients – the funds are not disbursed quickly as required by Bagehot's prescription. Thirdly and finally, especially in the wake of the scale of some recent crises and the IMF's difficulties in securing subscriptions from some member countries, it does not have the resources required to serve as a credible LoLR to sovereign entities and, of course, unlike national central banks it lacks the capacity to print the money required to perform the role.

There is a clear need for a global LoLR. National LoLRs, such as the central bank of most nations, cannot function as a LoLR for their nation's foreign currency borrowings, precisely because they cannot generate the currency in which the indebtedness is denominated.[46]

No domestic banking system would be stable without such a backstop so it is no surprise that the international system is not particularly stable.[47] The challenges in implementing an international LoLR are threefold:

(i) the fears of some sovereigns that the establishment of such an entity will result in some loss of sovereignty;

---

43. W. Bagehot, *Lombard Street: a description of the money market* (London, H.S. King & Co, 1873); S. Fischer, 'On the need for an International Lender of Last Resort' <www.imf.org/external/np/speeches/1999/010399.htm>, 4 December 2007.
44. H.S. Scott, *International Finance: Transactions, Policy & Regulation* (Foundation Press, 14th ed., 2007), p. 851.
45. B. Eichengreen, 'Bailing in the Private Sector: Burden Sharing in International Financial Crisis' (1999) *Fletcher Forum of World Affairs*, 57, 59; C. Lichtenstein, 'The Role of International Law in the 21st Century: The Mexican Crisis : Who should be a country's lender of Last Resort' (1995) *Fordham International Law Journal*, 1769.
46. See, generally, on two models for a global LoLR – one in which the global LoLR injects liquidity into the international financial system, and the other in which it supports national banking systems: O. Jeanne and C. Wyplosz, 'The International Lender of Last Resort: How Large is Large Enough?' (Working Paper No. WF/01/76, IMF, May 2001).
47. See generally J. Sachs, 'The International Lender of Last Resort : What are the alternatives?' <www.bos.frb.org/economic/conf/conf43/181p.pdf>, 4 December 2007.

(ii) the difficulty of ensuring that the LoLR lends only on adequate enforceable security so that exceptional moral hazard is not engendered by its activities;[48] and

(iii) the difficulty of providing the LoLR with the resources to do the job.

The sovereignty fears should be far less with a LoLR than with a global financial regulator. Indeed a LoLR detracts less from national sovereignty than even a global bankruptcy regime. After all, the LoLR would merely be serving as a lender to a troubled country – its loans need not be accepted and its existence would not require any reduction in the freedom to act of the country or its judicial system.

However, the provision of adequate security poses very real difficulties indeed. Oil exporting nations such as Mexico could charge future oil revenues to serve as collateral for such a facility. However non-oil exporters may well lack adequate realizable security on the scale required – it may be necessary to structure some sort of escrow arrangement under which, upon a loan being made by the LoLR, a set proportion of the nation's subsequent export earnings are redirected to a trusted third party to use to secure the loan(s). The difficulty is that in troubled times, which by definition will be the period after a LoLR has been called upon, developing nations invariably need all of their foreign exchange earnings to service existing debt and to acquire the imports needed by their domestic industries. To redirect a substantial proportion of foreign exchange from export earnings into re-paying the loans of the LoLR would typically be unsustainable. Accordingly, most countries are going to find the provision of adequate security for the amounts of loans likely to be needed from a LoLR to be extremely problematic, if not downright impossible. For this reason, and the associated massive moral hazard if adequate security is not provided,[49] it is difficult to conceive of an effective global LoLR.

9.5   A SOVEREIGN BANKRUPTCY REGIME

Adam Smith, the father of economics, identified the clear need for a sovereign bankruptcy regime over 200 years ago. In his words:

> When it becomes necessary for a state to declare itself bankrupt, in the same manner as when it becomes necessary for an individual to do so, a fair, open, and avowed bankruptcy is always the measure which is both least dishonourable to the debtor, and least hurtful to the creditor.[50]

---

48. F. Capie, 'Can there be an International Lender of Last Resort?' (1998) *International Finance*, 311, 314.
49. Moral hazard arises whenever a financial market actor does not bear the full risk of their actions. For a consideration of the moral hazard engendered by the IMF-organized bail-outs of Indonesia, Korea and Thailand in 1997 and the ways in which it contributed to Russia's economic meltdown in 1998 see Buckley, 'An Oft-Ignored Perspective on the Asian Economic Crisis: The Role of Creditors and Investors', 431.
50. A. Smith, *The Wealth of Nations*, Book V, Chapter III, p. 468 in the Edward Cannan edition, 1976.

Yet today there is still no machinery or rules in place to facilitate and regulate sovereign bankruptcy.

In 2002 Horst Kohler, then Managing Director of the International Monetary Fund, identified the same problem as Adam Smith, when he said, '[T]he present arrangements for resolving sovereign debt crises are not sufficiently transparent or predictable, and...they impose unnecessary costs on debtors, creditors, and the system as a whole.'[51]

Adam Smith and Horst Kohler agree on the problem, but propose different solutions.

This section analyses why Smith was right in advocating, when necessary, a 'fair, open, and avowed bankruptcy' as the best course for both debtors and creditors, and why the IMF was wrong when it proposed the Sovereign Debt Restructuring Mechanism as an adequate response to the problem of sovereign debt crises.

9.5.1 THE BENEFITS OF BANKRUPTCY REGIMES

At the national level, the principal benefits and purposes of a personal bankruptcy system are generally enunciated as being to divide the assets of an insolvent debtor fairly and rateably between its creditors, and to allow an insolvent debtor the opportunity to make a fresh start free from the burden of accumulated debt (provided the debtor has not engaged in dishonest or otherwise improper financial conduct). Sir Roy Goode has identified four objectives of *corporate* insolvency law: restoring the company to profitable trading, maximizing returns to creditors, providing a fair and equitable system for the ranking of claims and identifying the causes of company failures and imposing sanctions for culpable management.[52] All of the other literature on the topic is in similar terms.

What is missing from the literature is the notion that an effective insolvency regime will improve dramatically the allocation of credit within an economy, and thus make the economy more stable. This I have termed the 'systemic' aspect of bankruptcy – for without a bankruptcy regime, any economy will, as a system, be unstable.

The fairness aspects of bankruptcy are important. Internationally their absence has cost millions of lives. However, notwithstanding this appalling mortality, the systemic advantages of a bankruptcy system are arguably as, or even more, important at the international level. This is because the more immediate and real risk of loss under a global bankruptcy regime would tend to moderate capital flows to developing countries. An effective global sovereign bankruptcy regime in the

---

51. Horst Köhler, 'Reform of the International Financial Architecture: A Work in Progress' <www.imf.org/external/np/speeches/2002/070502.htm>, 4 December 2007.
52. R.M. Goode, *Principles of Corporate Insolvency* Law (London, Sweet & Maxwell, 1997), pp. 25–28.

1970s would have led to far less capital flowing south. The real prospect of massive loan losses would have sharpened banker's minds. When a Rockefeller said these loans were unsustainable,[53] bankers would have listened, for if he was right they would have been set to lose billions. Likewise, a genuine prospect of sovereign bankruptcy would have moderated the size of capital flows to Russia and Argentina.

These systemic advantages can help to ensure that the capital flows are more appropriate to the needs and capacities to repay of the respective debtors. Financial crises would thus be less frequent and less severe. Furthermore, in the event of a crisis, the workout would proceed more rapidly and efficiently and thus the workout costs to creditors and debtors would be reduced.

We take this systemic effect of bankruptcy for granted in domestic systems. If a bank makes a poor credit decision domestically and lends to a borrower who subsequently becomes insolvent, absent security, most of the money will be lost. Without the prospect of sovereign bankruptcy, lenders do not bear the full implication of poor lending decisions internationally and thus excessive extensions of credit are likely. When nations have unsustainable debts, they typically repay them through higher taxes and lower social services. This in nations where these measures translate into malnutrition, inadequate housing, inadequate or no health care, unsafe water supplies, etc. The debts of effectively bankrupt nations are repaid at the expense of the most basic human rights of their own citizens. We still have something very like debtors' prisons for highly indebted nations. The Latin American nations are still struggling to service the debt that was incurred in the 1970s in the debt crisis. That debt has been restructured, reduced, and transformed into Brady bonds, but some of these bonds won't be due to be repaid in full until 2024, and in the interim must be serviced, along with much of the debt incurred since the 1970s. Debt is a lifetime sentence for poor countries. The countries wages, in the form of foreign exchange earned from exports, are effectively garnished, often for thirty or forty years or more!

Given these are the human consequences of sovereign insolvency, and given the founder of economics as we know it could see so clearly that from time to time it would be necessary for nations to declare themselves bankrupt, why has there never been put in place any means for a country to do so?

9.5.2   WHY IS THERE NO GLOBAL SOVEREIGN BANKRUPTCY REGIME?

The answer to why there is no global sovereign bankruptcy regime has three elements to it:

(1) The lack, before the 1980s, of an overarching need for a sovereign bankruptcy regime.

---

53. See text accompanying note 8 in Chapter 3.

(2) The profound difficulties of creating international institutions and gaining widespread implementation of treaties.
(3) The perceived interests of the creditors.

Each element will be considered.

9.5.2.1 Absence of an Overarching Need – until Relatively Recently – for a Sovereign Bankruptcy Regime

Significant international financial crises are becoming more frequent and severe, as the growing interconnectedness of markets means that national crises, that once would have been limited to that one country, now routinely spread throughout their region, and often to the other emerging markets of the world.

In the 'good old days', developing countries had financial crises intermittently and there was simply no pressing need for a supranational institution to deal with them – the crises were insufficiently frequent to warrant it and were often quite limited in their geographic spread. Yet, the proliferation of crises since 1982 means today that, for the first time in history, any such institution would, if it were to exist, be consistently busy.

There are reasons for this recent proliferation of crises. The principal one is the convergence of financial markets under globalization. Until the 1970s most national financial systems functioned as relatively self-contained units: savings within an economy funded investment within that economy. The internationalization of finance since that time has meant ever-increasing capital flows, particularly portfolio capital flows of commercial banks and institutional investors, between nations. The spread of modern telecommunications has meant information travels quickly between nations and capital can react quickly to adverse developments in a country. All in all, contemporary capital flows swiftly into developing nations when prospects look good and there is a surplus of liquidity in the developed world, and as swiftly out of those nations when storm clouds gather, or prospects in the developed nations' markets look better.[54] As Michael Pettis, himself a former senior Wall Street banker, wrote, our contemporary international financial system is a Volatility Machine.[55]

9.5.2.2 Difficulties of Creating International Institutions

History teaches us to never underestimate the difficulty of establishing an international institution. Witness the abortive history of the precursor to the United Nations, the League of Nations, and the International Trade Organization. The IMF and World Bank came into existence after WWII, but due to subsequent US opposition the International Trade Organization was never formed, and only

---

54. Buckley, 'International Capital Flows, Economic Sovereignty and Developing Countries', p. 17.
55. Pettis, *The Volatility Machine*.

Global Measures to Improve the System

the treaty it was to administer, the General Agreement on Tariffs and Trade, was implemented.

The scale of accomplishment in establishing the IMF and World Bank should itself not be undervalued. It took a global cataclysm, preceded by the Great Depression, to summon the political will to make those ideas reality. And in the late 1980s and early 1990s it took years of failure by the US and E.U. to extend the GATT to protect intellectual property rights and trade in services to persuade them of the need for an International Trade Organization, and to allow the ITO to come into being, fifty years late, as the World Trade Organization.

Indeed, fifty years was roughly the gestation time also for the International Criminal Court that came into being in The Hague on 1 July 2002. The Nuremburg War Crimes Tribunal was an ad hoc international criminal court formed for the purpose of trying the Nazi war criminals of WWII, and at that time the need for a standing court was recognized and articulated. The realization of that idea took 56 years. An international sovereign bankruptcy regime would have saved millions of lives in the 1980s, and so the need for it was critical, but the idea wasn't seriously considered until the mid-1990s. Let us hope history is not a firm guide to the gestation periods of such organizations, and we don't have to wait until 2050 for a sovereign bankruptcy regime.

9.5.2.3 Perceived Interests of Creditors

The principal reason there is no global sovereign bankruptcy regime is because the creditors believe its absence works in their favour. The banks have argued vociferously against a bankruptcy regime internationally when they accept, and indeed welcome, them nationally. In the words of William Rhodes, Senior Vice-Chairman of Citibank:

> the existence of a formal bankruptcy mechanism, whether invoked or not, would cause uncertainty in the markets, deter potential lenders and investors, and drive up the countries' borrowing costs.[56]

This is nonsense. National bankruptcy regimes greatly enhance certainty and this serves generally to attract lenders and investors and diminish borrowing costs. There is no reason it would be any different internationally. In the IMF's words: 'In the domestic context, the existence of a bankruptcy law makes debt markets more efficient. . . . The same principle should hold for international capital markets.'[57]

On the other hand, there is no formal structure for the resolution of sovereign debt crises and each crisis typically casts a pall for many years on debtor country prospects and bank profits. Debtor countries suffer with no new capital and ever

---

56. Quoted in P. Hartcher, 'US reigns in IMF with tough debt rules', *Australian Financial Review*, 22 April 2002.
57. IMF, 'Proposals for a Sovereign Debt Restructuring Mechanism (SDRM) A Factsheet', <www.imf.org/external/np/exr/facts/sdrm.htm>, 6 March 2003, D.5.

increasing debt loads and banks suffer as in most cases they have to keep advancing new funds for years to enable the debtors to keep paying interest.[58]

William Rhodes is the world's most experienced banker in sovereign debt restructurings. He speaks as he does, presumably, because banks like the present arrangement under which, when a crisis hits, the poor in developing countries are consigned to the debtors' prisons of poverty, ill-health and ignorance so that the loans made by the banks can be repaid.

So what would a global sovereign bankruptcy regime entail?

9.5.3 THE DETAILS OF A GLOBAL SOVEREIGN BANKRUPTCY REGIME

The comprehensive approach would be to establish a sovereign bankruptcy court (or, at least initially, an ad hoc tribunal for each case) applying a body of rules and procedure. Presently, no court has jurisdiction over disputes between a sovereign state and citizens (such as banks or bondholders) of another sovereign state – the International Court of Justice deals only with disputes between sovereign states.[59] Many writers have advocated the establishment of a global bankruptcy regime as a way of allocating losses more fairly between lenders and borrowers and of improving the efficiency of the system. If implemented by a treaty between nations, such a court/tribunal and rules would require decades of planning and negotiations; however, it could be implemented almost immediately if implemented by agreement between the creditors and debtors of one nation in difficulty and facilitated by the IMF.[60]

The proposal which is closest to the domestic law in most countries is that developed by the Jubilee Framework.[61] This envisages a bankruptcy procedure based on Chapter 9 of the US Bankruptcy Code (which deals with municipal bankruptcies) and enforced by an ad hoc independent panel of experts convened for a specific proceeding. Chapter 9 of the US Code is the best model for any sovereign bankruptcy regime. It has worked effectively and efficiently in the bankruptcy of local municipalities within the US and already deals with the issues peculiar to the bankruptcy of governments.

---

58. Buckley, *Emerging Markets Debt* (London, Kluwer Law International, 1999), 33–34.
59. M. White, 'Sovereigns in Distress: Do They Need Bankruptcy?', *Brookings Paper on Economic Activity* (2002), 21. Arbitral tribunals, such as those under the auspices of the International Centre for the Settlement of Investment Disputes (ICSID), do deal with such disputes, but are, of course, not courts.
60. The two principal models widely discussed for any such transnational law are Chapters 9 and 11 of the US Bankruptcy Code. Raffer has made a strong case for Chapter 9 as the best precedent for international sovereign bankruptcies: see K. Raffer, 'Solving Sovereign Debt Overhang by Internationalising Chapter 9 Procedures' (2002) *Studien von Zeitfragen*. See also K. Raffer, 'Applying Chapter 9 Insolvency to International Debts: An Economically Efficient Solution with a Human Face' (1990) 18(2) *World Development*, 301; and K. Rogoff and J. Zettelmeyer, 'Early Ideas on Sovereign Bankruptcy Reorganisation: A Survey' (Working Paper No. WP/02/57, IMF).
61. A. Pettifor, 'Chapter 9/11? Resolving International debt crises – the Jubilee Framework for international insolvency', <www.jubileeplus.org/analysis/reports/jubilee_framework.html>, 26 September 2002 and 24 March 2003.

Under a Chapter 9 model, the decision upon whether to file for bankruptcy protection would be the debtors – as it is in domestic law – provided they are unable to service their debts and have either obtained the agreement of creditors or tried and failed to work out a plan with them. A nation's incapacity to service debts would be defined by reference to an inability to provide certain minimal human rights to their people. This capacity to initiate bankruptcy proceedings would be no incentive to go bankrupt, just as it is not in domestic practice. Filing for protection would initiate an automatic stay, for a period, on creditors' claims. The claim for protection would be determined by an independent tribunal appointed by the creditors and the debtors. For instance, the creditors could appoint two members to the tribunal, the debtor nation could likewise appoint two members, and the four members could then jointly appoint a fifth, to serve as their presiding member.[62]

Developing nations, and the international financial system, would both be best served by a carefully crafted set of bankruptcy rules, based on Chapter 9 of the US Bankruptcy Law, and applied and enforced by independent tribunals.

As alternatives to such a regime the major banks and banking industry associations proposed the mandatory inclusion of collective action clauses (CACs) in all sovereign bond documentation; and the IMF proposed its SDRM initiative. Each alternative will be considered.

9.6   COLLECTIVE ACTION CLAUSES

Collective action clauses are clauses in debt documentation by which creditors agree in advance to accept the determination of a majority, usually a super-majority of 75% of creditors, as to any variation of the terms of the debt. This removes many of the collective action problems inherent in bond debt, in which the bonds may be held by hundreds or thousands of creditors. It prevents the free-rider problem, in which small creditors may allow the others to restructure the debt, and then insist on repayment in full, on the original terms. It makes a debt workout with bonds more workable.

Bonds issued under UK and Japanese law traditionally had such clauses in them, and those issued under New York and German law did not. The same sovereigns issue in both New York and London. The leading research shows that collective action clauses (CACs) tend to lower the borrowing cost for more credit-worthy issuers and raise it for less credit-worthy issuers, but in neither case particularly significantly.[63] Presumably the more credit-worthy benefit from being able to take advantage of a more orderly restructuring process should it

---

62. *Ibid.*
63. B. Eichengreen and A. Mody, 'Would Collective Action Clauses Raise Borrowing Costs?' (Working Paper No. w7458, NBER, January 2000) <papers.nber.org/papers/w7458>, 4 December 2007; and J. Drage and C. Hovaguimian, 'Collective Action Clauses: An Analysis of Provisions Included in Recent Sovereign Bond Issues' <www.bankofengland.co.uk/publications/fsr/2004/fsr17art7.pdf>, 4 December 2007, p. 2.

ever become necessary, whereas for less creditworthy issuers, any provision that makes a rescheduling easier is resisted.[64]

In response to the strong encouragement of the US Treasury,[65] Mexico led the way in 2003 by issuing bonds with CACs under New York law. Since then, most emerging market countries issuing in the New York market have followed Mexico's lead while only a few have not.[66] CACs appear to have now become the market standard for new bond issues under New York law, bringing New York practice into line with that in London. The US and the other G-7 nations wanted to see CACs made mandatory in all sovereign bond contracts as an alternative to the SDRM approach and they now appear to have substantially achieved their goal. Mandatory CACs are better than nothing, so they should be the norm in bond documentation. However they are but a very partial solution to the problem, for two reasons:

(1) CACs do not remove the need for a sovereign bankruptcy regime.[67] They facilitate reschedulings, but do not afford debt relief when major debt relief is what is needed to allow a nation a fresh start and to permit it to honour most of the human rights of its people.
(2) The debt workout for the Debt Crisis took from 1983 to 1994 – a lost decade of development in Latin America and Africa – and this debt workout faced relatively few collective action problems. The restructurings were managed by steering committees of typically six to eight banks appointed to represent all of the lenders. These were not restructurings of bonds held by many creditors and the banks were highly susceptible to the moral suasion of their respective central banks, and it was this pressure, and this pressure only, that eventually led to the Brady Plan and some relief for debtors – but a decade too late for most debtors. Collective action problems are only a small part of the problem. The US Treasury's approach implicitly assumed they were most of the problem. One is tempted to believe the US proposal conveniently and cynically treated the collective action problems as being most of the problem precisely so as not to have to deal with the real issues.

The problem with CACs is not that they won't help, but that they won't help insolvent sovereigns become solvent again.

In September 2002 the national members of the International Monetary and Financial Committee Meeting of the IMF, agreed to proceed with the 'twin-track approach' of seeking to implement the IMF's SDRM proposal plus the US

---

64. Eichengreen and Mody, 'Would Collective Action Clauses Raise Borrowing Costs?'.
65. Statement of Under Secretary John B. Taylor Regarding the Decisions by Countries to Issue Bonds with Collective Action Clauses (CACs), 3 February 2004, <www.treas.gov/press/releases/js1144.htm>, 4 December 2007.
66. Drage and Hovaguimian, 'Collective Action Clauses: An Analysis of Provisions Included in Recent Sovereign Bond Issues', p. 2.
67. White, 'Sovereigns in Distress: Do They Need Bankruptcy?'.

Global Measures to Improve the System

Treasury's initiative of mandating the use of collective action clauses.[68] The SDRM proposal has always required US support as its implementation requires amendment of the IMF's constituent documents, and as this requires a 75% majority vote, the US has had a veto over any such change.

The SDRM was first proposed in a signal speech by Anne Krueger, First Deputy Managing Director of the IMF.[69] The IMF's proposed scheme, limited as it was, drew forth a strong reaction from creditors and the US Treasury, and in light of these criticisms the IMF revised its initiative considerably.

9.7 THE IMF PROPOSAL: THE SDRM

The IMF developed its Sovereign Debt Restructuring Mechanism (SDRM) proposal to address two problems it identified. The first is the absence of 'adequate incentives for orderly and timely restructuring of unsustainable sovereign debts'.[70] The general consensus is that developing country debtor governments tend to postpone initiating a restructuring of their debt until far later than is optimal from the perspective of their creditors and their own citizens. In the words of Anne Krueger:

> Like a patient with a toothache avoiding a trip to the dentist, a debtor country will all too often delay a necessary restructuring until the last possible moment, draining its reserves and increasing the eventual cost of restoring sustainability. Creditors suffer too, as the fear that some may be unfairly favored in a disorderly workout depresses the value of claims on the secondary market and, at worst, may block agreement on a necessary restructuring. All this can leave the international community with the unpalatable choice of accepting a disruptive and potentially contagious unilateral default, or bailing out private creditors and thereby contributing to moral hazard.[71]

---

68. 'Transcript of a Press Conference Following the International Monetary and Financial Committee Meeting', 28 September 2002, <www.imf.org/external/np/tr/2002/tr020928.htm>, 30 September 2002.
69. A. Krueger, 'International Financial Architecture for 2002: A New Approach to Sovereign Debt Restructuring' (Speech delivered at the National Economists' Club Annual Members' Dinner, Washington DC, 26 November 2001), <www.imf.org/external/np/speeches/2001/112601.htm>, 4 December 2007 ('Krueger I'); the proposal was substantially modified in A. Krueger, *A New Approach to Sovereign Debt Restructuring*, <www.imf.org/external/pubs/ft/exrp/sdrm/eng/index.htm>; delivered at 'Sovereign Debt Workouts: Hopes and Hazards' (Washington, DC, Institute for International Economics, 1 April 2002) <www.iie.com/papers/krueger0402.htm> ('Krueger II') and restated in A. Krueger, 'Preventing and Resolving Financial Crises: The Role of Sovereign Debt Restructuring' (Speech delivered at the Latin American Meeting of the Econometric Society, Sao Paolo, Brazil, 26 July 2002) < www.imf.org/external/np/speeches/2002/072602.htm> ('Krueger III'). See generally, on the Krueger proposals, White, 'Sovereigns in Distress: Do They Need Bankruptcy?', 20.
70. Krueger I.
71. See Krueger II.

The second problem is that without a bankruptcy type mechanism the only choices available when a nation is in serious financial trouble are a default (which is highly disruptive to the debtor and potentially destabilizing for the entire international financial system) or a bailout of the private creditors thereby, in Anne Krueger's words, 'contributing to moral hazard'.[72]

'Moral hazard' describes any system that protects parties from the consequences of their actions and thus holds out inducements to seek to profit from misbehaviour.[73] Two classic instances of moral hazard are the US Savings and Loan crisis brought on by lax prudential supervision and government insurance of S&L deposits and Russia's economic collapse of 1998 exacerbated by a massive prior inflow of foreign capital in reliance on the IMF bailing out Russia due to its geo-political significance, given the IMF had bailed out the East Asian countries the year before.[74]

The IMF's proposal as developed and modified had four principal elements:[75]

(1) Majority restructuring so as to circumvent the collective action problems that are particularly prevalent with bond financing and to remove the free-riding and rogue creditor problems.
(2) Deterrence of disruptive litigation – by providing for any amounts recovered to be deducted from any eventual residual claims.
(3) Protection of creditor interests by a restraint on the debtor paying non-priority creditors and by an IMF assurance of good economic conduct by the debtor to give the creditors an assurance the debtor will pursue policies that protect asset values and restore growth.
(4) Seniority for new lending, so as to attract it to the country.

The SDRM also involved the appointment of a Sovereign Debt Dispute Resolution Forum, described as independent even though its members would be nominated and endorsed by the Fund. The Forum would have had power to decide disputes between creditors and between creditors and debtors. However its role fell far short of that of a bankruptcy tribunal and the SDRM fell far short of the bankruptcy regimes that are an essential part of all national economic systems.[76]

The G-7 nations, at the behest of their banks, opposed the IMF's SDRM proposal and supported the far more limited, collective action clause approach of the US Yet the SDRM was very pro-creditor and would have certainly served the banks – my opposition to it was that it didn't go far enough and was in no sense

---

72. Krueger III.
73. C.W. Calomiris, 'The IMF's Imprudent Role as Lender of Last Resort' (1998) 17 *Cato Journal*, 275.
74. On the S&L Crisis see, Eichengreen and Mussa, 'Capital Account Liberalization: Theoretical and Practical Aspects', pp. 43–44 and on Russia's crisis, see R.P. Buckley, 'The Essential Flaw in the Globalisation of Capital Markets: Its Impact on Human Rights' (2001) 32 *California Western International Law Journal*, 125.
75. IMF, 'Proposals for a Sovereign Debt Restructuring Mechanism (SDRM) A Factsheet'; Krueger II.
76. A. Pettifor and K. Raffer, 'Report on the IMF's conference on the SDRM, 22 January 2003', unpublished report on file with author.

what is needed, a bankruptcy regime. The G-7 nations' banks[77] appear unable to learn the lessons of history or appreciate the benefits to themselves of a more enlightened approach. The debt crisis of 1982 was resolved in part by the Brady Plan. The Plan changed perceptions about Latin America as a destination for capital flows, and the fresh money allowed Latin American economies to begin growing again. The Plan also gave the banks readily tradable bonds, rather than illiquid loans, that permitted many banks to sell their exposure to investors comfortable with risk, and free up their own capital to move on and undertake new business. The Brady Plan proved to be a huge boon to banks, yet at the time they resisted it strongly, and only agreed to it under enormous pressure from their own national banking regulators.[78] The banks, in opposing a global sovereign bankruptcy regime, have got it wrong, again, from their perspective.

From my perspective, there were six problems with the SDRM initiative:

(1) The determination of whether a nation qualified for debt restructuring was to be made not by the Sovereign Debt Dispute Resolution Forum, as one would expect, but by 'the debtor and a super-majority of creditors'.[79]

(2) The determination of a nation's level of debt sustainability, from which the necessary amount of debt reduction would follow as a matter of logic, was to be made not by the Sovereign Debt Dispute Resolution Forum, as one would expect, but by the IMF.[80]

(3) The IMF will discharge this critical function while compromised by its status as a major creditor of the debtor, and presumably with one eye upon the recoverability of its own loans. That one should never be a judge in one's own cause is a fundamental principle of natural justice that the SDRM proposal ignored.

(4) The SDRM was to apply only to commercial bank debt and leave Paris Club debt and IMF and World Bank loans out of the equation. This meant that even considerable debt reductions by commercial creditors might be insufficient to return the debtor nation to viability as the overall debt burden on the nation would be insufficiently reduced.

(5) The stay on enforcement of claims that is a feature of all domestic bankruptcy regimes, was dropped from the SDRM proposal and replaced by the less effective 'Hotchpot rule' under which any amounts recovered by a creditor are deducted from the creditor's eventual entitlements.[81]

---

77. P. Blustein, 'IMF Crisis Plan Torpedoed', *Washington Post*, 3 April 2002, p. E-1; and 'G-7 Finance Ministers Adopt Financial Crises Action Plan', <www.fin.gc.ca/news02/02-034e.html>, 15 June 2002.
78. Buckley, 'The Facilitation of the Brady Plan: Emerging Markets Debt Trading from 1989 to 1993', 1802.
79. Krueger II.
80. K. Raffer, 'The IMF's SDRM – Another Form of Simply Disastrous Rescheduling Management?' in *Sovereign Debts at the Crossroads*, C. Jochnick and F. Preston (eds) (Oxford University Press, 2006).
81. See K. Raffer, 'To Stay or Not to Stay – A Short Note on Differing Versions of the SDRM', <www.jubileeresearch.org/news/raffer310103.htm>, 4 December 2007.

(6) The laws and rules that the Forum would apply were still to be drafted – so the IMF was in effect requesting support for a process the final form of which was uncertain.

Perhaps unsurprisingly, given it was a proposal of the IMF, the SDRM served to entrench the IMF in its role of international debt and economic crisis policeman by increasing the legal basis for that role – a role it has conspicuously failed to discharge well ever since it took it on in late 1982.

The SDRM proposal sought to render more efficient the current, haphazard debt restructuring process without addressing any of the inequities or power imbalances of the present system. In the IMF's words, 'We are not proposing a bankruptcy mechanism for countries, but simply a mechanism to facilitate debt workout negotiations between a debtor and its creditors'.[82]

Yet a bankruptcy mechanism is precisely what is needed. One purpose of a rules-based system is to redress power imbalances by the application of fair and just rules – to replace the law of the jungle under which the most powerful wins, with the rule of law under which justice should out. The SDRM failed this test. The critical issues in its rules would have been determined and applied not by an independent court, but by an interested party, the IMF itself. Futhermore, in seeking to render the current system more efficient it appeared to seek to do no more than entrench and enhance the power of the creditors.

The IMF attracted criticism for its unwillingness to extend the SDRM to debts owed to it. It argues it is not a commercial lender that seeks profit, but rather a creditor that lends at concessional rates precisely when others will not. There is some substance to this position, and as the IMF has pointed out, sovereign creditors adopt the same stance with less justification.[83] 'Official debt' is that extended by multilateral institutions such as the IMF and the World Bank and sovereign creditors. Poor nations traditionally strive hardest to avoid defaulting on official debt, on the basis that it will be the only source of funds when all others dry up. Notwithstanding the substance behind the IMF's claim, to push for a debt relief mechanism while exempting one's own claims from it, did not exhibit tremendous moral leadership.

9.7.1 Would the SDRM Have Served the Debtors?

If the SDRM would have served the debtors it would principally have done so by requiring and facilitating debt relief as part of the restructuring process, for debt relief allows insolvent nations to grow and develop again. However this wasn't likely as the SDRM was really just a process and the substantive issues, such as

---

82. International Monetary Fund, 'Proposals for a Sovereign Debt Restructuring Mechanism (SDRM) A Factsheet', <www.imf.org/external/np/exr/facts/sdrm.htm>, 4 December 2007, B.6.
83. Krueger III.

debt relief, were reserved for negotiated resolution between the creditors and the debtors.

Ultimately, the strongest argument for a sovereign bankruptcy regime and against the SDRM arises from the long-standing attitudes of creditors to debt relief. Throughout the 1980s the creditor community resisted vigorously all calls for debt relief as a response to the Latin American and African debt crisis – a crisis which for its resolution desperately required debt relief. As Donald Regan said, when Secretary of the US Treasury:

> I don't think we should just let a nation off the hook because we are sympathetic to the fact that they are having difficulty. As debtors, I think they should be made to pay as much as they can bear without breaking them. You just can't let your heart rule your head in these situations.[84]

The first Brady Plan restructuring, for Mexico in 1989, was a slow process as hundreds of banks resisted it strenuously, principally because it contained an element of debt relief. Many banks were reportedly 'disgusted' with the deal but in the end had to go along with it under intense pressure from their central bank regulators.[85] This is the standard approach of creditors to debt relief. It was the stance in the Argentina case – it took tremendous resolve and courage on the part of Argentina, and a prolonged default, for the creditors to accept meaningful debt relief.

An insight into creditor thinking in this regard can be gained from a letter from the chief executives of five financial market associations to Horst Kohler, then Managing Director of the IMF, expressing concerns over the IMF's SDRM proposal.[86] The financial market associations disagreed strongly with several of the key assumptions behind the SDRM, viz. that there are collective action problems preventing creditors as a group from reaching agreement on restructuring terms, that IMF bailouts have the effect of bailing out private creditors and that the SDRM would be analogous to domestic bankruptcy procedures. They even had the chutzpah to put the word 'unsustainable' in quotation marks when referring to an 'unsustainable' level of external debt.

To deny the existence of collective action problems among creditors was a very long bow to draw indeed in 2002 when this letter was written and most debt was, once again, appropriately, in the form of bonds.[87] From the perspective of the creditors who typically continue to receive interest in the years that debt restructurings take to work out, such delays might appear acceptable. However from the

---

84. As quoted in W.J. Quirk, 'Will an Underdeveloped Countries Debtors' Cartel Squeeze the Big Banks?' (1983) 47 *Business and Society Review*, 10.
85. 'Hurricane heading for Brady Plan' 794 *IFR*, 23 September 1989, 12; and 'Commercial bankers say Brady Plan is a non-starter' 795 *IFR*, 30 September 1989, 8.
86. Letter dated 6 February 2002 from the Securities Industry Association, Emerging Markets Traders Association, International Primary Market Association, International Securities Market Association and The Bond Market Association to Mr Horst Köhler <www.emta.org/ndevelop/imflettr.pdf>, 4 December 2007.
87. See L.C. Buchheit and G.M. Gulati, 'Sovereign Bonds and the Collective Will' (2002) 51 *Emory Law Journal*, 1317.

perspective of debtor country citizens who cannot find work or feed and educate their families in those years, such delays are utterly unacceptable.

To deny that IMF bailouts serve to bail out private creditors is even more outrageous. The IMF itself admits this is the consequence of the IMF organized loans to sovereign debtors in times of crisis – in fact, such a use of the funds is mandated by the terms of the bail-out loans.[88] The financial industry associations asserted that 'private creditors have and undoubtedly will continue to experience substantial losses on their exposure to emerging market sovereign debtors who have experienced payment difficulties'.[89] True, entirely true, and so what? No one asserts that bailouts completely protect creditors from losses. The problem is that bailouts shield creditors of short-term debt from much of the losses that an unfettered market would impose upon them – thereby encouraging the very type of debt, short-term debt, that is most volatility enhancing and least desirable from the debtor nation's perspective.

The third objection of the financial industry associations has substance: the SDRM is not analogous to domestic bankruptcy procedures (and that is precisely the great weakness with it).

Finally, putting the word 'unsustainable' in quotation marks so as to suggest that nations do not have unsustainable debts is simply unethical. The most impoverished nations today spend four to eight times more repaying debt than on health, education, sanitation and other basic needs and the total external indebtedness of developing countries is more than USD 2.7 trillion.[90] Such debt can only be serviced at the direct expense of the human rights, and often the very lives, of millions of people and can only be considered sustainable by those whose moral compass has gone utterly awry.

For as long as creditors adopt such positions, there is simply no prospect of negotiated justice for debtor nations from any restructuring whether pursued under a version of the SDRM or otherwise.

In any event, the SDRM initiative was shelved in at the Spring Meeting of the International Monetary and Financial Committee of the IMF.[91]

---

88. C.W. Calomiris and A.H. Meltzer, 'Fixing the IMF' (1999) 56 *The National Interest*, 88. See also H.S. Scott and P.A. Wellons, *International Finance: Transactions, Policy and Regulation* (University Casebook, 6th ed., 1999), pp. 1204–1205.
89. Letter dated 6 February 2002 from the Securities Industry Association, Emerging Markets Traders Association, International Primary Market Association, International Securities Market Association and The Bond Market Association to Mr Horst Köhler <www.emta.org/ndevelop/newfin.htm>, 2.
90. The total external indebtedness of developing countries in 2005 was USD 2,793 billion, see World Bank, *World Development Indicators 2007*, p. 187, <www.siteresources.worldbank.org/DATASTATISTICS/Resources/WDI07section4-intro.pdf>, 4 December 2007.
91. Communiqué of the International Monetary and Financial Committee of the Board of Governors of the International Monetary Fund, Washington, DC, 12 April 2003, 15, <www.imf.org/external/np/cm/2003/041203.htm>, 4 December 2007.

9.8 BENEFITS OF A GLOBAL SOVEREIGN BANKRUPTCY REGIME

So what advantages would a global bankruptcy regime with a highly developed, formal system of rules bring? Four come to mind.

(1) The unconscionable delays that occasion most sovereign debt workouts would be shortened, to the benefit of creditors and debtors.
(2) The appalling human suffering, and the state mandated infringements of basic human rights, that have accompanied the overwhelming majority of IMF Structural Adjustment Programs and Poverty Reduction Strategy Papers, would be dramatically ameliorated by the debt relief granted to sovereign debtors.
(3) Capital flows to less credit worthy developing countries would be ameliorated by the prospect of national insolvency. Reckless lending and reckless borrowing would be constrained – and this would be a good thing.
(4) The international financial system would be far more stable as capital would flow within it only after far more careful credit decisions than is now the case. This greater stability would benefit both creditors and debtors. In short, capital would tend to flow between economies more as it does today within economies (where the prospect of debtor bankruptcy plays its cautionary role).

The history of the past fifty years tells us that debtor nations usually continue to service their debts, even when as nations they are functionally bankrupt and can do so only by borrowing ever more debt.[92] Countries can always repay loans precisely because they can always increase taxes and reduce spending on health, education and nutrition – and at some point with poor countries such reductions in spending lead to unconscionable hardship.

National bankruptcy regimes seek to ensure the maximum return to creditors while ensuring the debtors have food, housing and the capacity to work. Humane nations tolerate nothing less. We rejected debtors' prisons centuries ago. The absence of an international bankruptcy regime means people starve, and live without adequate shelter, healthcare and education, while their country's wealth goes to service loans. Why is it that what is considered unacceptable within any developed nation, is considered acceptable by the international financial community when it applies in other, poorer, borrowing countries?

A global bankruptcy court or tribunal with a fully developed accompanying jurisprudence would be a tremendous asset to the world as it would moderate capital flows to developing countries and provide a way out from under unsustainable debt burdens for these countries.

---

92. See Buchheit and Gulati, 'Sovereign Bonds and the Collective Will'.

In the words of one commentator,

> In the absence of a strong push for a... global bankruptcy court, the losses to overall global economic efficiency from emerging market crises of liquidity quickly becoming crises of solvency (resulting in unnecessarily destroyed domestic economies), are likely to mount.[93]

The pressure from civil society for an effective global bankruptcy regime must be increased. Bankruptcy is an essential element of all domestic economic systems offering equity for debtors and creditors and systemic stability. As Adam Smith identified over 200 years ago, an effective bankruptcy regime is needed for sovereign states. It would provide major benefits in terms of fairness and systemic stability to the international financial system – benefits that will translate into a massive reduction of unconscionable human suffering. Sovereign bankruptcy is an idea whose time has come. Work is required to ensure it comes to pass.

9.8.1 CONCLUSION ON SYSTEMIC MEASURES

This chapter has considered the following range of measures to improve the international financial system:

(1) Reduce currency mismatches on national balance sheets by developing markets in local currency debt, in doing which there is a major role for the Paris Club and the international financial institutions.
(2) Implement a two-tier currency transactions tax to dissuade short-term speculative capital flows and enhance the stability of the international financial system, as well as raise the funds needed to substantially reduce global poverty and disease.
(3) Establish a global financial regulator with enforcement powers.
(4) Establish an effective global lender of last resort.
(5) Establish a global sovereign bankruptcy regime.

The systemic reforms that are achievable are working to remedy the structural flaw in national balance sheets by reducing currency mismatches, implementing a currency transactions tax, and establishing a global sovereign bankruptcy regime.

All three reforms need greatly enhanced research and advocacy efforts. Much more research needs to be done on how to minimize currency mismatches and on how to capture all relevant transactions with a currency transactions tax. The national balance sheet problem can be addressed nation by nation, although as this book has identified, it will probably only be effectively minimized when the Paris Club and international financial institutions begin to denominate restructured debt in local currency. The currency transactions tax requires a concerted effort by leading international financial centres and therefore probably awaits sufficiently

---

93. L.E. Armijo, 'The Political Geography of World Financial Reform: Who Wants What and Why?' (2001) 7(4) *Global Governance*, 379.

enlightened leadership to be in place at the same time in London, New York, Tokyo and Shanghai. But the arguments for this tax are persuasive, and the revenues it would raise are sorely needed to resist the spiraling inequality which history teaches us is the greatest threat to the political stability of any system. If, for instance, the leaders of London and New York agreed to implement such a tax, it would be interesting indeed to see whether other nations fell into line. It is not difficult to imagine a concerted campaign by aging rockers like Bono and Geldof generating sufficient political pressure to make it electorally very difficult for most nations not to follow New York and London's lead.

A global bankruptcy court would have to be created by international treaty among the affected nations – the home jurisdictions of the creditors and the debtor nations. Law reform by international treaty is usually grindingly slow. The International Criminal Court was some 55 years in the making. The World Trade Organization came into being 51 years after it was first proposed as the third of the Bretton Woods institutions. Even the Uniform Customs and Practice for Documentary Credits, which is only a set of standard terms for letters of credit, was in existence for some 40 years, and went through three revisions before gaining widespread usage and acceptance globally.[94] History is not on the side of expeditious reforms of this type.

A global bankruptcy regime seeks to achieve what is essential for the efficiency and stability of the international financial system and while this would most definitely enhance global prosperity and thus bank profitability in the long term, it will not necessarily enhance the bottom line for international banks in the short term. The long-term self-interest of the international banks would be best served, as it is domestically, by an efficient global bankruptcy regime and the more stable international financial system it would deliver. However, more research, and a major educative effort, will be required to prove this to the banks and until they accept and understand it, a global bankruptcy regime is less than likely.

An ad hoc global bankruptcy tribunal administering an agreed body of rules is the most realizable first step in the journey towards a permanent global bankruptcy court. This remains a major undertaking as a debtor nation and its creditors would have to agree to the rules that would be applied and the constitution of the tribunal that would apply them – and this difficulty is compounded by debtor nations typically having thousands of creditors each holding bonds. Nonetheless as collective action clauses become more widespread in sovereign bond documentation, as is occurring, these problems are diminished; and they are by no means insuperable.

While forming an ad hoc tribunal and reaching agreement on the applicable rules will prove a challenge for creditors and debtors, recent developments suggest some cause for optimism. Developing nations are displaying far more collective solidarity and strength in negotiations of the Doha Development Round of the WTO than has previously been the norm. The quite unprecedented discount for

---

94. See R.P. Buckley, 'The 1993 Revision of the Uniform Customs and Practice for Documentary Credits' (1995) 28 *George Washington Journal of International Law and Economics*, 265.

a middle-income country achieved by Argentina in the renegotiation of its external indebtedness in 2005 came about because of Argentina's resolution, and its accurate conceptualization of its own situation as one of insolvency. It will only be debtor nation strength and resolve that will bring creditors to the sovereign bankruptcy table and these are examples of debtor nation strength and resolve. So there remains some cause for hope that a global bankruptcy regime is realizable in the next decade or two provided the necessary research and advocacy efforts are increased soon.

Chapter 10
The Way Forward

As this book has demonstrated, the international financial system doesn't work well. Loans typically leave the exchange rate risk and interest rate risk with the party least able to bear them, and hedge them, the borrower. When crises occur, the system colludes with the international banks and the elite in the debtor nations, to have the debts assumed by the debtor nations themselves and these loans, often made to private sector corporations, end up being serviced by the common people paying higher taxes and receiving fewer government services.

In other words, the system favours the banks of the rich countries at the expense of the poor in the poor countries. This is utterly unsurprising. It is the role of law to protect the powerless and there is very little binding, mandatory law applicable to international capital flows. Major banks throughout history have regularly done things in developing countries they would never do at home, such as bribing treasurers to take loans their countries don't really need, or arranging sophisticated schemes by which loans to private corporations are eventually repaid by that corporation's sovereign.

So what to do about this?

In this book, in earlier chapters, I have considered a range of solutions, ranging from restructuring national balance sheets to minimize currency mismatches to the establishment of a sovereign bankruptcy regime to bring that most basic of commercial law institutions and market disciplines to the realm of international finance, through to the rich countries making far greater use of debt-for-development swaps to afford debt relief and increased levels of aid to poor nations, especially those excluded from the HIPC framework.

While these measures will all take time to implement, there is one measure that can be implemented almost immediately – and that is to stop the socialization of private sector debt.

10.1 THE SOCIALIZATION OF PRIVATE SECTOR DEBT

One of the depressingly consistent themes of the aftermath of each financial crisis is the socialization of private sector debt – a consequence which the IMF either engineers or to which it acquiesces.

After the debt crisis broke in 1982 the creditors persuaded each nation to represent all debtors within its borders in the rescheduling negotiations and to do so by bringing all the debts of those debtors under its sovereign guarantee. The first step was necessary. The second was not.

Bringing all debts under the sovereign guarantee improved the security of the creditors – particularly of the creditors who had made most of the loans to private sector corporations – and these just happened to be the major lenders who were sitting on the creditor steering committees and orchestrating the process.[1] Bringing corporate debts under the sovereign guarantee also represented an utterly unjustifiable charge on the common people of these countries – these loans were ultimately serviced by higher taxes and lower social services.

Fifteen years later in Asia the nature of the crisis was quite different, but the resolution of it was the same – the poor in the debtor countries were exploited – this time by a process engineered by the IMF. The IMF organized bailouts of Indonesia, Thailand and Korea. While described as IMF bailouts of the countries, they were in fact long-term loans made on condition they be used to repay creditors.[2] These loans thus became debts of the nation and the bailouts were of the creditors, not the debtor nations at all.[3] It took four years before bailouts were generally understood to be 'a welfare system for Wall Street'[4] as the funds flowed directly through to creditors.

To make matters worse the creditors with debts due typically held short-term bonds – and short-term debt is particularly destabilizing for developing countries. So the IMF bailouts encouraged precisely the type of debt that a stable system would discourage.

The idea was that the nations again would take responsibility for the indebtedness of corporations incorporated in the nation, use the loans obtained in the bailout to pay off the foreign creditors, and later recover the debts from the corporate debtors. The Indonesian government recovered some 30% of the value of the loans it incurred on behalf of the banking sector.[5] The other 70% became a charge on the Indonesian people. And these are large sums of money. The amount

---

1. Buckley, *Emerging Markets Debt: An Analysis of the Secondary Market*, 43.
2. J. Levinson, 'Living Dangerously: Indonesia and the Reality of the Global Economic System', (1998) 7 *Journal of International Law and Practice*, 437–441, 446.
3. Calomiris and Meltzer, 'Fixing the IMF', 88.
4. In the words of a senior G-7 official, quoted in C. Denny, 'IMF sheds no tears for Argentina', *The Guardian*, 29 April 2002.
5. Indonesia, Indonesia Financial Sector Monthly Report No. 42, Feb 2004, available at http://siteresources.worldbank.org/INTINDONESIA/Resources/Fin-Priv-Sector/FSReport-022004.pdf

of the IMF bailout now represents well over one-half of the total external sovereign indebtedness of Indonesia.[6]

After Argentina's economic implosion, the international financial community, with the assistance of a compliant Argentine government and the IMF, found two ways to socialize private indebtedness. The first is the familiar IMF bailout, in this case a massive USD 40 billion loan to Argentina in late 2000, that was required to be used to repay a mix of public and corporate debt.[7] The second was a new way to achieve an old end: having the people repay corporate debts. This technique was known as 'pesofication'.

Under pesofication, dollar-denominated bank loans and deposits were redenominated in pesos. Banks were required to convert their assets (such as loans) into pesos at a one-for-one rate and their liabilities (such as deposits) into pesos at a rate of 1.4 to 1. This generated huge losses for the banks for which the government sought to compensate them by a massive issue of government bonds of necessarily doubtful value.[8]

Thus the circle was completed in the usual way in such crises – the ultimate burden fell on the public purse. In the words of Pedro Pou, President of the Central Bank of Argentina until mid-2001, 'The government has transferred about 40% of private debt to workers...We are experiencing a mega-redistribution of wealth and income unprecedented in the history of the capitalist world.'[9]

To require the common people to repay corporation's debts, through increased taxes and reduced government services, is simply immoral. It is a massive interference with the market system that the IMF professes to support. In each of these crises, the market, through the mechanism of bankruptcy, would have allocated the costs of the poor lending and borrowing decisions upon the lenders and borrowers. The IMF, either as architect, or complicit partner, in each case allocated the costs of these poor decisions to parties who had nothing to do with them: the common people of the debtor nations.[10]

The IMF must stop facilitating bailouts in which anything other than sovereign debt is repaid – if poor countries choose to bail out their corporate sectors they should do so openly, and certainly not through the subterfuge of an IMF orchestrated loan. Likewise, debtor governments must resist the urgings of the IMF and the creditors to socialize private debt. Too often, developing country governments act in accordance with the interests of the small elite in their nation

---

6. As at December, 2006 Indonesia's total external sovereign debt was USD 75.8 billion and the bailout was for USD 43 billion. See on the level of sovereign debt: Bank Indonesia, Financial Statistics, available at <www.bi.go.id/web/en/Data+Statistik> and on the amount of the bail-out: IMF, IMF Fact Sheet, available at <www.imf.org/external/np/exr/facts/asia.pdf>, 13 Dec. 2007.
7. E. Hershberg, 'Why Argentina Crashed – And Is Still Crashing' (2002) 36 *NACLA Report on the Americas*, 32.
8. A. Gaudin, 'Thirteen days that shook Argentina – and now what?' (2002) 35 *NACLA Report on the Americas*, 6; and 'Latin Banks: Eyes on Brazil', (200) 8(18) *Emerging Markets Monitor*, 12.
9. As cited in Gaudin, 'Thirteen days that shook Argentina – and now what?'.
10. See generally Buckley, 'The Fatal Flaw in International Finance: The Rich Borrow and the Poor Repay', 59–64.

and of global capital, and not in the interests of their common people. This is partly because politicians and technocrats share the perspectives of the elite and international financiers, and partly because the elite and the politicians benefit from strong capital inflows and are insulated from the devastating effects of financial crises. For national governments to assume corporate debt in desperately poor countries is immoral. It rewards the rich in those countries at the direct expense of the poor. It is a practice that must stop and a practice the IMF must stop orchestrating.

It is so often the case that the costs of IMF policies are borne by the common people of poorer nations, it has caused me to challenge the very need for an international monetary fund.

10.2   THE FUTURE OF THE IMF

Beyond restructuring national balance sheets, imposing a currency transaction tax, facilitating sovereign bankruptcy, and stopping the socialization of private sector debt, there is one more improvement to the global financial system, more radical than any considered to date, and yet as sorely needed. It is to revisit the role of the IMF. The Fund served an important purpose in the 1950s and 1960s but by the late 1970s that purpose had gone. Since 1982 the IMF has made the plight of poor countries worse. To understand why, let's review some of the highlights of this book, starting with the founding of the Fund.

The Fund was founded, along with the World Bank, in 1945. In the words of its website:

> It was established to promote international monetary cooperation, exchange stability, and orderly exchange arrangements; to foster economic growth and high levels of employment; and to provide temporary financial assistance to countries to help ease balance of payments adjustment.[11]

This is a reasonable summary. But the website proceeds:

> Since the IMF was established its purposes have remained unchanged but its operations – which involve surveillance, financial assistance, and technical assistance – have developed to meet the changing needs of its member countries in an evolving world economy.

This is pure spin. The Fund's purposes have changed, utterly. They changed in the 1970s when most developed countries moved away from fixed, to floating, exchange rates and the core function of the Fund, the maintenance of exchange stability, was ceded by governments to the market.

The Fund's operations today do involve surveillance and financial and technical assistance, but these operations are primarily in the service of the prevention and management of developing country financial crises, not exchange stability.

---

11. IMF Website, <www.imf.org/external/about.htm>, 10 September 2007.

The Way Forward

As we saw, the debt crisis that engulfed Africa and Latin America in late 1982 gave the Fund a new lease of life – for the crisis allowed the Fund to reinvent itself as the manager of developing country crises. The IMF took on the critical role in the management of the debt crisis of directing the debtor nations' economic policies throughout the 1980s. Debtors needed new money, to at least service interest. Creditors, understandably, wanted some assurance that the debtor's economic policies that had contributed to the crisis had been changed. The commercial banks had firm views on the need for economic austerity by countries whose debt they were rescheduling. Yet considerations of national sovereignty made direct commercial bank involvement in the setting of local economic policies a political impossibility. The IMF was ideally placed, as an apparently independent international financial institution to determine and monitor the economic policies, going forward, of the debtor nations.

The IMF conditioned its loans upon domestic economic policy reform. The foreign commercial banks, in turn, conditioned their loans upon debtor nations securing the approval of the IMF for their policy packages. Thus was borne cross-conditionality – the practice by which foreign commercial banks would only extend new loans to debtor nations upon the new policies of those nations receiving the Fund's stamp of approval. This practice 'strengthened creditor solidarity and created close ties between the IMF and the commercial banks'.[12]

As early as 1983 the banks were describing the IMF's role in these terms:

> [A] fruitful co-operation is emerging between the commercial banks and the IMF ... without IMF persuasion of the borrowing countries to undertake needed adjustment and in the absence of Fund monitoring of the progress, the banks would be unwilling to advance sufficient additional credit.[13]

The cooperation of debtors with the IMF was indeed fruitful, for the banks. Adherence to IMF austerity programs permitted continued servicing of the debt so that by the end of the decade, the banks were in a much stronger state than in 1983 and the debtor nations in a much worse state.

It was, however, simply untrue to state that without IMF oversight of debtor economies the banks would not have advanced new money. This utterly overstated the strength of the banks' position. In 1983 the major banks would have advanced sufficient additional credit, irrespective of IMF involvement, as the consequence of not doing so was their own insolvency.[14] The debtors simply could not, unaided, service their debts. The banks had insufficient capital to withstand the losses if

---

12. MacMillan, 'The Next Sovereign Debt Crisis', 320. See also Green, *Silent Revolution – The Rise of Market Economics in Latin America*, pp. 36–37.
13. Statement by Rimmer de Vries, Senior Vice President, Morgan Guaranty Trust Company, before the Subcommittee on International Economic Policy of the Senate Foreign Relations Committee, Washington, DC, 19 January 1983 (reprinted in *World Financial Markets*, February 1983, 9).
14. Between 1982 and year-end 1988 exposure of the nine largest US commercial banks to Latin America decreased from 176.5% of their capital to 83.6%: Masuda, 'Mexico's Debt Reduction Agreement and the New Debt Strategy', 36–37.

the loans were not serviced. Advancing additional credit was simply a survival strategy for the major banks but, of course, their rhetoric did not disclose this fact.

The focus of the IMF reform programs was to permit the debtors to generate sufficient foreign exchange resources to stay current on their debts.[15] The policies imposed to achieve that goal typically included:[16]

- reductions in the budget deficit to limit inflation, and the need for foreign borrowing;
- limits on domestic credit expansion to control inflation;
- exchange rate devaluations to discourage imports and encourage exports; and
- generally a much reduced role for government and a much increased role for markets.

Other policies imposed on debtors, at times, included:

(i) higher income and sales taxes;
(ii) higher charges for state-produced goods and services such as electricity and water;
(iii) privatization of state-owned companies;
(iv) deregulation of the labour market; and
(v) reform of tariffs and import quota regimes.[17]

Another explicit aim, and effect, of the IMF's policies was to reduce protectionism in the Latin American countries. The Washington consensus is that economic growth is promoted through unilateral tariff cuts and reductions in import restrictions. Once again, this policy flies in the face of the experience of OECD countries. Britain in the nineteenth century, and the United States in the twentieth century, promoted free-trade 'because they were the most efficient producers of the highest value-added goods. They did not become so through free trade; they protected themselves for decades in order to achieve that end'.[18] John Kenneth Galbraith wrote of this nineteenth century protectionism in these terms:

> For Britain, the industrially most advanced of countries, free trade was of obvious advantage, and like laissez-faire, it acquired a strong theological aura. In Germany and the United States, on the other hand, economic interest was better served by tariffs. Accordingly, the most respected economists in

---

15. Askari, *Third World Debt and Financial Innovation – The Experiences of Chile and Mexico*, p. 21; Hannan and Hudgins, 'A U.S. Strategy for Latin America's Debts', 4.
16. Askari, *Third World Debt and Financial Innovation – The Experiences of Chile and Mexico*, p. 22; and Suratgar, 'The International Financial System and the Management of the International Debt Crisis', in *International Borrowing – Negotiating and Structuring International Debt transactions*, Bradlow (ed.) (International Law Institute, 1986), p. 494.
17. Green, *Silent Revolution – The Rise of Market Economics in Latin America*, pp. 45–46; and Hannan and Hudgins, 'A U.S. Strategy for Latin America's Debts', 4–5.
18. Castenada, *Utopia Unarmed*, (New York: Alfred A Knopf, 1993) at 464.

those countries... spoke vigorously for protection for their national 'infant industries'... from the products of the British colossus.[19]

Free trade and laissez-faire economics do indeed attract a theological aura; as do the economic theories of the IMF.[20] Ultimately, like all matters religious, one embraces the theology of the IMF by a leap of faith, not logical reasoning. The consequences of this theology since 1982 has literally been a matter of life, or more accurately, death for millions of people.

The IMF policy prescriptions for Africa and Latin America meant that the 1980s were a decade in which net capital flows from these nations were north-bound, a decade in which infrastructure crumbled, a decade, in Sub-Saharan Africa, in which life expectancy at the decade's end was shorter than at the beginning.[21] This entire process, and the policies it imposed on the debtor nations, became known as 'structural adjustment', a 'stunningly bland name'[22] for policies with a stunningly high human cost.[23]

In the early years of the debt crisis the Fund severely underestimated its magnitude[24] and the Fund's policies did little to alleviate the crisis. The debt crisis was eventually relieved for the banks by the Brady Restructurings of the early 1990s. The Brady process did less for the debtor nations than for the banks but brought some modest relief and encouraged genuinely new capital inflows into the region. Of particular importance in terms of the contribution of the IMF, is that the Brady Plan was devised initially in Sao Paulo and Mexico City and given the imprimatur and support of the US Treasury. The fingerprints of the IMF were nowhere to be found on the only creative measure brought to bear on the worst international economic crisis since World War II.

We have considered the East Asian crisis of late 1997. Asia's was a fundamentally different crisis from the debt crisis of 1982 in that the great majority of the troublesome indebtedness was of the private, not the public or quasi-public sector, and it was not a crisis caused by over-consumption. The Latin American nations had been borrowing, in part, to fund general government budgets. The East Asian governments had not been similarly seduced. Their fiscal policies were prudent. Furthermore, Asia's crisis occurred within 'a benign international environment with low interest rates and solid growth in output and exports'.[25] Asia's crisis was primarily a crisis of inadequate local prudential regulation and inadequate confidence in the region by global capital. It was a contractionary crisis – the

---

19. Galbraith, *The Culture of Contentment*, p. 46.
20. S. George, *A Fate Worse then Debt* (London, Penguin Books, 1987).
21. E.R. Bos (ed.), *Disease and Mortality in Sub-Saharan Africa* (Herndon, The World Bank, 2006), p. 12.
22. Green, *Silent Revolution – The Rise of Market Economics in Latin America*, p. 11.
23. See Bello, *Dark Victory: The United States, Structural Adjustment and Global Poverty*.
24. S. Edwards, 'The International Monetary Fund and the Developing Countries', (Working Paper No. 2909, NBER, March 1989).
25. The World Bank, *Global Development Finance 1998*, Vol 1 (Washington, DC, World Bank, 1998), pp. 4, 30.

exodus of global capital and loss of confidence in the region meant a steep decline in economic activity.

Notwithstanding all of these differences, the IMF ventured into Asia dispensing the policy prescriptions it believed had worked in Latin America in the 1980s and Mexico in 1995 – prescriptions of budgetary tightening and austerity. Austerity is always bad policy for a contractionary crisis. It is utterly ineffective in encouraging contracting economies to expand. At the time the Nobel laureate, Joseph Stiglitz, was the Chief Economist of the World Bank and he spoke out repeatedly to highlight the fundamental error in the Fund's response to the Asian crisis.[26] The vast gulf separating Stiglitz's views from those of the IMF can be seen in two quotations. Stiglitz said, economic pain 'should contribute to strengthening the economy, not exacerbating economic downturns.' Michael Mussa, the IMF's economic counsellor, responded that, 'Those who argue that monetary policy should have been eased rather than tightened in those economies are smoking something that is not entirely legal.'[27]

Joe Stiglitz was proven right by later events, but when it mattered the most, the IMF wouldn't listen to him.

The Reserve Bank of Australia approached the US Treasury to deliver essentially the same message as Stiglitz: the fiscal policies of the Asian economies had been in the main conservative and prudent, this was a contractionary crisis, a crisis of confidence, and expansion was needed to stimulate these economies, not the higher interest rates and budget tightening being prescribed by the Fund. The US Treasury took the message on board and managed to persuade the Fund, and so, about 15 months after the onset of the crisis, the IMF began to acquiesce to requests by national governments for more expansionary policy settings.

While the Fund eventually came around, the crisis was deepened by its initial misdiagnosis and considerable, otherwise avoidable, human suffering was the result. Furthermore, the Fund only altered its views to the extent of easing the austerity it had imposed. In the meantime, Malaysia had adopted more successful strategies that remain, to this day, outside the Fund's kitbag of policy options.

Malaysia refused IMF funding and advice and chose to chart its own way out of the Asian crisis. The policies Malaysia eventually settled upon were in sharp contrast to the Fund's. Malaysia imposed capital outflow controls to keep foreign capital within the country, and pegged the ringgit to the US dollar. With these policies in place, Malaysia was able to ease monetary policy and pursue expansionary fiscal policies, without being hampered by concerns about precipitate capital outflows. Suddenly Malaysia had created as close to a controlled laboratory experiment as one ever gets in economics. Thailand and Korea were seeking to exit the Asian Crisis using the Fund's policies, while Malaysia was

---

26. P. Passell, 'Critics: The IMF is misguided. Skeptics: Too much rot in Asia', *The New York Times*, 15 January 1998, D2; 'World Bank's Stiglitz criticises IMF on S.Korea', *Reuters News*, 17 March 1998.
27. E. Lachica, 'IMF-World Bank: Rethinking the Global Financial System – Oh, Brother: World Bank, IMF Jockey for Position' *The Asian Wall Street Journal*, 5 October 1998, 13.

The Way Forward 163

charting an utterly different course. (I leave Indonesia out of the analysis as its high debt levels means the nature of its problems were quite different and proved to be of longer duration).

All three economies recovered from the crisis, but Malaysia's recovery was more rapid, and its poor were harmed far less by its recovery policies than were the poor in countries following the IMF approach.[28] In the words of Kaplan and Rodrik, 'compared to IMF programs, we find that the Malaysian policies provided faster economic recovery . . . smaller declines in employment and real wages, and more rapid turn around in the stock market.'[29]

Yet the Fund's mistakes in East Asia, so clearly highlighted by Malaysia's taking the road less travelled, paled in comparison to its egregious errors in Argentina, which had been toasted as 'the best case of responsible leadership in the developing world'.[30] Argentina's severe recession which commenced at the end of 1998 was the product of policies which the IMF had developed or agreed with. As we have seen the crisis deepened until late 2001 when the IMF refused to extend further credit to the nation, believing its economic programs to be unsustainable, and as commercial lenders followed this lead, Argentina was denied access to capital and defaulted on its external debt of some USD 132 billion.

In the year from March 2001 to March 2002, total domestic Argentine financial assets shrunk from USD 126.8 billion to USD 41.5 billion. Between 1999 and early 2004, Argentina's poverty rate doubled from 27% to 54.7%; its per capita GDP halved from USD 7,800 to USD 3,800; and its external debt increased from 47.4% of GDP to 140% of GDP.[31] These figures translate into appalling human suffering – all as a result of policies with which the Fund agreed.

The IMF emerged from Argentina's collapse with its credibility in tatters. Never before had a country that had so faithfully followed the Fund's policies collapsed so severely, never before had the Fund's image been so badly damaged by a sovereign default.

The Fund has few friends. Criticism of the Fund's policy prescriptions have been sustained, fierce and unrelenting from the left ever since the early-to-mid 1980s, principally for the impact of its policies on the poor and because the Fund is seen, by the left, to be the handmaiden of the G-7 nations implementing their policies and those of their banking sectors. More recently, for perhaps the past 15 years, commentators from the right have joined battle criticizing the Fund for having lost its mission, purpose and relevance. Commentators from both sides of

---

28. R.P. Buckley and S. Fitzgerald, 'An Assessment of Malaysia's Response to the IMF during the Asian Economic Crisis' (2004) *Singapore Journal of Legal Studies*, 96.
29. E. Kaplan and D. Rodrik, 'Did the Malaysian Capital Controls Work?' (Working Papers, NBER, 2003), <papers.nber.org/papers/W8142>, 4 December 2007.
30. 'Chaos in Argentina', *The Nation*, 21 January 2002, 3; 'Argentina: A Poster Child for the Failure of Liberalized Policies? Interview with Lance Taylor', 28.
31. Hornbeck, *Argentina's Sovereign Debt Restructuring*.

politics and from developed and developing nations have argued for the Fund's fundamental reconceptualization or closure.[32]

In the late 1990s the Fund sought to respond to its critics. In 1999 it replaced the economic policies which it had been imposing upon developing nations in crisis, the so-called Structural Adjustment Policies (SAPs), with Poverty Reduction Strategy Papers. PRSPs were to be a new tool for poverty reduction, debt relief, and access to funding from donors.

According to the IMF, 'PRSPs are prepared by the member countries through a participatory process involving domestic stakeholders as well as external development partners, including the World Bank and the International Monetary Fund.'[33] PRSPs outline the economic, social, and structural programs to be used to reduce poverty. Instead of focusing on macroeconomic stability and growth like SAPs, PRSPs, as their name suggests, were to put poverty reduction at the core of the nation's economic policies.

Once approved, the PRSP forms the basis for future funding. Potential recipients of debt relief under the Heavily Indebted Poor Country (HIPC) Initiative and of loans under the IMF's Poverty Reduction and Growth Facility (PRGF) are required to produce a PRSP to be eligible.[34]

However, the change from SAPs to PRSPs was more an effort to rescue the Fund from its crisis of legitimacy than to respond to the needs of the poor in poor countries. If programs were truly national creatures, tailored to each individual nations' needs, one would expect some PRSPs to exhibit strategies that differ from the standard policy prescriptions of the past. But this is not the case – the PRSPs of different countries are strikingly similar. The macroeconomic policies under PRSPs have essentially been a continuation of the policies under SAPs and PRSPs don't contemplate alternative approaches to poverty reduction.[35]

The entire shift from Structural Adjustment to Poverty Reduction Strategy Papers was designed to blunt the criticisms but it failed because it was mere window dressing, the operative ideology of the Fund, and hence its policy prescriptions, had not changed.[36]

---

32. D. Lachman, A. Meltzer and C. Calomiris, 'Is the IMF Obsolete?', American Enterprise Institute for Public Policy Research, <www.aei.org/publications/filter.,pubID.26202/pub_detail.asp>, 18 September 2007. See also C.W. Calomiris, 'How to invent a new IMF', Hoover Institution Public Policy Inquiry, <www.imfsite.org/reform/calomiris2.html>, 18 September 2007.
33. International Monetary Fund, *Poverty Reduction Strategy Papers (PRSP)* <www.imf.org/external/np/prsp/prsp.asp>, 6 August 2007.
34. F. Steward and M. Wang, 'Do PRSPs empower poor countries and disempower the World Bank, or is it the other way round?' (Working Paper No. 108, QEH, October 2003), p. 5.
35. G. Dor, 'G8, Tony Blair's Commission for Africa and Debt' *Global Policy Forum*, 7 July 2005, 1; R. Gottschalk, 'The Macroeconomic Policy Content of the PRSPs: How Much Pro-Growth, How much Pro-Poor?' The Institute of Development Studies, University of Sussex (February 2004), p. 3; and Steward and Wang, 'Do PRSPs empower poor countries and disempower the World Bank, or is it the other way round?', p. 19.
36. R.P. Buckley, 'IMF Policies and Health in Sub-Saharan Africa', forthcoming, *Global Health Governance: Crisis and Challenges*, Kay and Williams (eds).

The Way Forward

In short, there has been a marked gap between Fund rhetoric and policies, as have been noted by the Independent Evaluation Office of the IMF.[37]

10.2.1 THE IMF AND POVERTY IN AFRICA

In 2000, Michel Camdessus, the Fund's Managing Director said:

> the greatest concern of our time is poverty... it is the ultimate systemic threat facing humanity.... If the poor are left hopeless, poverty will undermine the fabric of our societies through confrontation, violence, and civil disorder. We cannot afford to ignore poverty, wherever it exists, whether in the advanced countries, emerging economies, or the least developed nations. But it is in the poorest countries that extreme poverty can no longer be tolerated; it is our duty to work together to relieve suffering.[38]

The IMF has its own internal evaluation division, the Independent Evaluation Office, and in March, 2007, the IEO released an Evaluation Report, 'The IMF and Aid to Sub-Saharan Africa'.[39]

The Report concluded that there were differences of views among the Executive Board of the Fund about the IMF's role and policies in poor countries, and that

> lacking clarity on what they should do on the mobilization of aid,... and the application of poverty and social impact analysis, IMF staff tended to focus on macroeconomic stability, in line with the institution's core mandate and their deeply ingrained professional culture.[40]

In other words, some seven years after the Managing Director's speech cited above, seven years after the replacement of Structural Adjustment Programs with ***Poverty Reduction** Strategy Papers*, seven years after the establishment of the ***Poverty Reduction** and Growth Facility*, IMF staff were unclear on the priority to be give to poverty reduction and how to achieve it, and so sought to attain that which they knew how to attain, macroeconomic stability. In the first year or two of the introduction of new priorities and programs this would be understandable though regrettable. After seven years this is ridiculous. For an institution that is the subject of unremitting criticism for the impact of its programs and policies on poverty, and which has been maintaining steadfastly in all its press releases and public pronouncements since 2000 that poverty reduction is its highest priority, to still be trying to bed down new initiatives and priorities on poverty reduction over seven years after their introduction is utterly

---

37. Independent Evaluation Office of the IMF, 'The IMF and Aid to Sub-Saharan Africa', <www.imf.org/external/np/ieo/2007/ssa/eng/pdf/report.pdf>, 24 September 2007.
38. Camdessus, 'Development and Poverty Reduction: a Multilateral Approach'.
39. Independent Evaluation Office of the IMF, 'The IMF and Aid to Sub-Saharan Africa'.
40. *Ibid.*, vii.

unacceptable. In most corporate or government settings, one would expect such non-performance to result in the sacking of senior staff.

The Report also found that the Fund's policies have accommodated increased aid 'in countries whose recent policies have lead to high stocks of reserves and low inflation', but 'in other countries additional aid was programmed to be saved to increase reserves or to retire domestic debt'.[41] Yet virtually no sub-Saharan African countries have strong foreign exchange reserves and low inflation rates. So extra aid was routinely channelled by the Fund into foreign exchange reserves or into the repayment of debt in most poor African countries. Such an approach has two flaws:

(1) It diverts extra aid away from healthcare, education or other social welfare expenditures; and
(2) It risks being a 'self-fulfilling prophecy' as diverting aid flows into reserves and debt reduction is likely to dissuade donors from giving more aid.[42] Most donors want to give aid to directly assist suffering people, not to improve the macroeconomic profile of the nation in which they live.

This is a perfect illustration of the damage that the Fund's obsession with the macro-economic profile of a country can do.

10.2.2   THE FUND'S INABILITY TO REINVENT ITSELF

When Malaysia was charting its own course out of the Asian crisis and imposing capital outflow controls, the Executive Director of the Fund, Michel Camdessus was Malaysia's sternest critic. In speech after speech around the world he admonished Malaysia in terms such as:

> investor confidence has been damaged by the capital controls, and some official sources of external finance have dried up. Neither source is likely to recover until the overall stance of policies is modified.[43]

The extraordinary feature of this episode is not that Michel Camdessus was wrong, there has been nothing unusual about that at all in the IMF's performance since 1982. The extraordinary and laudable feature is that as quickly as 12 months after the Fund's Managing Director was delivering withering attacks on Malaysia's use of capital controls, members of the Fund's staff felt able to write a balanced

---

41. *Ibid.*, 32.
42. PRS Watch: A Eurodad newsletter, 16 August 2007.
43. M. Camdessus, 'Economic and Financial Situation in Asia: Latest Developments', paper delivered to the Asia Europe Finance Ministers Meeting, Frankfurt, Germany, <www.imf.org/external/np/speeches/1999/011699.htm>, 4 December 2007.

and generally positive assessment of Malaysia's use of capital controls and to conclude that:

> preliminary evidence suggests that the controls have been effective in realizing their intended objective of reducing the ringgit's internationalization and helping to contain capital outflows.[44]

Furthermore, in the IMF's review of Malaysia's policies between 1997 and 2000 other staff members wrote that:

> Market assessment turned more positive, however, as it became clear that Malaysia's macroeconomic policies were not out of line, that the undervalued pegged exchange rate was contributing to the rapid recovery of exports and output, and that financial sector reforms were being vigorously pursued.[45]

And in yet another publication, the staff noted that the 'successful experience of the 1998 controls so far is largely due to the appropriate macroeconomic policy mix that prevailed at that time'[46] and that the controls were effective because they 'were wide ranging, effectively implemented, and generally supported by the business community'.[47]

So the IMF, through the work of its research department, has a proven capacity to be self-critical, a fundamental requirement for an organization's ability to learn from experience, change and adapt. The Fund enhanced this capacity in 2001 by establishing the Independent Evaluation Office, the report of which into Aid in Africa has already been considered. The IEO states that it is 'fully independent from the Management of the IMF and operates at arm's length from the Board of Executive Directors, representing the 185 member countries of the IMF.'[48]

In its own words:

The IEO's overarching mission is to improve the IMF's effectiveness by:

- Enhancing the learning culture of the IMF and enabling it to better absorb lessons for improvements in its future work.
- Helping build the IMF's external credibility by undertaking objective evaluations in a transparent manner.
- Providing independent feedback to the Executive Board in its governance and oversight responsibilities over the IMF.
- Promoting greater understanding of the work of the IMF.[49]

---

44. Ariyoshi, Habermeier, et al, 'Country Experiences with the Use and Liberalization of Capital Controls', pp. 104–105.
45. International Monetary Fund, 'Malaysia: From Crisis to Recovery', 3 <www.imf.org/external/pubs/nft/op/207/index.htm>, 14 September 2007.
46. *Ibid.*, 6.
47. International Monetary Fund, 'Malaysia: Selected Issues' (1999), 18.
48. See homepage of the Independent Evaluation Office at <www.ieo-imf.org/about/>, 11 September 2007.
49. See IEO Mission and Values page available at <www.ieo-imf.org/about/mission.html>, 11 September 2007.

Since its inception, the IEO has issued 25 Evaluation Reports.[50] Each has been an extensive, detailed, reasoned document, some more forthright and direct than others, but most tending to be relatively clear and critical in their findings.

For example, the Summary of Major Findings, Lessons and Recommendations of the Report on the Evaluation of Poverty Reduction Strategy Papers and the Poverty Reduction Growth Facility, 6 July 2004,[51] states, inter alia, that:

- [M]ost PRSPs fall short of providing a strategic road map for policymaking, especially in the area of macroeconomic and related structural policies.
- On balance, joint staff assessments do not perform adequately the many tasks expected of them.
- Success in embedding the PGRF in the overall strategy for growth and poverty reduction has been limited in most cases – partly reflecting shortcomings in the strategies themselves.[52]

These are not the words of bureaucrats seeking to be coy or to obfuscate. These are honest assessments of the Fund's policies and achievements. So why is there so little evidence that these honest and frank assessments have had any real impact on altering the policies and culture of the Fund?

Indeed, why, and how, could the Fund staff have been unsure throughout the first six years of the new millennium of the priority to be afforded to poverty reduction in Africa and therefore have reverted to structural adjustment because it is what they knew best? Why is an organization unable to learn and change and adapt when its staff have sufficient intellectual freedom to adopt positions in direct opposition to those recently taken by their Managing Director and its internal evaluation office regularly critiques its performance in honest, unflattering terms?

For Joseph Stiglitz, the answer has four parts. In his view, the Fund's economists:

(i) 'frequently lack extensive experience in the country [and] are more likely to have firsthand knowledge of its five-star hotels than of the villages that dot its countryside';[53]
(ii) are not nearly as good or bright as they think they are;
(iii) tend to use poor economics; and
(iv) 'close themselves off from outside criticism and advice.'

---

50. See Independent Evaluation Office of the IMF, IEO Publications, <www.imf.org/external/np/ieo/pap.asp#1>, 14 September 2007.
51. Available at <www.ieo-imf.org/eval/complete/eval_07062004.html>, 24 September 2007.
52. Available at <www.ieo-imf.org/eval/complete/pdf/07062004/summary.pdf>, 24 September 2007.
53. J. Stiglitz, 'The Insider – What I learned at the world economic crisis' (2000) *The New Republic*, April 17 and 24, 57.

The Way Forward

In his words, the Fund's economists:

> work hard, poring over numbers deep into the night. But their task is impossible. In a period of days or...weeks they are charged with developing a coherent program sensitive to the needs of the country....
>
> IMF experts believe they are brighter, more educated, and less politically motivated than the economists in the countries they visit. In fact, the economic leaders from those countries are pretty good – in many cases brighter or better-educated than the IMF staff, which frequently consists of third-rank students from first-rate universities. (Trust me: I've taught at Oxford, MIT, Stanford, Yale and Princeton and the IMF almost never succeeded in recruiting any of the best students.)[54]

Notwithstanding the respect I have for Joe Stiglitz and his intimate first-hand knowledge of the World Bank as its former Chief Economist, I wonder whether he quite has this right. One doesn't need to be among the brightest graduates of a first-rate university to know that austerity will make a contractionary crisis worse or that Argentina cannot peg its currency to that of the US dollar indefinitely without its currency risking becoming severely overvalued. A competent students of Economics 101 knows these things.

Stiglitz's explanations, written in anger at the human suffering he'd seen the IMF's policies cause, are to my mind a little too pat. Of course I agree with him that the Fund's fly in-fly out model tends to deny their experts the local knowledge they need to craft appropriate policies, and tends to reinforce the staff's tendency to make unwarranted assumptions about the strength or even existence of local institutions such as the rule of law. And I also agree that the Fund tends to close itself off from outside criticism and advice and that 'in government,...openness is most essential in those realms where expertise seems to matter most'.[55]

But on the other issues, I don't think it is just that the Fund's experts are not bright enough and use out-dated and poor economic models. I think the core problem is that the IMF has become a fundamentalist organization. It subscribes utterly to market fundamentalism – the belief that markets will always best and most efficiently allocate resources and provide the needed services. This is why the IMF can divert desperately needed donations intended for schools and health clinics in Africa into the repayment of external debt or into bolstering foreign exchange reserves – because the Fund staffers really believe that if they get the macroeconomic profile right, the market mechanism will ride to the rescue and fix the country's problems. This is why the IMF can require poor African countries to privatize their healthcare systems and stop subsidizing much needed drugs for their people – because staff believe that if you just let the market handle healthcare, it will do the job right. This belief trumps the consistent experience in Africa that privatization of healthcare results in good hospitals for the small, affluent middle

---

54. *Ibid.*
55. *Ibid.*, 60.

classes in the cities and no care in rural areas whatsoever. This belief trumps what Fund staffers would see if they looked outside their windows in Washington DC at America's own, essentially privatized, healthcare system that so badly serves America's poor. For fundamentalist beliefs trump all objections based on reality. Once into the realm of fundamentalist belief, evidence becomes marginalized.

Fund officers who subscribe to this world view get promoted, those who do not, languish in minor roles. The leadership of the Fund hires in its own image and promotes in its own image, as do most organizations. In this case, however, the core belief of the organization is utterly unconnected to reality. At the end of Chapter 5, I recommended three major reforms the Fund could make to its policies and internal culture to make itself more effective and relevant.

If the Fund is to continue, those three major reforms need to be made. However, the Fund's original function disappeared in the 1970s. Many of its current technical data-gathering and analysing roles are also performed by the World Bank, and the Fund's efforts largely duplicate those of the Bank. The central current role of the Fund is as the economic crisis manager for poor nations. This it performs poorly, I would argue, disastrously. In light of the Fund's proven inability to reinvent itself, and its embedded culture of market fundamentalism, the real answer is to close the organization. There is no reason, given the history of the Fund's performance to believe it can fundamentally reform itself. The IMF is an idea whose time has come, and gone.

List of References

'1997 Debt Trading Volume Survey'. Emerging Markets Traders Association, 25 February 1998.
Adams, P. 'Iraq's Odious Debts' (Cato Institute Policy Analysis No. 526, 2004).
Amann, E. & W. Baer. 'Anchors Away: The Costs and Benefits of Brazil's Devaluation'. Working Paper. University of Illinois at Urbana-Champaign College of Business, 2002. <www.business.uiuc.edu/Working_Papers/papers/02-0122.pdf>.
Anayiotos, G. & J. de Piniés. 'The Secondary Market and the International Debt Problem'. *World Development* 18 (1990).
Argy, V. *The Postwar International Money Crisis: An Analysis*. London: George Allen & Unwin, 1981.
Ariyoshi, Habermeier, et al. 'Country Experiences with the Use and Liberalization of Capital Controls'. IMF Paper. January 2000. <www.imf.org/external/pubs/ft/capcon/index.htm>, 29 February 2000.
Armijo, L.E. 'The Political Geography of World Financial Reform: Who Wants What and Why?' *Global Governance* 7, no. 4 (2001).
Arner, D.W. *Financial Stability, Economic Growth, and the Role of Law*. Cambridge: Cambridge University Press, 2007.
Aronson, J.D. 'International Lending and Debt'. *The Washington Quarterly* 6, no. 4 (1983).
'Asia's Financial Markets: Capitalising on Reform'. Canberra: Dept of Foreign Affairs and Trade, East Asia Analytical Unit, 1999.
Askari, H. *Third World Debt and Financial Innovation: The Experiences of Chile and Mexico*. Paris: Development Centre of the OECD, 1991.
Astor, H. & C. Chinkin. *Dispute Resolution in Australia*, 2nd edn. Butterworths, 2002.
Auerback, R.M. 'Sovereign Debt: Default and Restructuring of Debts Owed to Private Creditor' *Journal of International Banking Law and Regulation* 18 (2003).

Ayuso, J. & R. Blanco. 'Has Financial Market Increased during the 1990s?' Paper presented at the International Financial Markets and the Implications for Monetary and Financial Stability conference of the Bank for International Settlements. Basel, 25–26 October 1999.

Bagehot, W. *Lombard Street: A Description of the Money Market.* London: H.S. King & Co, 1873.

Bailey, N. Comments in *Comity, Act of State, and the International Debt Crisis: Is There an Emerging Legal Equivalent of Bankruptcy Protection for Nations.* Proceedings, Seventy-Ninth Annual Meeting, The American Society of International Law.

Bergsman, J. & W. Edisis. 'Debt-Equity Swaps and Foreign Direct Investment in Latin America'. Discussion Paper No. 2. International Financial Corporation, 1989.

Block, F. 'Controlling Global Finance'. *World Policy Journal* (1996).

Bos, E.R. (ed.). *Disease and Mortality in Sub-Saharan Africa.* Herndon: The World Bank, 2006.

Brady, N. 'Remarks to a Third World Debt Conference'. Sponsored by the Brookings Institute and the Bretton Woods Committee, 10 March 1989. Reprinted in *Department of State Bulletin*, May 1989.

Braithwaite, J. & P. Drahos P. *Global Business Regulation.* Cambridge: Cambridge University Press, 2000.

Brooks, J.N. 'Participation and Syndicated Loans: Intercreditor Fiduciary Duties for Lead and Agent Banks under US Law'. *Butterworths Journal of International Banking and Financial Law* (June 1995).

Brooks World Poverty Institute, University of Manchester. 'Ending World Poverty'. <povertyblog.wordpress.com/implementing-the-mdgs-and-other-statistics/>, 12 December 2007.

Brown, H. & A. Marriott. *ADR Principles and Practice*, 2nd edn. Sweet & Maxwell, 1999.

Buchheit, L.C. 'Tightening Controls on International Lending by US Banks'. *International Financial Law Review* (May 1983).

Buchheit, L.C. 'The Background to Brady's Initiative'. *International Financial Law Review* (April 1990).

Buchheit, L.C. 'Whatever Became of Old New Money?' *International Financial Law Review* (December 1990).

Buchheit, L.C. 'Moral Hazards and Other Delights'. *International Financial Law Review* (April 1991).

Buchheit, L.C. & G.M. Gulati. 'Sovereign Bonds and the Collective Will'. *Emory Law Journal* 51 (2002).

Buckley, R.P. 'The 1993 Revision of the Uniform Customs and Practice for Documentary Credits'. *George Washington Journal of International Law and Economics* 28 (1995).

Buckley, R.P. 'Debt Exchanges Revisited: Lessons from Latin America for Eastern Europe'. *Northwestern Journal of International Law and Business* 18 (1998).

Buckley, R.P. 'The Law of Emerging Markets Loan Sales'. *Journal of International Banking Law* 14 (1999).
Buckley, R.P. 'The Practice of Emerging Markets Loan Sales'. *Journal of International Banking Law* 14 (1999).
Buckley, R.P. *Emerging Markets Debt: An Analysis of the Secondary Market.* London: Kluwer Law International, 1999.
Buckley, R.P. 'An Oft-Ignored Perspective on the Asian Economic Crisis: The Role of Creditors and Investors'. *Banking and Finance Law Review* 15 (2000).
Buckley, R.P. 'A Tale of Two Crises: The Search for the Enduring Lessons of International Financial Reform'. *UCLA Journal of International Law and Foreign Affairs* 6 (2001).
Buckley, R.P. 'The Essential Flaw in the Globalisation of Capital Markets: Its Impact on Human Rights'. *California Western International Law Journal* 32 (2001).
Buckley, R.P. 'International Capital Flows, Developing Countries and Economic Sovereignty'. In *Yearbook of International Economic and Financial Law 1999.* London: Kluwer Law International, 2001.
Buckley, R.P. 'The Fatal Flaw in International Finance: The Rich Borrow and the Poor Repay.' *World Policy Journal* XIX, no. 4 (Winter 2002/2003).
Buckley, R.P. 'Iraqi Sovereign Debt and Its Curious Global Implications'. In *Beyond the Iraq War: The Promises, Perils and Pitfalls of External Interventionism*, edited by Heazle & Islam. London: Edward Elgar, 2006.
Buckley, R.P. 'The Facilitation of the Brady Plan: Emerging Markets Debt Trading from 1989 to 1993'. *Fordham International Law Journal* 21.
Buckley, R.P. 'A Force for Globalisation: Emerging Markets Debt Trading from 1994 to 1999'. *Fordham International Law Journal* 30, no. 2 (2007).
Buckley, R.P. 'IMF Policies and Health in Sub-Saharan Africa'. In *Global Health Governance: Crisis and Challenges*, edited by Kay & Williams, forthcoming.
Buckley, R.P. & P. Dirou. 'How to Strengthen the International Financial System by Improving Sovereign Balance Sheet Structures'. *Annals of Economics and Finance* 2 (2006).
Buckley, R.P. & S. Fitzgerald. 'An Assessment of Malaysia's Response to the IMF during the Asian Economic Crisis'. *Singapore Journal of Legal Studies* (2004).
Buira, A. *An Alternative Approach to Financial Crises.* Princeton: Princeton University, 1999.
Bustelo, P., C. Garcia & I. Olivie. 'Global and Domestic Factors of Financial Crisis in Emerging Economies: Lessons from the East Asian Episodes'. Working Paper No. 16, Instituto Complutense De Estudios Internationales, November 1999.

Calderon, C. & R. McCarthy. 'New Money for Old'. *LatinFinance* 20 (1990).
Calomiris, C.W. 'The IMF's Imprudent Role as Lender of Last Resort'. *Cato Journal* 17 (1998).

Calomiris, C.W. 'How to Invent a New IMF'. Hoover Institution Public Policy Inquiry. <www.imfsite.org/reform/calomiris2.html>, 18 September 2007.

Calomiris, C.W. & A.H. Meltzer. 'Fixing the IMF'. *The National Interest* 56 (1999).

Calomiris, C.W. & A. Powell. *Can Emerging Market Bank Regulators Establish Credible Discipline? The Case of Argentina, 1992–1999*. Working Paper No. 7715. NBER, 2000. <www.nber.org/papers/w7715>.

Calverley, J. & I. Iversen. 'Banks and the Brady Initiative'. In *Third World Debt: Managing the Consequences* edited by Griffith-Jones. London: *IFR* Publishing Ltd, 1989.

Camdessus, M. 'Development and Poverty Reduction: A Multilateral Approach'. Address by the Managing Director of the IMF at the Tenth United Nations Conference on Trade and Development. Bangkok, Thailand, 13 February 2000.

Camdessus, M. 'Economic and Financial Situation in Asia: Latest Developments'. Paper delivered to the Asia Europe Finance Ministers Meeting. Frankfurt, Germany. <www.imf.org/external/np/speeches/1999/011699.htm>, 4 December 2007.

Capie, F. 'Can There Be an International Lender of Last Resort?' *International Finance* (1998).

Caramazza, F. & J. Aziz. 'Fixed or Flexible? Getting the Exchange Rate Right in the 1990s'. <www.imf.org/external/pubs/ft/issues13/Issue13.pdf>, 17 March 2000.

Casey, M. 'The Economy: IMF Chief Presses Argentina on Spending, Debt'. *The Asian Wall Street Journal*, 2 September 2004.

Castenada. *Utopia Unarmed*. New York: Alfred A. Knopf, 1993.

'Changing Geopolitics of Energy – Part IV: Regional Developments in the Gulf, and Energy Issues Affecting Iran, Iraq, and Libya'. Washington: Center for Strategic and International Studies (CSIS), 1998.

Chow, H. 'Crawling from the Wreckage'. *Emerging Markets Investor* 4 (July/August 1997).

Clark, J. 'Debt Reduction and Market Reentry under the Brady Plan'. *FRBNY Quarterly Review* 18, no. 4 (Winter 1993–1994).

Comley, B. & D. Turvey. 'Debt Management in a Low Debt Environment: The Australian Government's Debt Management Framework'. Working Paper 2005-02. Commonwealth of Australia Treasury Department, 2005.

Conover, C.T., Comptroller of the Currency. Evidence to Subcommittee on Financial Institutions Supervision. Regulation and Insurance of the House Committee on Banking, Finance and Urban Affairs, Washington, DC, 21 April 1983.

Corden, M. *The Asian Crisis: Is There a Way Out?* Singapore: Institute of Southeast Asian Studies, 1999.

Corsetti. G., P. Pesenti & N. Roubini. *What Caused the Asian Currency and Financial Crisis? Part II: The Policy Debate*. Working Paper No. W6834. NBER. Available at <ssrn.com/abstract=227609>.

List of References

Crutsinger, M. 'IMF Grants Argentina Debt Extension'. New York: *Associated Press Online*, 9 May 2002.

Cuddington, J. 'Capital Flight, Estimates, Issues and Explanations'. Princeton Essays in International Finance No. 58.

Dawson, F.G. *The First Latin American Debt Crisis: The City of London and the 1822–1825 Loan Bubble*. New Haven, CT: Yale University Press, 1990.

De Brouwer, G. 'The IMF and East Asia: A Changing Regional Financial Architecture'. In *The IMF and Its Critics*, edited by C. Gilbert & D. Vines. Cambridge: Cambridge University Press, 2003.

de Janvry, A. & E. Sadoulet. 'Growth, Poverty and Inequality in Latin America: A Causal Analysis, 1970–1994'. Inter-American Development Bank Conference on Social Protection and Poverty, February 1999.

de Ruyter van Steveninck, R. 'Import Substitution and the Debt Crisis in Latin America'. *Tinbergen Institute Research Bulletin* 3, no. 2 (1991).

de Vries, R., Senior Vice President, Morgan Guaranty Trust Company. Statement before the Subcommittee on International Economic Policy of the Senate Foreign Relations Committee. Washington, DC, 19 January 1983 (reprinted in *World Financial Markets*, February 1983).

de Vries, R., Chief Economist, Morgan Guaranty Trust Company. 'Economic and Trade Adjustment in the United States and Other Industrial Countries and the LDC Debt Issue: Problems and Prospects'. Statement to the Asahi-Zeit Symposium. Tokyo, 29–30 March 1988.

Debs, R.A., D.L. Roberts & E.M. Remolona. *Finance for Developing Countries: Alternative Sources of Finance – Debt Swaps*. New York and London: Group of Thirty, 1987.

Delamaide, D. *Debt Shock*. London: Weidenfeld & Nicholson, 1984.

Delaume, G.R. 'The Foreign Sovereign Immunities Act and the Public Debt Litigation: Some Fifteen Years Later'. *American Journal of International Law* 88 (1994).

Dellapenna, J.W. *Suing Foreign Governments and Their Corporations*. New York: Transnational Publishers, 1988.

Denny, C. 'IMF Sheds No Tears for Argentina'. *The Guardian*, 29 April 2002.

Denny, C. 'Firefighters Turn on Tap Again'. *The Guardian* (United Kingdom), 12 August 2002.

Dodd, R. 'Sovereign Debt Restructuring'. *The Financier* 14, nos 1–4 (2002). <www.financialpolicy.org/dscsovdebt.pdf>, 6 April 2005.

Dor, G. 'G8, Tony Blair's Commission for Africa and Debt'. *Global Policy Forum*, 7 July 2005.

Dornbusch, R. 'Panel Discussion on Latin American Adjustment: The Record and Next Steps'. In *Latin American Adjustment: How Much Has Happened*, edited by J. Williamson. Washington, DC: Institute for International Economics, 1990.

Dornbusch, R. 'A Bail-out Won't Do the Trick in Korea'. *Business Week*, 8 December 1997.

Dornbusch, R. 'Debt Problems and the World Macroeconomy'. In *Developing Country Debt and the World Economy*.

Drage, J. & C. Hovaguimian. 'Collective Action Clauses: An Analysis of Provisions Included in Recent Sovereign Bond Issues'. <www.bankofengland.co.uk/publications/fsr/2004/fsr17art7.pdf>, 4 December 2007.

Eaton & Gersovitz. 'Debt with Potential Repudiation: Theoretical and Empirical Analysis'. *Review of Economic Studies* 48, no. 2 (1984).

Eavis, P. 'The Crossover Factor'. *Emerging Markets Investor* 4 (1997).

'Economic Outlook, Argentina Quarterly Forecast Report'. London: Business Monitor International, 2002.

Edwards, S. 'The International Monetary Fund and the Developing Countries'. Working Paper No. 2909. NBER, March 1989.

Edwards, S. *Real Exchange Rates, Devaluation and Adjustment*. Cambridge: MIT Press, 1989.

Edwards, S. 'How Effective Are Capital Controls?' Working Paper No. 7413. National Bureau of Economic Research (NBER), November 1999. <www.nber.org/papers/w7413>, 20 March 2000.

Eichengreen, B. *Toward a New Financial Architecture: A Practical Post-Asia Agenda*. Washington, DC: Institute of International Economics, 1999.

Eichengreen, B. 'Bailing in the Private Sector: Burden Sharing in International Financial Crisis' *Fletcher Forum of World Affairs* (1999).

Eichengreen, B. 'Financial Instability'. Paper prepared on behalf of the Copenhagen Consensus, 2004.

Eichengreen, B. 'Capital Controls: Capital Idea or Capital Folly?'. <www.econ.berkeley.edu/~eichengr/policy/capcontrols.pdf>, 4 December 2007.

Eichengreen, B. & R. Hausmann. 'Exchange Rates and Financial Fragility in Federal Reserve Bank of Kansas City'. New Challenges for Monetary Policy, Symposium Proceedings. Jackson Hole, 26–28 August 1999.

Eichengreen, B. & R. Hausmann. *Original Sin: The Road to Redemption*. USA: John F. Kennedy School of Government.

Eichengreen, B., R. Hausmann & U. Panizza. 'Currency Mismatches, Debt Intolerance and Original Sin: Why They Are Not the Same and Why It Matters'. Working Paper 10036. National Bureau of Economic Research, 2003.

Eichengreen, B. & A. Mody. 'Would Collective Action Clauses Raise Borrowing Costs?' Working Paper No. w7458. NBER, January 2000. <papers.nber.org/papers/w7458>, 4 December 2007.

Eichengreen, B. & M. Mussa. 'Capital Account Liberalization: Theoretical and Practical Aspects'. Occassional Paper No. 172. IMF, 1998.

Eichengreen, B. & R. Portes. 'After the Deluge: Default, Negotiation, and Readjustment during the Interwar Years'. In *The International Debt Crisis in Historical Perspective*, edited by B. Eichengreen & P.H. Lindert. Cambridge: MIT Press, 1989.

Endres, A. *Great Architects of International Finance: The Bretton Woods Era*. London: Routledge, 2005.

Espinosa-Vega, M.A., B.D. Smith & C.Y. Yip. 'Barriers to International Capital Flows: Who Should Erect Them and How Big Should They Be?' Working Paper No. 99-6. Federal Reserve Bank of Atlanta, July 1999.

Faini, R. & E. Grilli. 'Who Runs the IFIs?' CEPR Discussion Paper No. 4666. Available from <ssrn.com/abstract=631010>.
Feldstein, M. 'A Self-Help Guide for Emerging Markets'. *Foreign Affairs*, March/April 1999.
Feldstein, M. 'Argentina's Fall'. *Foreign Affairs* 81 (2002).
Ferguson, J. *Venezuela in Focus: A Guide to the People, Politics and Culture*. London: Latin American Bureau, 1994.
Fields, G.S. 'Growth and Income Distribution'. In *Essays on Poverty, Equity and Growth* edited by G. Psacharopolous. Oxford: Pergamon Press, 1991.
Fischer, S. 'On the Need for an International Lender of Last Resort'. <www.imf.org/external/np/speeches/1999/010399.htm>, 4 December 2007.
Fisher & Ury. *Getting to Yes*. Boston: Houghton Mifflin, 1991.
Fraust, L. 'Debt Plan Spurs Interest in Securitizing LDC Loans'. *The American Banker*, 28 March 1989.
'The Future of the International Financial Architecture: A Council on Foreign Relations Task Force'. New York: Council on Foreign Relations, 1999.

Galbraith, J. *The Sunday Times*, 25 October 1987.
Galbraith, J.K. *The Culture of Contentment*. Boston: Houghton Mifflin, 1992.
Garran, R. 'Korea Crisis'. *The Australian*, 19 November 1997.
Gaudin, A. 'Thirteen Days That Shook Argentina – And Now What?' *NACLA Report on the Americas* 35 (2002).
Gengatharen, R. 'Destabilising Financial Flows: Are Capital Controls the Solution?' *LAWASIA Journal* (1999).
George, S. *A Fate Worse then Debt*. London: Penguin Books, 1987.
George, S. 'A Short History of Neo-liberalism: Twenty Years of Elite Economics and Emerging Opportunities for Structural Change'. Paper presented at the Conference on Economic Sovereignty in a Globalizing World. Bangkok, 24–26 March 1999. <www.zmag.org/CrisesCurEvts/Globalism/george.htm>, 4 December 2007.
Giles, C. & F. Tiesenhausen Cave. 'International Economy'. *Financial Times*, 13 June 2005.
Goldman, M.B. 'Confronting Third World Debt: The Baker and Brady Plans'. *Backgrounder* No. 559, 22 January 1987. Washington, DC: The Heritage Foundation, 1987.
Goldstein, M. & P. Turner. *Controlling Currency Mismatches in Emerging Markets*. Washington, DC: Institute for International Economics, 2004.
Golub, S.S. 'The Political Economy of the Latin American Debt Crisis'. *Latin American Research Review* 26, no. 1 (1991).
Goni, U. 'Argentina Collapses into Chaos'. *The Guardian* (United Kingdom), 21 December 2001.

Goode, R.M. *Principles of Corporate Insolvency Law*. London: Sweet & Maxwell, 1997.

Gottschalk, R. 'The Macroeconomic Policy Content of the PRSPs: How Much Pro-Growth, How Much Pro-Poor? The Institute of Development Studies, University of Sussex, February 2004.

Green, D. 'Hidden Fist Hits the Buffers'. *New Internationalist*, October 1995.

Green, D. *Silent Revolution: The Rise of Market Economics in Latin America*. London: Cassell, 1995.

Green, D. 'Let Latin America Find Its Own Path'. *The Guardian* (United Kingdom), 5 August 2002.

Griffith-Jones, S. 'A History of Debt Crisis Management'. In *Third World Debt: Managing the Consequences*, edited by S. Griffith-Jones. *IFR*, 1989.

Gruben, W. & S. Kiser. 'Why Brazil Devalued the Real'. Federal Reserve Bank of Dallas. <www.dallasfed.org/eyi/global/9907real.html>.

Gwynne, S.C. 'Adventures in the Loan Trade'. *Harpers'*, September 1983.

Habito, C.F. & E.L. Beja, Jr. 'Beating the Odds? The Continuing Saga of a Crisis-Prone Economy'. Part of the *Civil Society Monitoring of the Medium Term Philippine Development Plan (MTPDP)*, 2006.

Hannan, E.W. & E.L. Hudgins. 'A US Strategy for Latin America's Debts'. *The Backgrounder*, No. 502, 7 April 1986. Washington, DC: The Heritage Foundation, 1986.

Hari, J. 'Aid and Debt Relief a Waste of Money? Try Telling That to the People of Tanzania'. *The Independent*, 15 June 2005.

Hartcher, P. 'US Reigns in IMF with Tough Debt Rules'. *Australian Financial Review*, 22 April 2002.

Hausmann, R & R. Rigobon. 'IDA in UF: On the Benefits of Changing the Currency Denomination of Concessional Lending to Low-Income Countries'. Harvard University, 2003. <siteresources.worldbank.org/INTDEBTDEPT/RelatedPapers/20263430/IDA_UEF_Benefits-of-changing.pdf>, 4 December 2007.

Hay, J. & N. Paul. *Regulation and Taxation of Commercial Banks during the International Debt Crisis*. US Annex 1.Washington, DC: World Bank, 1991.

Healey, M. & E. Seman. 'Down, Argentine Way'. *The American Prospect* 13 (2002).

Hershberg, E. 'Why Argentina Crashed – And Is Still Crashing'. *NACLA Report on the Americas* 36 (2002).

Hornbeck, J.F. 'Argentina's Sovereign Debt Restructuring'. CRS Report for Congress, 19 October 2004.

Hotland, T. 'RI, Germany Agree US$29.25m Debt Swap Deal'. *The Jakarta Post*, 15 May 2004.

Huhne, C. 'Some Lessons of the Debt Crisis: Never Again?' In *International Economics and Financial Markets: The AMEX Bank Review Prize Essays*. Oxford: Oxford University Press, 1989.

Independent Evaluation Office (IEO) of the IMF. 'Report on the Evaluation of the Role of the IMF in Argentina: 1991–2001'. <www.imf.org/External/NP/ieo/2004/arg/eng/index.htm>.
Independent Evaluation Office of the IMF. 'IEO Mission and Values'. Available at <www.ieo-imf.org/about/mission.html>, 11 September 2007.
Independent Evaluation Office of the IMF. 'IEO Publications'. <www.imf.org/external/np/ieo/pap.asp#1>, 14 September 2007.
Independent Evaluation Office of the IMF. 'The IMF and Aid to Sub-Saharan Africa', <www.imf.org/external/np/ieo/2007/ssa/eng/pdf/report.pdf>, 24 September 2007.
'Indonesia Financial Sector Monthly Report'. No. 42. February 2004. Available at <siteresources.worldbank.org/INTINDONESIA/Resources/Fin-Priv-Sector/FSReport-022004.pdf>.
'Indonesia's Foreign Debt: Imprisoning the People of Indonesia'. International NGO Forum on Indonesian Development (INFID), 2000. <www.odiousdebts.org/odiousdebts/index.cfm?DSP=content&ContentID=2385#_ftnref9>, 18 February 2005.
International Monetary Fund. 'Malaysia: Selected Issues'. (1999).
International Monetary Fund. 'Does Currency Denomination of Debt Hold Key to Taming Volatility? *IMF Survey* 33 (2004).
International Monetary Fund. 'Watchdog Faults Argentina, but Also IMF', *IMF Survey*. Washington, DC, 2004.
International Monetary Fund. 'Factsheet: Gold in the IMF'. <www.imf.org/external/np/exr/facts/gold.htm>, 5 April 2005.
International Monetary Fund. 'Articles of Agreement of the International Monetary Fund'. <www.imf.org/external/pubs/ft/aa/index.htm>, 3 July 2007.
International Monetary Fund. 'How the IMF Helps to Resolve Economic Crises'. <www.imf.org/external/np/exr/facts.crises.htm>, 3 July 2007.
International Monetary Fund. 'What Is the IMF?' <www.imf.org/external/pubs/ft/exrp/what.htm>, 3 July 2007.
International Monetary Fund. 'Poverty Reduction Strategy Papers (PRSP)'. <www.imf.org/external/np/prsp/prsp.asp>, 6 August 2007.
International Monetary Fund. IMF Website. <www.imf.org/external/about.htm>, 10 September 2007.
International Monetary Fund. 'Malaysia: From Crisis to Recovery'. <www.imf.org/external/pubs/nft/op/207/index.htm>, 14 September 2007.
International Monetary Fund. 'Communiqué of the International Monetary and Financial Committee of the Board of Governors of the International Monetary Fund'. Washington, DC, 12 April 2003, <www.imf.org/external/np/cm/2003/041203.htm>, 4 December 2007.
International Monetary Fund. 'The HIPC Initiative: Delivering Debt Relief to Poor Countries'. <www.imf.org/external/np/hipc/art0299.pdf>, 4 December 2007.
International Monetary Fund. 'IMF Conditionality: A Factsheet'. <www.imf.org/external/np/exr/facts/conditio.htm>, 4 December 2007.

International Monetary Fund. 'IMF Lending'. <www.imf.org/external/np/exr/facts/howlend.htm>, 4 December 2007.
International Monetary Fund. 'IMF Quotas: A Fact Sheet 2004'. <www.imf.org/external/np/exr/facts/quotas.htm>, 4 December 2007.
International Monetary Fund. 'Policy Statement on IMF Technical Assistance'. <www.imf.org/external/pubs/ft/psta/index.htm>, 4 December 2007.
International Monetary Fund. 'Proposals for a Sovereign Debt Restructuring Mechanism (SDRM): A Factsheet'. <www.imf.org/external/np/exr/facts/sdrm.htm>, 4 December 2007.
International Monetary Fund. 'Sovereign Debt Restructurings and the Domestic Economy Experience in Four Recent Cases'. <www.imf.org/external/NP/pdr/sdrm/2002/022102.pdf>, 4 December 2007.
International Monetary Fund. 'IMF Fact Sheet'. <www.imf.org/external/np/exr/facts/asia.pdf>, 13 December 2007.
International Monetary Fund Economic Forum. 'Financial Markets: Coping with Turbulence'. <www.imf.org/external/np/tr/1998/TR981201.htm>, 5 October 1999.
'Internet Usage Statistics'. Internet World Stats. <www.internetworldstats.com/stats.htm>, 12 December 2007.
Irwin, G. & D. Vines. 'International Policy Advice in the East Asian Crisis: A Critical Review of the Debate'. In *Capital Flows Without Crisis? Reconciling Capital Mobility and Economic Stability*, edited by D. Dasgupta, M. Uzan & D. Wilson. London: Routledge, 2001.

James, H. 'Deep Red: The International Debt Crisis and Its Historical Precedents'. *The American Scholar* (Summer 1987).
James, H. *International Monetary Cooperation since Bretton Woods*. Oxford: International Monetary Fund and Oxford University Press, 1996.
Jeanne, O. & C. Wyplosz. 'The International Lender of Last Resort: How Large Is Large Enough?' Working Paper No. WF/01/76. IMF, May 2001.
Jeffery, S. 'Crisis in Argentina'. *Guardian Unlimited* (United Kingdom), 4 January 2002.
Jenks, L. *The Migration of British Capital to 1875*. New York: Knopf, 1927.
Jolly, R. Deputy Executive Director for Programmes, United Nations Children's Fund, testimony before the House Committee on Banking, Finance and Urban Affairs hearings on the *International Economic Issues and Their Impact on the U.S. Financial System*, 4 January 1989, 101st Congress First Session.
Jorgensen, E. & J.D. Sachs. 'Default and Renegotiation of Latin American Foreign Bonds in the Interwar Period'. In *The International Debt Crisis in Historical Perspective*, edited by Eichengreen and Lindert.
Joyce, J.P., 'Through a Glass Darkly: New Questions (and Answers) about IMF Programs'. Working Paper 2002–04. Wellesley College, 2002.

Kamel, S. & E. Tooma. 'Exchanging Debt for Development: Lessons from the Egyptian Debt-for-Development Swap Experience'. Economic Research

Forum and Ministry for Communication and Information Technology (MCIT). Egypt, September 2005.

Kandler, S. 'Local Currency Markets Offer Promise and Risk'. *Emerging Markets Debt Report* 10, 3 February 1997.

Kaplan, E. & D. Rodrik. 'Did the Malaysian Capital Controls Work?' Working Papers, NBER, 2003. <papers.nber.org/papers/W8142>, 4 December 2007.

Kaufman, H. 'Protecting against the Next Financial Crisis: The Need to Reform Global Financial Oversight, the IMF, and Monetary Policy Goals'. *Business Economics* 34 (1999).

Kelly, P. 'IMF Tightens the Screws on Suharto'. *The Australian*, 11 March 1998.

Keynes, J.M. *The General Theory of Employment Interest and Money*. London: MacMillan, 1967.

Kiguel, M. 'Structural Reforms in Argentina: Success or Failure?' *Comparative Economic Studies* XLIV, no. 2 (2002).

King, R.G. & R. Levine. 'Finance and Growth: Schumpeter Might Be Right'. *The Quarterly Journal of Economics* 108, no. 3 (1993).

King, R.G. & R. Levine. 'Finance, Entrepreneurship and Growth'. *Journal of Monetary Economics* 32 (1993).

Klein, N. 'Revolt of the Wronged'. *The Guardian* (United Kingdom), 28 March 2002.

Köhler, H. 'Reform of the International Financial Architecture: A Work in Progress'. <www.imf.org/external/np/speeches/2002/070502.htm>, 4 December 2007.

Konz, P. 'The Third World Debt Crisis'. *Hastings International and Comparative Law Review* 12 (1989).

Kremer, M. & S. Jayachandran. 'IMF Seminar: Odious Debt'. <www.imf.org/external/np/res/seminars/2002/poverty/mksj.pdf>, 17 February 2005.

Krueger, A. 'International Financial Architecture for 2002: A New Approach to Sovereign Debt Restructuring'. Speech delivered at the National Economists' Club Annual Members' Dinner. Washington, DC, 26 November 2001. <www.imf.org/external/np/speeches/2001/112601.htm>, 4 December 2007 ('Krueger I').

Krueger, A. 'A New Approach to Sovereign Debt Restructuring'. Delivered at 'Sovereign Debt Workouts: Hopes and Hazards'. Washington, DC, Institute for International Economics, 1 April 2002. <www.imf.org/external/pubs/ft/exrp/sdrm/eng/index.htm>; <www.iie.com/papers/krueger0402.htm> ('Krueger II').

Krueger, A. 'Crisis Prevention and Resolution: Lessons from Argentina'. Paper presented at the NBER Conference on 'The Argentina Crisis'. Cambridge, 17 July 2002. <www.imf.org/external/np.speeches/2002/071702.htm>.

Krueger, A. 'Preventing and Resolving Financial Crises: The Role of Sovereign Debt Restructuring'. Speech delivered at the Latin American Meeting of the Econometric Society. Sao Paolo, Brazil, 26 July 2002. <www.imf.org/external/np/speeches/2002/072602.htm> ('Krueger III').

Krugman, P. 'Saving Asia: It's Time to Get Radical'. *Fortune*, 7 September 1998.

Krugman, P. 'Analytical Afterthoughts on the Asian Crisis'. <web.mit.edu/krugman/www/MINICRIS.htm>, 4 December 2007.

Lachica, E. 'IMF-World Bank: Rethinking the Global Financial System – Oh, Brother: World Bank, IMF Jockey for Position'. *The Asian Wall Street Journal*, 5 October 1998.

Lachman, D., A. Meltzer & C. Calomiris. 'Is the IMF Obsolete?' American Enterprise Institute for Public Policy Research. <www.aei.org/publications/filter., pubID.26202/pub_detail.asp>, 18 September 2007.

Larson, G.W. 'Default on Foreign Sovereign Debt: A Question for the Courts?' *Indiana Law Review* 18 (1985).

Lastra, R. 'The Bretton Woods Institutions in the XXIst Century'. In *The Reform of the International Financial Architecture*, edited by R. Lastra. London: Kluwer Law International, 2001.

Lee, S.H. & H.M. Sung. 'The Reactions of Secondary Market Prices of Developing Country Syndicated Loans to the Brady Plan'. Paper dated 15 January 1993.

Levine, R. & S. Zervos. 'Stock Markets, Banks, and Economic Growth'. *The American Economic Review* 88, no. 3 (1998).

Levinson, J. 'Living Dangerously: Indonesia and the Reality of the Global Economic System'. *Journal of International Law and Practice* 7 (1998).

Levinson, J. 'The International Financial System: A Flawed Architecture'. *Fletcher Forum of World Affairs* 23 (1999).

Lewis, C. *America's Stake in International Investments*. Washington, DC: Brookings Institute, 1938.

Lichtenstein, C. 'The Role of International Law in the 21st Century: The Mexican Crisis – Who Should Be a Country's Lender of Last Resort?' *Fordham International Law Journal* (1995).

Lindert, P.H. & P.J. Morton. 'How Sovereign Debt Has Worked'. In *Developing Country Debt and the World Economy*, edited by J.D. Sachs. Chicago: University of Chicago Press, 1989.

Lustig, N. 'Crises and the Poor: Socially Responsible Macroeconomics'. Presidential Address to the Fourth Annual Meeting of the Latin American and Caribbean Economic Association. Santiago, Chile, 22 October 1999. <www.lacea.org/Conferences_files/presidential.pdf>, 4 December 2007.

MacMillan, R. 'The Next Sovereign Debt Crisis'. *Stanford Journal of International Law* 31 (1995).

Makin, C. 'Doesn't Anybody Remember Risk?' *Institutional Investor*, April 1994.

Mann, F.A. *The Legal Aspect of Money – with Special Reference to Comparative Private and Public International Law*, 5th edn. Oxford: Clarendon Press, 1992.

Mansor, A.M., et al. 'The IMF and Recent Capital Account Crises: Indonesia, Korea, Brazil'. Independent Evaluation Office Report, International Monetary Fund, 2003.

Marichal, C. *A Century of Debt Crises in Latin America*. Princeton, NJ: Princeton University Press, 1989.

Marquis, C. 'Russia Sees Iraqi Debt Relief as Link to Oil, US Aides Say'. *New York Times*, 17 January 2004.
Masuda, A. 'Mexico's Debt Reduction Agreement and the New Debt Strategy'. *EXIM Review* 11, no. 1 (1991).
Mathieson, D. & L. Rojas-Suarez. 'Liberalization of the Capital Account: Experiences and Issues'. Occasional Paper No. 103. IMF, March 1993.
McCarthy, R. 'After Brady: The Debt Dust Settles'. *LatinFinance* 24 (1991).
McCoy, C.F. & P. Truell. 'Lending Imbroglio: Worries Deepen Again on Third World Debt as Brazil Stops Paying'. *Wall Street Journal*, 3 March 1987.
McKinnon, R. & G. Schnabl. 'The East Asian Dollar Standard, Fear of Floating, and Original Sin'. Working Paper No.11. Hong Kong Institute for Monetary Research, 2003.
Mekay, E. 'Debt Relief Weighted Down by IMF Burden'. *Global Policy Forum* (2004). <www.globalpolicy.org/socecon/develop/debt/2004/1123imfiraq.htm>, 18 February 2005.
Meyer, L.H. 'Lessons from the Asian Crisis: A Central Banker's Perspective'. Working Paper No. 276. Levy Economics Institute, 1999.
Montagnon, P. 'An Impasse That Is Difficult to Resolve'. *Financial Times* (Peru), 26 September 1986, special supplement.
Monteagudo, M. 'The Debt Problem: The Baker Plan and the Brady Initiative – A Latin American Perspective'. *The International Lawyer* 28, no. 1 (1994).
Morgan Guaranty Trust. *World Financial Markets* (June/July 1987).
Mossberg, W.S. & P. Truell P. 'Another Round: Bush Aides Are Likely to Offer a Plan Soon on Third World Debt'. *The Wall Street Journal*, 9 March 1989.
Mullin, K. 'Yield: The Opium of Global Investors', 1200 *IFR*, 12 September 1997.

North, D.C. *Institutions, Institutional Change and Economic Performance*. Cambridge: Cambridge University Press, 1990.
Norton, J.J. 'Are Latin America and East Asia an Ocean Apart? The Connecting Currents of Asian Financial Crises'. *NAFTA Law and Business Review of the Americas* 4 (1998).

O'Reilly, B. 'Cooling Down the World Debt Bomb', *Fortune*, 20 May 1991.
OECD. *Prudential Supervision in Banking*. Paris: OECD, 1987.
OECD. 'Compendium of Patent Statistics, 2007'. <www.oecd.org/document/10/0,3343,en_2649_34451_1901066_1_1_1_1,00.html>, 13 December 2007.
Office of the Superintendent of Financial Institutions, Canada. 'Guideline: Exposure to Designated Countries, EDC 1990-10'. Part E, reproduced in *Regulation and Taxation of Commercial Banks during the International Debt Crisis*, by Hay & Paul.
Onishi, N. 'Japan Open to Forgiving Iraqi Debt – If Others Do So'. *New York Times*, 29 December 2003. <www.benadorassociates.com/article/866 >, 16 February 2005.

Paris Club. 'Paris Club Agrees to Reduce Burundi's Debt by 67% in Net Present Value'. Press Release, 4 March 2004.

Paris Club. 'The Paris Club and the Republic of Iraq Agree on Debt Relief'. Press Release, 21 November 2004.
Paris Club. 'Debt Swap Reporting: Rules and Principles'. (2006). <www.clubdeparis.org/en/public_debt.html>, 20 April 2006.
Paris Club. 'The Evian Approach'. <www.clubdeparis.org>, 4 December 2007.
Partnoy, F. 'Why Markets Crash and What Law Can Do about It'. *University of Pittsburgh Law Review* 61 (1999–2000).
Passell, P. 'Critics: The IMF Is Misguided. Skeptics: Too Much Rot in Asia'. *The New York Times*, 15 January 1998.
Pastor, R.A. 'The Debt Crisis: A Financial or a Development Problem?' In *Latin America's Debt Crisis: Adjusting to the Past or Planning for the Future*, edited by R.A. Pastor. Boulder and London: Lynne Rienner Publishers, 1987.
Pereira, L.C. *Solving the Debt Crisis: Debt Relief and Adjustment*. Statement delivered before the House Committee on Banking, Finance and Urban Affairs hearings on the 'Lesser Developed Countries' Debt Crisis'. 101st Congress First Session, 5 January 1989.
Pettifor, A. 'Chapter 9/11? Resolving International Debt Crises – the Jubilee Framework for International Insolvency'. <www.jubileeplus.org/analysis/reports/jubilee_framework.html>, 26 September 2002 and 24 March 2003.
Pettifor, A. & K. Raffer. 'Report on the IMF's Conference on the SDRM, 22 January 2003'. Unpublished report on file with author.
Pettis, M. 'Can Financial Crises Be Prevented?' Unfinished paper, June 1998.
Pettis, M. *The Volatility Machine: Emerging Economies and the Threat of Financial Collapse*. Oxford: Oxford University Press, 2001.
Pettis, M. 'Reengineering the Volatility Machine: How the IMF Can Help Prevent Financial Crises'. *World Policy Journal* (Fall 2003).
Pinstrup-Andersen, P. 'Food Security and Structural Adjustment'. Statement delivered before the House Committee on Banking, Finance and Urban Affairs hearings on the *International Economic Issues and Their Impact on the U.S. Financial System*. 101st Congress First Session, 4 January 1989.
Platt, G. 'Mexican Virus Fells Emerging Markets but Prognosis Good Among Healthiest'. *Journal of Commerce*, 4 May 1995.
Poon, S.H. 'Malaysia and the Asian Financial Crisis: A View from the Finance Perspective'. *African Finance Journal*, Special Issue (1999).
Power, P.J. 'Sovereign Debt: The Rise of the Secondary Market and Its Implications for Future Restructurings'. *Fordham Law Review* 64 (1996).
'PRS Watch: A Eurodad Newsletter'. 16 August 2007.
Pyo, H.K. 'The Financial Crisis in Korea and Its Aftermath: A Political Economic Perspective'. In *Capital Flows Without Crisis? Reconciling Capital Mobility and Economic Stability*, edited by D. Dasgupta, M. Uzan & D. Wilson. London: Routledge, 2001.

Quirk, W.J. 'Will an Underdeveloped Countries Debtors' Cartel Squeeze the Big Banks?' *Business and Society Review* 47 (1983).

List of References

Raffer, K. 'Applying Chapter 9 Insolvency to International Debts: An Economically Efficient Solution with a Human Face'. *World Development* 18, no. 2 (1990).

Raffer, K. 'Solving Sovereign Debt Overhang by Internationalising Chapter 9 Procedures'. *Studien von Zeitfragen* (2002).

Raffer, K. 'International Financial Institutions and Financial Accountability' *Ethics and International Affairs* 18 (2004).

Raffer, K. 'The IMF's SDRM: Another Form of Simply Disastrous Rescheduling Management?' In *Sovereign Debts at the Crossroads*, edited by C. Jochnick & F. Preston. Oxford: Oxford University Press, 2006.

Raffer, K. 'To Stay or Not to Stay: A Short Note on Differing Versions of the SDRM'. <www.jubileeresearch.org/news/raffer310103.htm>, 4 December 2007.

Rajam, R. 'Odious or Just Malodorous?' *Finance and Development* (December 2004).

Rajan, R.S. 'The Southeast Asian Currency and Financial Crisis: Review of Experiences and Implications for IMF Policy'. Working Paper No. 1, The Institute of Policy Studies. Singapore, 1998.

Rasche, P.W. 'Argentina: Test Case for a New Approach to Insolvency?' *Studien von Zeitfragen*, 5 January 2002.

Reinhardt, C., K. Rogoff & M. Savastano. 'Debt Intolerance'. Working Paper No. 9908. NBER, 2003. <www.nber.org/papers/w9908>.

Reinhart, C.M. & R.T. Smith. 'Temporary Controls on Capital Inflows'. Working Paper No. 8422. NBER, August 2001.

Republic of Argentina v. Weltover, Inc. 504 US 607 (1992).

'Review of the Commonwealth Securities Market'. Discussion paper prepared for the Commonwealth Debt Management Review. Commonwealth of Australia Treasury Department, 2002.

Rhodes, W.R. Testimony, Federal News Service, 21 March 1990.

Rodrik, D. 'Development Strategies for the Next Century'. 2000. Available at <siteresources.worldbank.org/INTABCDEWASHINGTON2000/Resources/rodrik_japan.pdf>.

Rodrik, D. & A. Velasco. 'Short-Term Capital Flows'. Working Paper No. W7364. NBER, September 1999.

Rogoff, K. 'The IMF Strikes Back'. <www.imf.org/external/np/vc/2003/021003.htm>, 4 December 2007.

Rogoff, K. & J. Zettelmeyer. 'Early Ideas on Sovereign Bankruptcy Reorganisation: A Survey'. Working Paper No. WP/02/57, IMF.

Rohter, L. 'Giving Argentina the Cinderella Treatment'. *The New York Times*, 11 August 2002.

Rojas-Suarez, L. 'Toward a Sustainable FTAA: Does Latin America Meet the Necessary Financial Preconditions?' Unpublished paper.

Rousseau, P.L. & R. Sylla, 'Emerging Financial Markets and Early U.S. Growth'. Working Paper No. 7448. National Bureau of Economic Research, December 1999.

Rubin, R.E. 'Treasury Secretary Robert E. Rubin Remarks on Reform of the International Financial Architecture to the School of Advance International Studies'. Press Release, 21 April 1999.

Sachs, J.D. (ed.). *Developing Country Debt and the World Economy*. Chicago: University of Chicago Press, 1989.

Sachs, J.D. 'A Crash Foretold: Argentina Must Revamp Its Society and Economy for a High-Tech World'. *Time International*, 14 January 2002.

Sachs, J.D. 'The International Lender of Last Resort: What Are the Alternatives?' <www.bos.frb.org/economic/conf/conf43/181p.pdf>, 4 December 2007.

Sanger, D.E. 'IMF Reports Plan Backfired, Worsening Indonesia Woes'. *New York Times*, 14 January 1998.

Santayana, G. *Life of Reason* (1950–1956), vol. I, ch. xii.

Santiso, C. 'Good Governance and Aid Effectiveness: The World Bank and Conditionality'. *Georgetown Public Policy Review* 7 (2002).

Santos, A.G. 'Beyond Baker and Brady: Deeper Debt Reduction for Latin American Sovereign Debtors'. *NYULR* 66 (1991).

Schinasi, G.J. 'Responsibility of Central Banks for Stability in Financial Markets'. Working Paper No. WP/03/121. IMF, June 2003.

Schlesinger, S. *Act of Creation: The Founding of the United Nations*. Cambridge: Westview Press, 2004.

Scott, H.S. *International Finance: Transactions, Policy & Regulation*, 14th edn. Foundation Press, 2007.

Scott, H.S. & P.A. Wellons. *International Finance: Transactions, Policy and Regulation*, 6th edn. University Casebook, 1999.

Securities Industry Association et al. Letter dated 6 February 2002 from the Securities Industry Association, Emerging Markets Traders Association, International Primary Market Association, International Securities Market Association and The Bond Market Association to Mr. Horst Köhler. <www.emta.org/ndevelop/imflettr.pdf>, 4 December 2007.

'Selected Statistics on World Oil', HBS Case Services, No. 380–144.

Sen, A. 'Global Doubts as Global Solutions'. Alfred Deakin Lecture. Melbourne, 15 May 2001. <www.abc.net.au/rn/deakin/stories/s296978.htm>, 4 December 2007.

Sgard, J. 'The Renegotiation of Sovereign Debts and the Future of Financial Multilateralism'. Paper presented at the Fifth Pan-European Conference of the Standing Group on International Relations. The Hague, 9–11 September 2004.

Skiles, M.E. 'Latin American International Loan Defaults in the 1930s: Lessons for the 1980s?' Research Paper No. 8812 given at the Federal Reserve Bank of New York. New York, April 1988.

Sloan, R.D. 'The Third World Debt Crisis: Where We Have Been and Where We Are Going'. *The Washington Quarterly* (Winter 1988).

Smith, A. *The Wealth of Nations*, Book V, Chapter III. Edward Cannan edition, 1976.

Soros, G. *Open Society: Reforming Global Capitalism*. London: Little, Brown & Company, 2000.
Soros, G. Address to The Asia Society Hong Kong Center 11th Annual Dinner. Hong Kong, 19 September 2001. <www.asiasociety.org/speeches/soros.html>, 4 December 2007.
Soulard, A. 'The Role of Multilateral Financial Institutions in Bringing Developing Companies to U.S. Markets'. *Fordham International Law Journal* 17 (1994).
Spahn, P.B. 'The Tobin Tax and Exchange Rate Stability'. *Finance & Development* (June 1996). <www.worldbank.org/fandd/english/0696/articles/0130696.htm>, 4 December 2007.
Stabler, C. 'Mideast Oil Money Proves Burdensome'. *The Wall Street Journal* (New York), 6 June 1974.
Stallings, B. *Banker to the Third World: U.S. Portfolio Investment in Latin America, 1900–1986*. Berkeley and Los Angeles: University of California Press, 1987.
Stay, J. 'Reform of the International Financial Architecture: What Has Been Written?' In *International Financial Governance Under Stress Global Structure vs National Imperatives*, edited by Underhill & Zhang. Cambridge, 2003.
Steward, F. & M. Wang. 'Do PRSPs Empower Poor Countries and Disempower the World Bank, or Is It the Other Way Round?' Working Paper No. 108. QEH, October 2003.
Stiglitz, J. 'Statement to the Meeting of Finance Ministers of ASEAN Plus 6 with the IMF and the World Bank'. Kuala Lumpur, Malaysia, 1 December 1997.
Stiglitz, J. 'The Insider – What I Learned at the World Economic Crisis'. *The New Republic* (2000).
Stiglitz, J. *Globalisation and Its Discontents*. London: Penguin, 2002.
Stiglitz, J. 'Dealing with Debt: How to Reform the Global Financial System'. *Harvard International Review* 25 (2003).
Sudo, P.T. 'Chase Announces Plan to Fortify LDC Reserve'. *The American Banker*, 24 January 1989.
Sugisaki, S. 'Economic Crises in Asia'. Address delivered at the 1998 Harvard Asia Business Conference. Harvard Business School, 30 January 1998.
Suratgar. 'The International Financial System and the Management of the International Debt Crisis'. In *International Borrowing: Negotiating and Structuring International Debt transactions*, edited by Bradlow. International Law Institute, 1986.
Sutherland, P. 'Managing the International Economy in an Age of Globalisation'. The 1998 Per Jacobsson Lecture. Annual meeting of the IMF and the World Bank.
Sweeney, E. 'Argentina: The Current Crisis in Perspective'. *America* 186 (2002).

Tarnoff, C. 'Iraq: Recent Developments in Reconstruction Assistance'. CRS Report for Congress, 20 December 2004.

Taylor, J.B. Statement Regarding the Decisions by Countries to Issue Bonds with Collective Action Clauses (CACs), 3 February 2004. <www.treas.gov/press/releases/js1144.htm>, 4 December 2007.

Teather, D. 'Argentina Orders Banks to Close'. *The Guardian* (United Kingdom), 20 April 2002.

Thomas, J.P. 'Bankruptcy Proceedings for Sovereign State Insolvency'. United Nations University World Institute for Development Economics Research, Discussion Paper 2002/109. <www.wider.unu.edu/publications/dps/dps2002/dp2002-109.pdf>, 7 April 2005.

Tobin, J. 'A Proposal for International Monetary Reform'. *Eastern Economic Journal* 4 (1978).

Torres, J.F. & R. Landa. 'The Changing Times: Foreign Investment in Mexico'. *Int'l Law & Pol* 23 (1991).

Toussaint, E. 'The Odious Debt of Russia, the New Oligarchs, and the Bretton Woods Institutions'. <www.cadtm.org/spip.php?article536>, 4 December 2007.

Tran, M. 'Argentina Scrambles to Avoid Financial Collapse'. *Guardian Unlimited* (United Kingdom), 22 April 2002.

United Nations. 'UN Millennium Development Goals (MDG)'. <www.un.org/millenniumgoals/>, 4 December 2007.

United Nations. Report of the High Level Panel on Financing for Development. Available at <www.un.org/reports/financing/report_full.htm#appendix>.

United Nations Centre on Transnational Corporations. *Debt Equity Conversions: A Guide for Decision-Makers*. New York: United Nations, 1990.

United Nations Economic Commission for Latin America and the Carribbean & United Nations Centre on Transnational Corporations (ECLAC/CTC). *Transnational Bank Behaviour and the International Debt Crisis*. Santiago, Chile: United Nations, 1989.

US Department of Commerce. *Statistical Abstract of the United States 1998*, 118th edn.

US Department of the Treasury Office of Public Affairs. 'Factsheet: US-Philippines Debt-Reduction Agreement Under the Tropical Forest Conservation Act (TFCA)'. TFCA Debt Swap Signing Ceremony with Philippines, 19 September 2002.

US International Trade Commission (USITC). *The Effect of Developing Country Debt-Servicing Problems on U.S. Trade*. A Report to the Subcommittee on Trade of the House Ways and Means Committee, Investigation No. 332–234, USITC Pub. No. 1950.

UK Treasury. 'Executive Summary: Debt Relief Beyond HIPC'. (2005).

Van Dormael, A. *Bretton Woods: Birth of a Monetary System*. London: MacMillan Press, 1978.

Vankudre, P. 'Brady Bonds'. *LatinFinance* 26 (1991).

Vasquez, I. 'Why the IMF Should Not Intervene'. <www.cato.org/speeches/sp-iv22598.html>, 4 December 2007.
Viscio, I. 'The Recent Experience with Capital Flows to Emerging Market Economies'. *OECD Economy Outlook* 65 (1 June 1998).
Voorhees, 'Doses of Reality'. *LatinFinance* 40 (1992).

Wade, R. 'The Coming Fight over Capital Controls'. *Foreign Affairs* 113 (22 December 1998).
Wade, R. & F. Veneroso. 'The Gathering World Slump and the Battle over Capital Controls'. *New Left Review* 231 (1998).
Walford v. Miles 2 AC 128, 138 [1992].
Wallman, K.M.H. 'The Politics of Default: Politically Motivated Sovereign Debt Default and Repudiation'. *Texas International Law Journal* 20 (1985).
Warby, M. 'Review'. *The Australian Financial Review* (22 September 2000).
Wee, L.C. 'Debt-for-Nature Swaps: A Reassessment of Their Significance in International Environmental Law'. *Journal of Environmental Law* 6 (1994).
Weissman, R. 'Twenty Questions on the IMF'. In *Democratizing the Global Economy*, edited by K. Danaher. Common Courage Press, 2001.
Wellons, P.A. *World Money and Credit: The Crisis and Its Causes*. Boston: Division of Research, Harvard Business School, 1983.
Wellons, P.A. *Passing the Buck: Banks, Governments and Third World Debt*. Boston: Harvard Business School Press, 1987.
White, M. 'Sovereigns in Distress: Do They Need Bankruptcy?' *Brookings Paper on Economic Activity* (2002).
Williamson, J. *Curbing the Boom-Bust Cycle: Stabilizing Capital Flows to Emerging Markets*. Washington, DC: Institute for International Economics, 2005.
Wolfson, B. 'Paving the Paper Trail'. *LatinFinance* 26 (1991).
Woodroffe, J. & M. Ellis-Jones. 'States of Unrest: Resistance to IMF Policies in Poor Countries'. <www.globalpolicy.org/socecon/bwi-wto/imf/2000/protest.htm>, 19 February 2005.
World Bank. *World Development Report*. New York: Oxford University Press, 1985.
World Bank. *World Debt Tables, 1994–1995*. Washington, DC: World Bank.
World Bank. *Global Development Finance 1997*. Washington, DC: World Bank, 1997.
World Bank. *Global Development Finance 1998*. Washington, DC: World Bank, 1998.
World Bank. *Global Development Finance 2002*. Washington, DC: World Bank, 2002.
World Bank. 'About Us'. <www.worldbank.org/about>, 15 October 2003.
World Bank. *2004 World Development Indicators*. Washington, DC: World Bank, 2004.
World Bank. 'HIPC: Debt Relief for Sustainable Development'. <www.worldbank.org/hipc/about/hipcbr/hipcbr.htm>, 15 February 2005.

World Bank. 'World Bank History'. <web.worldbank.org>, 3 July 2007.
World Bank. *Global Development Finance 2007*. Washington, DC: World Bank, 2007.
World Bank. *World Development Indicators 2007*. <www.siteresources.worldbank.org/DATASTATISTICS/Resources/WDI07section4-intro.pdf>, 4 December 2007.
World Trade Organization. 'The WTO...in Brief'. <www.wto.org/english/thewto_e/whatis_e/inbrief_e/inbr00_e.htm>, 15 October 2003.
Wroughton, L. 'IMF Approves Aid for Iraq, Pushes for Debt Relief'. <www.globalpolicy.org/security/issues/iraq/contract/2004/0929imf.htm>, 18 February 2005.

Index

A

Africa, 8, 11, 16, 20, 22, 27, 41, 66-7, 127, 144, 159, 161, 164-5, 167-9
Aid, 165-7
Argentina, 2, 11, 14, 21-2, 25, 34, 48, 50-1, 75-84, 99, 101-3, 114-9, 149, 154, 156-7, 163
Argentine crisis of 2001, 21, 76-7, 81-4, 114, 117, 157, 163
Arner, Douglas, 98, 135
Asian economic crisis of 1997, 55, 57, 59, 61, 63, 65, 67, 69, 71, 73, 132

B

Baker, James A, 40, 87
Baker Plan, 39, 40, 43, 46
Bank for International Settlements, 18, 29, 98, 126
Brady Plan, 39-43, 45-7, 49, 51-4, 66, 75, 114, 147, 149, 161
Brazil, 2, 11, 22, 24-5, 31, 45-6, 48, 50-2, 56, 77, 93, 103, 107-8, 113-4, 117-8, 125
Bretton Woods, 3-10, 13, 40, 89, 104, 153

C

Camdessus, Michel, 165-6
Capital
  controls, 5, 8, 9, 12, 14, 17, 21, 61, 63, 78-80, 97, 104-12, 127-8, 163, 166-7
  flight, 33-4, 62, 69, 104, 109, 111

Causes of capital flows, 58-9
Chile, 12, 19, 21, 35, 50, 94, 103, 107-8, 123, 127, 160
China, 12, 16, 57, 61, 101, 105
Collective Action Clauses, 143-5, 153
Corruption, 33-4, 77, 79, 80
Currency mismatches, 121, 123-6, 128-30, 132, 152, 155

D

Debt
  buy-backs in the late 1980s, 35, 93, 141
  crisis of 1982, 21, 23, 25, 27, 29, 31, 33, 35, 37, 56, 75, 147, 161
  policy for developing nations, 99
  relief, 1, 22, 41, 45-6, 48, 66, 80, 83, 85-93, 95, 118-9, 128, 130, 144, 148-9, 164
    HIPC initiative, 85-6, 91
    for Iraq, 85, 87-91, 93, 95
Debt-equity swaps, 94-5
Debt-for-development exchanges, 93-4
Dollarization, 125

E

Ecuador, 52, 54, 114-5, 119
Exchange rate policies, 97, 101
  fixed, 5, 61, 64, 99, 101-4, 124-5, 130
  floating, 101

G

Galbraith, JK, 160
Global financial regulator, 132, 135, 137, 152
Globalization, 14-9, 133, 140
  impact on volatility of capital markets, 18, 121-2, 124, 127-8, 131-2, 140

H

Highly indebted poor country initiative (HIPC), 85-6, 88, 91-3, 155, 164
History of sovereign loans, 115

I

IMF, 4-8, 10-2, 19-21, 40, 52, 61-3, 66-73, 76-81, 83-92, 98-9, 104-11, 114-5, 123-5, 135-8, 140-51, 156-70
  in Argentina, 75-6, 78-81, 115, 163
  in Asian Crisis of 1997, 11, 19, 22, 103, 126
  in debt crisis of 1982, 56
  in peso crisis of late 1994, 19, 56, 58, 63, 99, 102-3, 114, 132
Independent Evaluation Office of the IMF, 79, 83, 124, 165, 168
Indonesia, 20, 22, 56-7, 59-63, 69, 70, 79, 86, 92-3, 95, 98-9, 102, 110, 114, 125, 137, 156-7
International Development Association (IDA), 129
International Trade Organization, 6, 140-1
Iraq's indebtedness, 40, 85-95

K

Keynes, JM, 3-5, 14, 62-3, 110
Kohler, Horst, 138, 149
Korea, 15, 22, 40, 56-7, 60-3, 68-9, 71, 79, 98-100, 103, 110, 114, 125, 127, 137, 162
Krugman, Paul, 106

L

Lender of last resort, 14, 20, 121, 132-7, 146, 152
Liberalization of financial sector, 5-6, 8-9, 19, 60-1, 98, 106

M

Malaysia, 12, 22, 55-6, 62-3, 71, 105-10, 162-3, 166-7
Mexico, 20-1, 25, 27, 31, 34-7, 41-6, 48-9, 54-6, 58, 63, 77, 99, 100, 102-3, 114, 144, 159-62
Moral hazard, 60, 66, 69, 93, 136-7, 145-6
Mulford, David, 43, 45-6

N

National balance sheets, 122, 127, 152, 155, 158

O

OPEC oil dollar recycling, 26-7, 36, 58
Original Sin, 123-6, 128-30

P

Paris Club, 41, 83-4, 86-90, 94, 101, 122, 130-2, 147, 152
Pesofication, 157
Pettis, Michael, 58-9, 122, 125-6, 131, 140
Philippines, 22, 47-8, 55, 57, 63, 90, 93, 95, 105, 110
Poverty in Africa, 165
Poverty Reduction Strategy Papers, 151, 164-5, 168
Prudential regulation, 60, 78-9, 97-8, 161

R

Reserve Bank of Australia, 162
Rockefeller, David, 23
Russian crisis of 1998, 21, 66, 69, 76-7, 100, 103, 115, 132, 146

S

Seigniorage, 125
Sen, Amartya, 16
Socialization of private sector debt, 155-6, 158
Sovereign
  bankruptcy regime, 79, 121, 132, 137-42, 144, 147, 149, 151-2, 155
  bond markets, 65

Index

Sovereign Debt Restructuring Mechanism (SDRM), 141, 145-6, 148
Stiglitz, Joseph, 12, 89, 162, 168-9
Structural Adjustment Programs, 151

T

Taiwan, 61, 112, 127
Thailand, 21-2, 55-7, 60-3, 67, 69, 79, 98-9, 101-2, 107-8, 110, 114, 137, 156, 162
Triffin, Robert, 8, 10

V

Venezuela, 2, 34, 39, 47-9
Volatility Machine, 122, 125-6, 131, 140

W

Wolfensohn, James, 85
World Bank, 3-8, 12-4, 34, 40-2, 48, 52, 56-8, 62-3, 82-3, 85-7, 91-2, 94, 129, 140-1, 161-2, 164
World Trade Organization, 6, 13, 141, 153